VIDEOSYNCRATIC

VIDEOSYNCRATIC by JON SPIRA

ISBN PAPERBACK: 978-0-9957356-0-6
ISBN E-BOOK: 978-0-9957356-1-3

First published 2017 by Jon Spira

First edition March 2017

VIDEOSYNCRATIC

A book about life.

In video shops.

JON SPIRA

CONTENTS

FOREWORD

by
SUSIE DENT

You'd expect a lexicographer to be attracted to a place called 'Videosyncratic'. Clever shop names don't come around too often. I still remember my double take at the new white lettering emblazoned across the window, and at the two sofas flanking its front door. Imagine a store where you were actually *invited* to sit down: idiosyncratic indeed.

I did a lot of perusing and pondering on those blue sofas – the latter while my enthusiastic daughter browsed the extensive children's section every Friday. She knew it as the Batman shop, her nod to the great man's inclusion (complete with a videotape-head) in the line of movie icons sketched above the door. A Batman shop, no less, in which Edward Scissorhands rubbed shoulders with the Famous Five and the Clangers.

This is how I came to know Jon Spira, amongst the most wonderfully eclectic collection of films I'd ever come across – then or since. Films that were frequently older than any Blockbuster cut-off date. Films that were classic, crazy, cult – often all three. Above all, films that Jon and his team seemed to know off by heart – and if they didn't, they'd be able to tell you why. Talking movies was in their blood and, unlike the BOGOF mentality of other video shops, they didn't care two hoots if you never bought popcorn – renting *Rocky* or *The Graduate* was enough to endear you to them forever. (That said, I'm repressing the knowledge that their system frequently carried a sentence or two about particular customers, along the lines of 'Insufferable Cow', or 'Life's too short to engage this man in conversation'. I'm hoping my own rubric wasn't along the lines of 'Dictionary Diva'.)

And so to this book, which I love. If Alfred J Prufrock measured out his life in coffee spoons. Jon has measured his in video tape. Every event in his life is unspooled like the tape of an old and cherished VHS, and every episode rings with the echoes of a favourite film. This is a man who, while his friends were enjoying cigarettes and whisky, was always happiest with a bag of peanuts and *The Last Waltz*.

Videosyncratic is a memoir both of one man's passion and of the rise and fall of the video industry, the story of dreams fulfilled and then toppled. It's funny, unexpected, and unwaveringly honest. Above all, it's a reminder for every cinephile of the pulse-quickening, dizzying feeling of standing in a video shop and peering into the hundreds of stories it had to offer. Those were special days. Life ain't all sunshine and rainbows, as Rocky Balboa knew, but videos, and Videosyncratic, made it a far better place.

"Whenever you rent, or buy, a video, you need to be sure that the film you choose is suitable for the audience at home. To help you, there are certificates given to films which tell you broadly what the film is like. This film has been classified 15, which means it's unsuitable for anyone younger than that. It's an offence for a shop to supply a 15 film to anyone below that age, so don't ask them to break the law. 15 films may have a fairly adult theme or contain scenes of sex, violence or drugs which, while not *particularly* graphic, are unsuitable for younger teenagers. They may also contain sexual swearwords. Video certificates are there to give *you* the chance to make an *informed* choice. They allow you to have peace of mind and be entertained. Thanks for listening. Enjoy the film"

Simon Bates, 1990.

Some names have been changed
to protect the litigious.

INTRODUCTION

Do you know the film Metropolis? This is not an obscure film and never has been. It's still regularly referenced as a masterpiece and is widely regarded as being the root of cinematic science fiction and the birthplace of moving image dystopia. So, this is one of the few enduring films from early cinema which is still widely seen as relevant today. Five separate generations of my family could have seen this film.

If my great-grandfather had wanted to watch Metropolis, upon its release in 1927 he'd have had to get dressed. He'd have had to wear a suit, maybe a hat, present a basic veneer of respectability and leave the house. He'd then probably have had to head down to the Marble Arch Pavilion in London, this was where the film had it's UK premiere. There, he would have had to sit through newsreels, shorts, potentially even a line of tiller girls, all accompanied by the obnoxiously 'charming' pipes of the Wurlitzer down the front before he could see the film. A few months after it's initial release, it's unlikely he'd be able to see it again.

If my grandfather had wanted to watch Metropolis in London in the 1940s, here's what he would have had to do – He'd have to get on a bus or in a taxi or walk himself down to his local cinema. In the 1940s, his local cinema would not have been likely to be showing a film from 1927, so he'd have to jump on the underground to get down to South Bank (which didn't yet exist) to visit the National Film Theatre (which also didn't yet exist) to catch it in a programme of repertory or 'revival' cinema (which, conceptually, you've guessed it, didn't yet exist). It's unlikely that my grandfather saw Metropolis.

If my dad had wanted to watch Metropolis in London in the 1960s, here's what he would have had to do – he, indeed, probably could have, and possibly did, see it at the NFT on the South Bank – both of which now happily existed. Or he could have joined a film society at his university and petitioned for a screening which would likely have been on a heavily scratched 16mm film print. It wouldn't have been an easy thing but at least once a year, if he kept his ear to the ground, he could probably have got to see the film if he was prepared to travel around the UK a bit. If he had the money or inclination, he might have been able to have tracked down and purchased a heavily truncated 4-reel 8mm print to watch on a shitty little noisy projector at home.

If my children (who don't yet exist) wanted to watch Metropolis today, they could stay in bed and just type 'Metropolis' into google on their phone. On Youtube alone, they could pick between a ton of different versions to watch for free. And many, many versions of Metropolis now exist – different versions released in different countries with different intertitles and many, many different musical scores – some official, many not. Were they respectful children, they could pay £4.99 to instantly download the current 150 minute version on iTunes – a 2010 restoration featuring 25 minutes of previously unseen footage discovered in a 16mm negative print found in Buenos Aires two years earlier. If they had the compunction to actually get out of bed and wander downstairs, they could put on the limited edition steelbook blu-ray and also enjoy the option to see the much maligned, but actually rather magnificent 1980s version which had been scored by Giorgio Moroder featuring performances by Adam Ant, Freddie Mercury and Bonnie Tyler. It also has a running time of just 118 minutes, which will doubtless be preferable to the attention span of a generation who don't have to get on a bus and sit through an entire Tiller girl performance just to experience the magic of the moving image.

Obviously, the way my non-existent children engage with film is also the way that I largely do now. If I want to see Metropolis, although I'd draw the line at watching it on my phone, I'm only ever a couple of clicks away on the TV from it. But this is new to me. And not entirely comfortable. There was a time when the notion of being able to watch any film that had ever been released, essentially for free, instantly, wherever I was in the world, in the palm of my hand would have been my greatest dream. But I wouldn't have reckoned on the cost of such luxury. The loss of video shop culture.

My culture.

From the age of seven to the age of thirty four, video shops were a massive part of my life. In those years, I progressed from wide-eyed customer to lacklustre till jockey to frustrated manager to gleeful owner. If as a young man I had wanted to watch Metropolis – and I did – I had to rent it from a video shop.

Video shops are only a couple of years gone now and I don't see anyone missing them. Perhaps people are still too enamoured with the thrill of our instant digital gratification. Perhaps they were sick of dragging themselves across town only to deal with surly staff and late fees. Perhaps the inevitable beam of retro nostalgia has yet to fall across the humble video shop. But I think about them often and there is a boarded-up video shop in my heart which is unlikely to re-open.

This book is about video shops and the time I spent in them.

PROLOGUE

In Oxford's historic Covered Market, there's a milkshake concession – just a hole in the wall on the periphery, small enough to fit a bored looking student in a jaunty hat, a fridge and a couple of blenders. They'll crumble biscuits or Maltesers into your milkshake for you. How is that not a choking hazard? Even if they blended it for ages, wouldn't it just turn into porridge? It doesn't sound nice to me, I haven't had one.

A few miles away, in Headington, a commuter's paradise on the London Road, a short walk to the bus that will whip you into the nation's capital faster than the buses in the nation's capital whip their own residents into the nation's capital, sits the tantalisingly-named Project X. Next to a depressingly busy Starbucks, a mysterious nondescript 'art studio' whose windows have been closed-blinded for over a decade and a half. I've never seen anybody go in or come out.

Six hours, 12 minutes north of Project X, the staff of Cafe Artista presumably spend many hours chasing chairs and tables carried by the fierce Edinburgh wind down Marchmont Road and cursing the management who thought that Parisian-style pavement seating was a clever idea this far north.

The chaos goes unnoticed across the road at number 136, where Marchmont's more refined residents peruse the shelves of Cork & Cask for a cheeky Rioja or a Hebridean pale ale, it's all bright and clean in there now. But it wasn't so long ago a far more insalubrious clientele moved through this shop, spending far less money for far bleaker products.

Across town, Lucifer Lighting hides down a rarely-explored side street. A double-fronted old shop with huge windows displaying antique lighting – crystal chandeliers, Georgian candlesticks, candelabras, it looks like it's been here for decades but it's been only a few years.

Back in Oxford, on the decreasingly hip and diverse Cowley Road, there's a Sainsbury's Local. It's not hard to miss, 2 minutes from the big Tesco and round the corner from the other Sainsbury's Local. You know, the one by the branch of Subway which is down the street from the other branch of Subway. It's right by the KFC. That KFC that's opposite the Chicken Cottage right by the Nando's. You can't miss it. I haven't been to that Sainsbury's Local. I don't spend a lot of time on Cowley Road any more. I used to. I spent some of the best years of my life there. Diagonally opposite the Sainsbury's Local, there's a big independent record shop. The last of its kind in Oxford. No more record shops. It wasn't a record shop then, though. And these days, when the flour and eggs are swept from Oxford's streets following that graduation ceremony, there's not a student left on the Cowley Road who would remember what was there before it or how it was linked to a posh yet funky restored furniture shop 3 miles away.

As a man who hates poetry, I've always found something deeply poetic – in a positive sense – about empty old shops. A time-worn sign above the door, junk mail piled up so high behind it that an estate agent would have a hard time getting in. Dusty old shelves, sun-faded posters. There's a story to each of them of long-spent dreams and underpaid mundane routine but they're places where people met and talked and interacted for a fixed period of time before scattering off around the world, paths never to cross again. The rusty signs, the peeling paint and the kebab-grease smeared windows at least serve as a memorial to what once happened there. Regeneration is inevitable, important and increasingly sad as you get older and see your world pass into the hands of the next generation.

You know this is a book about video shops so you probably connected the dots paragraphs ago. Yes, these places were all video shops. They were the video shops of my life.

Video shops, remember them? They were everywhere for a while. It's the only industry I can think of which has come and gone in my lifetime. I haven't even seen a gutted shell of a Blockbuster for a year or two. We don't consume films like that anymore. We download them or we select them from menus on our TV screens. We drop them into our basket in supermarkets or we buy them cheap from Amazon. Can you imagine walking across town on a Saturday night with a couple of mates and spending an hour walking around a shop looking at covers of things you will borrow for a few hours and then forget to bring back the next day? It seems archaic now, even to me. And my life was video shops. From the beginning to the end (of the industry, not my life. This is a book, not a protracted suicide note).

I went to the London Film Festival last year, I had tickets for the UK premiere of Christopher Guest's new film Mascots. It was on Netflix two days later. For a good few years there, between the cinema release and the television debut, the video shop was pretty much your only chance to see a film at all. But more than that, the video shop was a strange and wonderful place. A place you went only for a treat. A place filled with the extreme peaks and valleys of culture – Jean Luc Godard and Adam Sandler were only ever a shelf or two apart. It was a place staffed and frequented by every type of freak imaginable. A place where people went to chat and argue and learn and offer perspective.

I was there, right in the thick of it, from the joyous birth of the industry to its phlegmy death rattle.

Video shops made me the man I am today.

Whether that's a good or a bad thing, I couldn't possibly say.

CHAPTER 1

ELECTRIC DREAMS
1983 – 1985

This story begins in the first week of June, 1983. I was seven and I remember it with the clarity of a 34 year old VHS tape. In other words, it's fuzzy but I think I can just about make out the essentials. I remember it because it was the first time two monumentally exciting things happened in the space of a week. There wasn't a lot of monumentally exciting stuff for a seven year old in the suburbs of Oxford in the early eighties.

The first thing that happened that week was the cinema release of Return of The Jedi. Like every other thirty-something man who doesn't care for football, I don't remember life without Star Wars. It was always there. My life was Star Wars figures, annuals, scrapbooks, toothbrushes and thermos flasks but I'd never seen a Star Wars film in the cinema. I'd been way too young to see the first one there and Empire came out when I was 4 and my dad, despite being a huge Star Wars fan hadn't taken me to see it. This would be the first time I was old enough to understand one in the cinema. Old enough but not intelligent enough. Didn't have a clue what was going on, but I loved it. So, yeah, that was monumental. But perhaps even more monumental, for a family with a couple of film nuts in it was what happened later that week.

My dad had a rare midweek day off and had put it to good use. He picked my big sister and I up from school, deposited us in the living room and asked 'what's different in here?' My sister immediately squealed with joy but my parents swiftly told her to not say anything until I'd figured it out. Unfortunately for them, they were depending on an alertness and awareness of surroundings that eludes me to this day. It was a long wait which ended only when my father twisted my body towards the TV and pointed my head to the big grey slab sat on the new TV stand, that I also hadn't noticed, beneath it.

And there it was, the Ferguson Videostar. The only person I knew who had a Video

Cassette Recorder at home was Paul Sanders and his dad was a journalist for a video magazine. This was better than Paul Sanders' one. It didn't have that clunky, but admittedly awe-inspiring, toploading system – this one took the tape straight out of your hands once half-inserted in the sexy new 'frontloader'. 'It's a frontloader', I'd brag in the playground for the next few weeks. There were SO many exciting things about this new arrival in the Spira household, it's hard to actually know where to begin. I think a lot of people have forgotten what the world was like in pre-VCR Britain, swaddled as we are in our cosy internet blanket of downloadable content. With our bulging satellite TV nappies and our Netflix pacifiers. We are mollycoddled babies screaming out for instant cultural gratification. In the early 80s, you had to be a man. Even if you were a woman or a child. If you wanted to be entertained, you had to hunt for it. You had to wait patiently. You had to… buy magazines. The Radio Times for the BBC listings *and* the TV Times for the ITV ones. You couldn't even get your bloody *listings* in one place.

And there were only three TV channels. broadcasting for about 12 hours a day.

Nostalgia tells us that it was pure class with endless Morecambe and Wise, Leonard

Rossiter and Robin Day but I remember it being mainly darts and cartoons – neither of which I ever cared for. This box liberated a family from televisual hegemony. Not only could you record programmes to watch *whenever you felt like it* (apparently at the dawn of home video, thieves knew to target any house that still had a cathode ray glow emanating from behind the living room curtains post-National Anthem) but you could rent films on tape to watch.

Films! Like in the cinema! At the risk of definitely patronising you, can you even remember what it was like watching films back then? You could see them in the cinema for a couple of weeks and then they vanished forever. There was a window of three years before you could expect to see them appear on TV and even then it would be big films at Christmas, Bond films on bank holidays and black and white films on BBC 2 in the afternoons and that was your lot. No download, no retail websites, you couldn't even see the trailers on youtube or track the information down on the IMDB.

They just vanished into the ether.

Every year an increasingly grumpy man called Leslie Halliwell released a book of all the films he'd ever seen and that was about as comprehensive as it got. These were epitaphs for films you were unlikely to happen across ever again. Films just disappeared.

But not anymore.

Now you could hire them and watch them in your own house. A mind blowing cultural revolution. We were promised that Dad would join a 'Video Library', for that is what they were then called, and rent our first film that very Sunday. There was still plenty to be excited about before then. Not least our first ever remote control. Dad had generously waited to test this until we were all assembled and it was good. We sat on the sofa and whooped as he pressed a button and magically the machine two feet away whirred into life. 'Let's see what the range is' he suggested through furrowed brow. We stood behind the sofa, it still worked. We backed into the open dining room behind it – still worked. Through the french doors and into the garden – it STILL worked. Satisfied with its range capabilities, father handed remote control to son as Michaelangelo's God handed life to Adam. Son pointed remote control at sister and frantically pressed buttons to try to zap her. Father took remote control back and told son that it was dangerous and he could have given his sister cancer. Son fostered lifelong mistrust of anything wireless.

I would say that that week dragged on but it didn't, the novelty of watching news broadcasts from days earlier and the mighty distraction of Return of the Jedi with the promise of ewok action figures ("Do you think they'll be furry, Dad?" "They'll probably just repackage unsold teddy bears") filled my mind until Sunday presented itself. Dad's first choice for family viewing couldn't have been smarter – as a household we loved the TV show 'Fame'. I liked it because that guy Bruno had curly hair. A child of simple tastes. We'd never seen the Alan Parker film the series had been based on, though – so what could be better? What my father had not – and could not – have considered, though, was that this was the era of video known retrospectively by video nerds as 'pre-cert'. Meaning the British Board of Film Classification had yet to be mandated to rate home videos. You see, it turned out that Fame, eventually to be rated 15, contained a scene, very early on, in where a girl unleashes a tirade of F-bombs. My parents froze at the first one, at the second, my mum started chanting my dad's name as he fumbled for the remote control. I didn't see the rest of that film for a good 20 years. I don't think there was even any more swearing in it than that but our first Sunday film afternoon was a resounding failure and the popcorn didn't even trouble the microwave.

This was the Spira family's first brush with home censorship and probably the first time the issue of film classification had been presented to me.

When home videos first emerged, the government saw no need to censor them or demand age classification ratings. This made sense since all of Britain's parents were responsible, nurturing people and none of its children were resourceful little buggers with a macabre fascination for gory dismemberment. What could possibly go wrong? A certain level of B-movie marketing hyperbole clashed with a hysterical Daily Mail readership spearheaded by the tireless campaigner for decency and moral media standards Mary Whitehouse and quickly the 'Video Nasty' scandal washed over the UK.

Considered by some to be an insidious evil that threatened to invade every home in the country with a malevolent agenda, Mary Whitehouse also appealed to others as the last bastion of moral decency. To me, in retrospect, it was all a bit silly. Both sides had a case to answer. The legion of industrious independent video labels that had sprung up were desperately competing for sales and the way they did this was the way showmen had for centuries – by promising the most sick, depraved and horrific sights and being sure to collect their money on admission. Generally the box art for these films was far nastier than anything contained within them, which were principally cheap and shitty drive-in movies. Obviously Whitehouse and her cronies in government weren't going to actually sit down and watch them so fought to get them banned on the basis of the distributors' own hyperbole.

Video shops were getting raided by police on a bizarre and arbitrary basis (legendarily, one retailer had his whole stock impounded for owning a copy of 'The Best Little Whorehouse in Texas' which over-eager coppers eventually found to be an inoffensive Burt Reynolds comedy which, ironically was a story concerning a business targeted on charges of indecency) and nobody really knew what was going on. The Director of Public Prosecutions eventually drew up a list of films he wished to prosecute for breaking the Obscene Publications Act. Caught up in that list were some bonafide classic films which would go on to be recognised as excellent and influential pieces of film-making – notably The Evil Dead and Shogun Assassin.

Of the 72 films on that list, 39 were eventually released uncut, 23 were released with some cuts (usually just a few seconds here and there) and only 10 remain unavailable in the UK, mostly because when classification came in, their distributors didn't bother to get them re-released. I tend not to err on the side of my fellow film geeks over the whole Video Nasty thing. I don't think it was ridiculous, I think it's rather nice that people were worried enough about what children might find themselves exposed to through this new technology that they kicked up a fuss. It's easy in retrospect to point out what cheesy fun those films were but that's done from an adult perspective, adults do have a responsibility to protect kids from things they aren't ready to see, so I certainly have no problem with classification which at least arms the parents with a broad idea of suitability. It would have been helpful that Sunday afternoon and I'd argue that film classification remains helpful to many people now.

I only once visited that first video library but the image of it is burned into my memory. It was on the outer rim of the Covered Market – a bizarre, architecturally beautiful anomaly hidden in the very centre of Oxford. It was little more than a hole cut in the wall with a man sat inside it. To the left of the hole was a window with maybe 20 video boxes displayed in a grid. Presumably the newest or most popular.

In my mind, all video rental cases in this era were from Warner Brothers. I know this to be untrue, of course, but the design of the WB boxes is, probably purely for nostalgic reasons, one of my favourite pieces of graphic design ever. A satisfyingly large box (I never really understood later on why someone deemed it necessary to package retail videos in a slightly smaller box whilst the majestic sized rental one was still in production) with a black matt paper cover slipped behind the thin layer of plastic wrapping the box. On the front of the cover, top centre was the logo – a little blue blob with three smaller white blobs (two long and diagonal, one short and diagonal) which made a little globular 'W' Then a white line cut horizontally right across the cover. Beneath this, In bold white capital letters WARNER HOME VIDEO. For some reason, the first 'A' had no left side and was run into the first 'W', also, the two 'R's didn't fully connect to themselves. Hard to explain, really – maybe pointless – but it's all of great cultural historical significance to me. Then another clean white line. Below the second white line was a large image which dominated the cover. Some of them (my favourites) would frame the film's poster image here. Others would contain a still from the film and the film's title above it in simple (could that be 'Arial'?) font. Below this would be the film's credit block and, incase you'd missed it at the top, another assertion that this was 'FROM WARNER BROS' and they put the logo there at the bottom as well, in case you'd forgotten what it looked like. The logo was also big on the top of the spine of the case and even bigger at the bottom of the back. The backs of these cases looked a bit like the backs of old opera albums my parents owned – black on white, text dense offerings which included a big section detailing 'THE CAST'. These boxes would often be lovingly finished off by the application of a metallic circular sticker on the cover proclaiming 'RRP: £89.95' the shops never removed these and my mind is always thrown immediately back to them now when I see one of those hip hop people on the street walking around in their baseball caps with that round metallic label still on so you could be in no doubt of the expense of the investment. British rental video – in so many ways, a precursor to the 'bling' culture which now engulfs us. I loved those boxes. I still do. I don't own many VHS anymore but when I came to close my own video shops 27 years later, the only VHS I rescued for my own collection were the WB big black box pre-certs which I had spent so many years tracking down. I will always cherish those.

Where was I? Yes, the Covered Market! So, to the left of the hole was the display of covers. Behind the chap at the counter, were hastily erected MDF shelves containing rows of videos ready to be rented. Back then, you paid an annual fee to be a member of a video library, a tenner a year, I believe, and also, if you were clever, paid an additional £5 insurance fee so if your machine chewed up a tape you wouldn't be saddled with a ninety quid bill. Of course, if your machine did chew up a tape, you simply respooled it, fast forwarded or rewound the tape to an unchewed point and practised a defiant yet aloof 'it played fine for us!'

Talking of fines – of which we shall undoubtedly do a fair bit in our time together, let's pause for a moment to remember the long-departed 'rewind fee'. If you didn't rewind your tape before return, the shop would levy a 20p fee on you. Within the industry, they even sold 'rewinders' – little machines that would rewind a tape at the speed of sound, testing the rigidity of the tape's bond to the spool as it slammed into finish. Rewinders became a bizarre little culture of their own, hitting a zenith in the mid-90's when you could even buy them in the shape of sports cars.

But, what a wonderful thing – an annoyance which has been cast forever into the ether – the moment where you open up the video box and realise that the tape inside *isn't rewound*. Ugh, the pain of waiting sometimes two whole minutes for the tape to rewind – in the knowledge that once it is, you'd still have to fast forward through the copyright warnings and trailers.

On the counter of the video shack sat a pile of paper. This pile was for you, the customer, a monthly updated printed list of every video they had in their inventory. As I remember it, three sheets of A4, stapled in the top left corner, double spaced, wide margined.

This was not an impressive shop. It was perfunctory, ugly even, but what it represented is almost impossible to convey in this age of everything on-demand. You could take any film you wanted home and watch it whenever you wanted. You could watch it three times in a row. And, for the first time in fucking cinema or televisual history, if you needed a wee, you could STOP the film and miss nothing. You could also pause the film, but there was a real anxiety in the early newly-developed pause function which made you feel like you were in some way inconveniencing the VCR by using it as it anxiously flickered, stretched and strained to be allowed to flow free.

So, as unimpressive as this shop was, it was genuinely magical to me. I already loved films but they were treats – a couple of times a month we'd be taken to see a film at the cinema, at the mercy of what was on and what my parents were willing to tolerate. Occasionally, but not usually outside of the festive period, a decent film would appear on TV. But now, there was a place to go which had films just sat waiting for me. I fell in love with the very concept of a video shop in a way that, just like real love, would go on to shape the entire course of my life.

Although principally intended as a way for my parents not to miss certain TV pro-grammes and a cheap alternative to family outings to the cinema, the VCR swiftly changed the dynamics of family life. Where the TV had once been an object of interest to different family members at different times of the day, drifting towards and away from it depending what was on, it was now in regular demand. Mainly, I suspect, by me – the child who could lobby for his own agenda tirelessly and vociferously even when he was unsure of what his own agenda was. The TV was no longer an object interesting for short bursts on Saturday mornings, Sunday evenings and weekday afternoons, it had the potential now to render books, socialising, family interaction and, essentially, the entire outside world totally obsolete. My parents struggled valiantly, as did those of my friends, unaware that the healthy socialising they thought they were encouraging was really just the shunting of a group of small boys around Headington to sit in front of a variety of different televisions.

The epidemic spread fast. Within a year, every family had a VCR and, presumably, the family power struggles that went with it.

Let us pause again to remember another departed icon of 80's family life – the collection of tatty-cardboard-sleeved E-180's clearly – even angrily – labelled in defiant ownership of a family member. Often modified with an instruction and warning. 'MUM'S TAPE – DO **NOT** TOUCH. I mean it' and in tiny writing it detailed what was on it along with the crossed-out names of what it had previously contained. I wish I still had my tape. There was a magic to the functional VHS tapes we all had, not the ones we kept things we cared about on, the one we used just when we needed to tape something and then tape over. The crappy timer function of the VCR, or an over-running live programme meant you'd find the last 3 minutes of a sitcom you'd wanted to see which would segue into the first bit of an odd documentary which would be wiped by a noisy wall of static into the end of a music video which you'd decided to record as it came on but the time it took to get the tape into the machine and recording meant you missed most of it, that would flicker to black then flicker up into a Christmas Special of a show you didn't really like which would be accidentally recorded over half of a film you'd wanted to see but hadn't fast forwarded past when you'd started recording the Special. Layer upon layer of video. Old trailers for long-forgotten TV movies, old adverts (my favourites being the 'Why Do Do-It-All Do It?' and Birdseye Steakhouse 'Will it Be Chips or Jacket Spuds' song-based adverts which both, interestingly (to me), featured cockney-for-hire Daniel Peacock whose career peak was screaming 'TOTHETREEEEEEEEEEES' in Robin Hood: Prince of Thieves). I'd imagine, you could tell everything you needed to know about a person by perusing their old E-180.

Dad was, and remains, a huge film fan and films were, and still are, something that bond us and provides part of the foundation of our relationship. He would tape films he thought I should see if they were on late at night and leave the tapes on top of the telly for me. I became obsessed very quickly. Seeing Close Encounters of the Third Kind was a huge moment for me. I think it was the first non-kids film that I connected with. It still had the magic of spaceships and aliens but it felt grown up too. The scene where the scientists nick someone's globe from their office and roll it down the corridor to work out where the aliens would land was this perfect dichotomy of something very grown up yet infused with a childish glee. Of course, that is pure Spielberg and he quickly became my favourite director.

As my film obsession grew, my parents had to tackle the issue of censorship – what could I handle? What was suitable? Would I ever shut up if they said no? They settled on a progressive yet eccentric policy. In regards to more grown-up films; I could watch whatever I wanted, on the proviso that Dad would watch it first to ascertain what was and wasn't suitable and then would watch the film with me, jumping up to block the screen and fast forward during the unsuitable bits. This must have been exhausting and infuriating to him. It was baffling and frustrating to me. What a trooper, though. He never just refused to let me watch anything. Years later, I'd watch these films again, thinking I knew them and then be outraged by a moment of unexpected violence or shagging. Similar things were happening across Headington in the homes of my friends (although I suspect their parents just said 'yes' or 'no' rather than the more complicated 'jump up and smother the screen with your belly' form of censorship my dad employed). But not quite similar enough. We quickly realised that different parents had different thresholds and different foibles about different films. This sparked off a network of small boys trotting through the suburbs, finding homes prepared to screen films contraband to their own. At Paul's house, I saw the scene in You Only Live Twice where the girl gets eaten by piranhas – a scene so lacking in graphic violence that I probably wouldn't have actually understood what had happened to her if Dad hadn't told me why he was jumping-and-blocking. Richard Jones came to my house specifically to watch Raiders of the Lost Ark, which had been banned in his due to the bit where the Nazis faces melt off. I really have no idea why face-melting was deemed acceptable in my house. Perhaps being a Jewish household the melting, specifically, of Nazis was deemed in some way actually quite appropriate.

I spent a lot of time when I was 8 years old thinking about videos and that little video shop in the Covered Market. Flicking through each month's hand-typed list of their current stock. My dad really indulged my burgeoning film obsession and suffered at the hands of my preferences, as parents will, sitting through endless hours of crap. He only once put his foot down, though. It wouldn't be until I was in my thirties that I would finally see the film I begged and begged him to let me watch as an 8 year old. Cannon and Ball's The Boys in Blue. Good call, Dad.

I'm sure any amateur psychologists out there could explain it in a patronising and backhanded manner but… the die was cast. By 8, my life was irrevocably dedicated to film. Dedicated to video. Dedicated to video shops. They were my earliest focus for my excitement and passion and intrigue and wonder. The thrill of standing in a shop full of films has never left me, has never even dulled. To this day, I find it hard to visit London without popping in to the BFI shop on South Bank, where that dizzy sense of being surrounded by thousands of windows into thousands of worlds and stories still quickens my pulse. Carefully choosing one, taking it to the counter, having a chat with whoever's behind the counter – I know them all – and then putting it in my bag, bringing it all the way home, watching it and then shuffling my shelves around to accommodate it in its correct alphabetical position in my own collection of all the films that have mattered to me since I was a small child. There's security there. The feeling many get from eating beans on toast is on my shelf in the form of a Silent Running (please don't confuse that with Cool Runnings) Blu-Ray. That old tattered teddy bear so many have clung on to is, to me, seeing Blue Peter presenter Peter Duncan die horribly in Flash Gordon. Some people go to the football on a Saturday to relive the magic of their youths, I'll wait until after 11pm and slide along to my local indie cinema for an old 35mm print screening of Aliens. A film I already own on Blu-Ray, DVD and VHS. Some guys might wind down after a punishing week with a cigar and a bottle of whiskey. I'm fine with some peanuts and The Last Waltz.

When you love film, it doesn't just transport you to another world. It transports you back to where you were, who you were, when you first saw it. Hours sat with friends now missing or lost. Sunday afternoons on the sofa with your family. Youthful fumblings with girls in cinemas. Heated debates with friends in pubs which no longer exist. You remember the awe of your first Kubrick film. The delight of your first Ghibli experience. The uncontrollable giggles of your first Monty Python flick. I suppose to some people, these are just the disposable moments used as distraction from a plodding life. To others of us, they are touchstones, full of art, magic and warmth. And that's why, despite the outward appearance of many of those shabby little filth-pits, the video shop will always be my favourite place.

CHAPTER 2

AMERICAN BEAUTY AND VIDEO NASTIES

1985 – 1987

As 1985 rolled in, we were a family on the move. We said goodbye to the 1960's suburban new-build I'd grown up in and hello to a 1980's suburban new-build 10 minutes round the corner. It was a cul-de-sac of double-garaged family homes in a better-to-do area. Gone would be the gangs of teenage boys running across the back wall of the garden. Gone would be the psychotic family across the road who would scream at each other every night until once a month the police would come to arrest the father. Gone would be the noisy parties and occasional brawls and all of the colour provided by living so close to a couple of estates.

Along with the new house came a new school. Now 9 years old, it was time for Middle School (Oxford, until fairly recently, didn't do the Primary/Secondary thing, we did First/Middle/Upper) and with that came a certain relaxing of parental stand-ards. The Jump-and-block palaver ended badly when Dad acquiesced to my demand of watching David Lynch's Dune. Uncertain of judging what might actually damage me and incapable of understanding – let alone conveying – the story, he flopped back on to the sofa, said 'Just tell me if it gets too much' and fell asleep.

By this time, everybody had a video recorder and the place to be on a Saturday night was Bogart's. A cultural shift had taken place in the UK and on Saturday nights, you either went out or you stayed in with a video. Or you went out to someone else's house who'd rented a video. It was really all about renting videos in the suburbs and if you lived in Headington and weren't going out, you'd head to Bogart's. Bogart's Video. Our first membership card. Sepia, laminated, on one side our name and membership number, which in my head is number 57, but how would I remember that? On the other, the logo – an art-deco style film noir man in a hat with BOGART'S written in that half-blocky-half-fine Al Capone style writing. One of the more flamboyant of the 5 fonts available in the 80's. Like every new and exciting shop in the 80's, Bogart's rocked a suspended polystyrene ceiling, lush carpet tiles and a neon sign. Hollywood. It was a big shop and you could really browse. I don't think they had as many as a thousand videos but it seemed like a lot. Dad would take me and my sister down there after dinner and we'd spend a good amount of time perusing and choosing. These were still somewhat in the days where video itself was a novelty so it was more about the quality of the film than how recently it was released but, once we'd exhausted film history, we tore into the new releases too.

The clever families would phone up on a Monday and book the film they wanted to see for the Saturday. This meant you could eat a leisurely dinner and swan in of a Saturday evening, waiting your place in line as everyone in front of you asked for exactly the same film and got rebuffed as it was sat behind the counter with your name on it. My family were clever. In video rental terms, at least.

My mum was clever enough to realise Bogart's potential as not just a video shop, but a creche facility whilst she got the shopping done, knowing that I'd happily spend hours entranced merely by cover art. And I was. I think I was a very sheltered child and was constantly surprised by the world's ever expanding capability for nastiness. My first school had been a Church of England – endlessly confusing for this little Jew – Middle England idyll. It was very jolly and small and middle class. There was basically no ethnic diversity. I was friends with the only boy of Asian origin in the school, where I think I'm right in saying he received no racism, just an occasional air of exotic awe. It was all very… nice.

Middle school was a very different affair. It was situated on the wrong side of the roundabout, right on the gateway to a pretty notorious area of pre-fab social housing. The kids we were mixed in with were by no means bad kids – although some of them would go that way eventually – they had just had a kind of rougher start and their parents were less concerned with preserving the notion of innocence. These were the kids who had seen the video nasties. In fact, I don't think they'd seen much else. A conversation about films in this environment would inevitably lead into the relating of stories of a depraved nature which I could barely fathom.

One boy spent a lunchtime detailing to me the film 'I Spit On Your Grave', the notion of the things he described tortured my mind. Why would people do that? Why would people film that? Why would people watch that? I've still never seen that film, it's taken on mythical proportions in my mind but the curiosity has never got the better of me, knowing what I do about it. I still can't see why anybody would choose to watch it. Even the title disturbed me deeply. The title actually shocked and troubled me. *Spitting*. On someone's *grave*. Disgraceful. As I got older and my film knowledge deepened, I found out that the lead actress was Buster Keaton's granddaughter Camille and that just made it all the worse. Imagining a heart-broken, pale-faced Buster watching her cutting off willies left, right and centre, a single tear rolling down his cheek. Anyway, this is what 9 year old boys in Barton were watching.

In the back corner of Bogart's was the horror section. I felt an uneasy attraction to it. I wouldn't stand in front of it. I'd stand near it, facing away, and steal the occasional glance. There are now coffee table books of VHS horror cover art of the 80's – and rightly so – the mixture of grotesque and pantomime was captivating but dirty and wrong and anxiety-fuelling. It was invigor-ating to steal a glance and then cleansing to scuttle back to the safety of the comedy or sci-fi sections and the wholesome optimism they offered.

I was still very young when I learned to understand the value of film, the point of it. Like music, films are there to balance you out. To shake you up. They're uppers and downers and adventures and roller coasters. They can be quiet and warm or loud and cold. They can energise or calm. They transport you to places you wouldn't or couldn't go and illustrate the whole spectrum of human experience. How could that not be something people could get obsessive about or addicted to?

My father loved film and yet he sold linen. This baffled me. Why would somebody devote their life to the sale of linen? Admittedly, he was the manager of all the shops he worked in, but why linen? When given the choice of things to do, why had he picked linen? It would be a good decade before I'd come to understand how adult life works and that a life in linen had been chosen in no small part so that his kids could have the luxury of choice in their own futures. But I saw other people's dads doing more interesting things and quickly decided they were the ones to follow. That year, I made good friends with a kid called Simon whose dad, Mr Edwards, owned a couple of video shops called 'Movies' in parts of town we never visited – Jericho and Cowley Road. Although I rarely saw the shops, I couldn't believe how lucky Simon was. I guess occasionally my Dad's career delivered – I always had *duvet covers* of the latest films. But Simon's dad seemed to bring home an endless bounty of posters, badges, stickers and, of course, films. He drove a flash car, too. A Jag or something. He'd drive us to cubs at 80mph to make us all scream. I thought he was brilliant and I wanted to be like him. On one car journey, I told him that when I was grown up, I wanted to own my own video shop. 'You should!' he smirked, before fixing me an icy glare and said 'But don't even think about doing it in Oxford'.

These early video shops were the province of the entrepreneur. In the 80's, long before the internet would ravage high street retail and when supermarkets just sold food, not so many people thought globally, or even nationally. You could make a good living locally if you served a need for the community and didn't have too much competition. Video shops were a completely new business idea. A new business model, utterly modern and relevant to that moment in history. Each one was completely different. This was the era before vac-formed plastic walling, displaying cases at jaunty angles, became de rigueur, nobody really knew what a video shop looked like, so they just did their own thing. Every video shop had its own incredibly distinct personality, its own magic. Some were skeezy, smokey porn and horror holes, others were rainbow-coloured celebrations of Hollywood. Wherever we visited in the world, it was the video shop I wanted to see.

They were springing up all over the place and Bogarts had competition now. Directly across the road, next to the 'Not The Moulin Rouge' Cinema, with it's enormous can-can dancer legs kicking out of the crazy pink facade, sat Oxford Video. A stoic and curiously understated video shop. Video library. It felt more like a library. It was much smaller than Bogarts and had, to my nine-year-old mind, rubbish films in comparison – mainly black and white or foreign language. Ugh. Staffed by a sour-faced middle-aged woman, whom I assume owned it, I really couldn't see the point in it. Mum and Dad would rent films from there occasionally but my memories of it at that point were mainly having my face pressed up against the window looking out over the road to Bogarts.

I suppose the thing that was most attractive about Bogarts was how incredibly American it felt. To a little British boy in the mid-80's, there was little more enticing than America.

Life almost felt like a pursuit of all things American. Oh, America. The land of consumerist, glitzy promise. I had yet to visit the place yet felt like some kind of castaway from its shores. You got glimpses of it on TV, kids there seemed a lot happier. They all lived in converted attic rooms and ate chocolate bars far more exciting than our Topics and Walnut Whips. They drank root beer and cherry soda whilst we made do with Dandelion & Burdock and Top Deck Shandy. They ate pizza instead of chips. They didn't even call chips chips, they called them fries and they called crisps chips. Which was all very exciting. Anything American was good. Coke, Pepsi, Marvel Comics… I think that was about all we got. I yearned to visit America. My parents best friends lived there and occasionally would sent packages with comics and little toys for us. I got my first Transformer – Bumblebee (back when he was a VW beetle, not a flashy sportscar, I'll have you know) – months before they appeared on these shores and consumed a post-Star Wars generation of developing geeks. I told anyone who would listen that I wanted to live in America. America apparently heard me.

It started tentatively. Headington's first dose of Americana was the rather quaintly named 'The American Pizza Company' which appeared in a puff of smoke and changed all of our lives. Pizza up to that point was what is now charmingly known as 'Cheese and Tomato flavoured pizzas' and can now only be found in the freezer sections of the lower-brow supermarkets. A splodge of stodge, about the size of a CD with a wipe of tomato (flavoured) sauce and sprinkling of questionable cheese. This would be served with baked beans and crinkle-cut chips as a huge 'fuck you' to the notion of low-carb. This new 'American' pizza was something else. Huge, flat, with crazy choices of toppings. Family treats and friends' birthday parties became merely chances to create the most unholy food combinations. My favourite was one of the delicacies the establishment themselves had created and named – the Miami Vice. A pizza with extra mozzarella, green peppers, onion, pineapple and tuna. Fruit, fish, dairy, bread and tomato sauce – who'd have ever thought those things would go together? They didn't. I just enjoyed the look of amused disgust on my dad's face as I ate it.

Although my school was Church of England, I had been excused going to actual church services after it had been established that, not unlike Damian Thorne, I had a tendency to cry, scream and thrash about on holy ground. It had been a considered move of my folks to enrol their Jewish kids into secular schools to help us integrate, it worked well for my sister, but made no sense to me. Having been told at home in no uncertain terms that Jesus was a false prophet, being carted into a church and expected to venerate the guy caused me anxiety, well, psychosis, really. So, church days were half-days for me. My mum picked me up from school one lunchtime, as my classmates filed off to pray, and we walked into Headington to pick up some shopping. As we came to the corner of London Road and Windmill Road, I froze. Someone had… someone had put… someone had put a 7-Eleven in my village! An actual, real, 7-Eleven. Like in America! Like in all American films. A bloody 7-Eleven! It was like a dream or something. We went inside and it was… American. In the pride of place was the giant self-service SLURPEE machine, churning the frozen chemical slop of the gods. I had my first ever Slurpee. I had my first ever brain-freeze.

The Americanization of our shores had begun and, ironically, Bogarts was to be the first victim of it. One day, it was gone. Replaced by a gleaming new video shop, a branch of the UK's first national chain, branded in garish yellow with red lettering – RITZ had arrived.

CHAPTER 3

THE ENORMOUS CARDBOARD JAMES BELUSHI

1987 – 1991

I liked Ritz. Mainly for the reason we like things today – instant gratification. Ritz bought more copies of each new film than anybody else. Twenty or thirty copies.

It was a bit more corporate, but we all loved that then. The dawn of plastic vac-formed walling had arrived and videos would never again be displayed side-on or face-on. Oh no, these were the days of diagonal exhibition. How could one truly judge a film on its spine or cover alone?

There were two eighties comedies I remember renting out endless times; a film my friend Darren had discovered called Moving Violations, of which I remember nothing except the fact it was a comedy about a driving school which had us crying with laughter. The other was a film that I spent most of 1987 obsessing over called 'Walk Like a Man'.

'87 marked the year the Spira family finally hit America. I practically hyperventilated when my folks sat us down to tell us, and they planned the perfect trip. 3 weeks, coast-to-coast. We started in New York and ended in L.A. Where, of course we visited Disneyland and Universal Studios (where Dad in pursuit of what turned out to be an indecipherable photo performed the best jump-and-block of his career denying me my only chance to see Jaws lunge at me in person. This is still a sore point between us). I was so wired and overstimulated that I barely slept throughout the whole trip. We had the full experience, we binged on Reese's Pieces, went square-eyed to MTV, discovered breakfast pancakes, generally over-consumed our way from sea to shining sea. There were just two opportunities for cinema visits and on both of them, Dad somewhat-unbegrudgingly acquiesced to my choices. We both marvelled at the concept of people eating actual buckets of popcorn drenched in melted butter. We shared a 'small' popcorn, which was a good 50% bigger than what constituted a large in the UK. The first film I chose for us was The Garbage Pail Kids Movie. This has since become enduring proof of what a generous, self-sacrificing man my father was. The Garbage Pail Kids – a collectable sticker line of vile satirical renderings of Cabbage Patch Dolls (interestingly, GPK were the work of Maus author Art Spiegelman) was not an obvious candidate for film adaptation. The film itself, an interminable hour and a half of midgets in horrible animatronic suits being watched over by an avuncular Anthony Newley – why Anthony Newley???? – was, obviously a massive piece of shit. I didn't realise that. I think Dad did. It's the only time I've ever see him actually sulk. Despite that experience, he also let me choose the second film and I opted for the equally abysmal Walk Like a Man.

Telling the story of Bobo, an heir to millions who got lost in the forest as a baby and raised by wolves, I realise now that Walk Like a Man was, in fact, the not-entirely-inevitable slapstick remake of the previous year's Greystoke: The Legend of Tarzan. Bobo was played by Howie Mandel, now best known as the host of the American version of Deal or No Deal. Before I get lost in a sinister daydream imagining a loin-clothed Noel Edmonds dashing about the streets of Edwardian London, I should make it clear that it was not a good film. Anyway, those days were behind me.

I was 11, my sister Janis was 14, so my parents finally reclaimed their social lives and left us to our own devices on Saturday nights with money for an 'American' pizza and a video, on the proviso that Janis was in charge. Jan had little tolerance for the films I wanted to watch, but that was OK because I was fascinated by the films she picked. They weren't films I probably would have chosen myself but I fell in love with them. The films of John Hughes and The Brat Pack. The films that I had loved up to that point took place in other galaxies, time periods or realms of reality. All I cared about were creatures and ghosts, occasionally intrigued by the glimpses of incidental Americana – what cereal the characters were eating, how old they had to be before they could drive, the fact that they all really did seem to have attic bedrooms.

The first Hughes film we watched was The Breakfast Club and it captivated me. So *this* is what kids my sister's age got up to. This is what being a teenager was like, you got to be nasty and sarcastic and tell the teachers to fuck off. You got to smoke and dance and, as demonstrated by Emilio Estevez, shout so loud as to smash a glass window (I still don't quite understand what he does there). During that period, we watched all of the classic Hughes films – Pretty in Pink, Sixteen Candles, Some Kind of Wonderful (my favourite of them), then the comedies – Weird Science, Ferris Bueller and all of the subsequent brat pack spin-off films St Elmo's Fire (which I just didn't understand at all with its yuppie politics and vested Rob Lowe sax solos) right through to Mannequin and the risible Men at Work, which I imagine was the most painful premiere Martin Sheen ever had to attend.

The Breakfast Club stuck with me in particular, though and I went on to spend most of my teens trying in some way to channel Judd Nelson despite being English, overweight and middle class. Basically, I wore a denim jacket and Doc Martens. I still wear Docs, maybe that's my concession to Judd who went on to betray me by becoming a loathsome right-winger in St Elmo's Fire. Since then he's popped up in the occasional supporting role and still to this day lets down my inner teenager by acting generally like some kind of buffoon or wimp. A couple of months ago, I was watching a terrible straight-to-DVD film called The Bigfoot Wars (oh, come on – how could anybody resist that title? Wars! With Bigfeets!!! – of course, there was no war, barely a skirmish, and there were, like, three Bigfeet at most) and suddenly there was Judd, in a brief cameo as a doctor. "Oh, Bloody HELL, Judd!" I shouted at the screen. "You're better than this!!!!" Perhaps I'm wrong.

As fanciful as they were in their depiction of 'average teenage life', the Hughes movies nudged me out of my more childish tendencies and, although I burned a torch for blockbuster movies pretty much up until the first X-Men movie (which I saw with a friend who was coming down from a cocaine binge, dribbling nacho cheese and occasionally croaking 'cool', for some reason that was the straw that broke my event movie back) I was now interested in seeing a broader spectrum of movies.

By '88 my folks had given up on any notion of regulating my viewing. That dream had passed after I won The Battle of Jaws 2 (that's the battle to watch Jaws 2, not the second battle to watch Jaws, which I finally watched mere days after the battle for Jaws 2 had been won) and my mother threw her hands up and said 'Fine, watch what you want, don't come crying to us if you have nightmares'. I was pretty good at self-regulating and never had much time for slasher movies, anyway. When I finally developed an interest in horror films a couple of years later, I was more prone to testing my boundaries with the Cronenbergs and Clive Barker films, the slightly more highbrow stuff, which fascinated me but didn't seem nearly as disturbing as the Peter Greenaway films I was seeing late at night on Channel 4.

I spent a lot of time in Ritz. I idolised the staff who were all cool, rocker-looking guys who bragged about getting to see the films ages before they were released. These were the coolest people in my world. They were nominally adults but they didn't act like any grown-ups I knew. They just watched movies and smoked fags and insulted each other and all of their customers. They also had dibs on all of the posters. I got wise to this and managed to ingratiate myself with them to the point that any posters they didn't want went straight to me. I wasn't even selective, a film poster was a film poster, the walls, eventually even the ceiling of my bedroom were plastered with them. I had a similar wheeze going on at the cinema in town, although they charged me £1 a poster – it was well worth it, though, because those posters were massive. The majesty of the British Quad Cinema Poster. 30 x 40 inches, landscape format. Nowhere else in the world are posters this size and shape manufactured but to this day, Britain holds out against the eternal threat of the portrait format American one-sheet poster (27x40 inches). Video posters were A2 and printed on shittier paper, but that was fine. A poster was a poster and I loved them. I was woken up most nights by a quad poster breaking free its blu-tack grip and landing softly on my head. I blamed my mother for not allowing me to use pins or staples, her steadfast response remained 'why do you need posters on your *ceiling*?'

One day, I thought it was time to go for broke. The posters were great but what I truly wanted, the thing that would make my heart sing, the object of my youthful lust and wonder, were the standees. The enormous cardboard cut-outs. My bedroom was barely big enough to fit a single bed and a desk but I didn't care. I'd make it work. They told me to write my name and phone number on the back of any standees I wanted and they'd call me the day they were getting rid of them. I struck gold with my first haul – a Schwarzenegger standee! Unfortunately it was for his not-entirely-classic buddy film Red Heat. I schlepped it a mile and a half home. It was six foot tall and four foot wide. I hadn't even seen the film. I didn't care. Once in my bedroom, it blocked out the window, denying me any natural light and, as anyone familiar with the film has probably already worked out, meant that alongside Arnie, I had an enormous cardboard Jim Belushi in my bedroom. Which is weird. Things got progressively weirder as it became apparent that I was unable to say no to ANY standee I was offered, I ended up with a Cry Freedom one, a massive Arachnophobia one (bizarrely, the marketing for the UK video release of Arachnophobia used the same brilliant artwork as its cinema release but removed the spider, rendering it a pointless painting of a town bathed in moonlight. Despite knowing and hating this, I still allowed this 7ft x 4ft piece of cardboard dominate my living space) and eventually a really enormous one for a Gene Hackman film called BAT 21 which, to this day, I have never seen. The madness mercifully stopped after I'd let slip to a couple of guys at school how I was getting them. Every standee in the shop ended up a battle with names and numbers surreptitiously crossed out and usurped. It all came to a head in an ugly battle over the Police Academy V (that'd be Assignment Miami Beach) standee. The Ritz staff decided that enough was enough and called time on free standees. It was for the best. What I lost in free cardboard, I regained in daylight.

I was a Ritz guy through and through. I'd collect and pore over their glossy in-house magazine and would write letters to head office if I couldn't get the posters I wanted –

usually ignored, but once struck gold when they send me a whole goodie bag of Spaceballs paraphernalia. Eventually, I struck gold and had a drawing I'd done of E.T. Published in their letters page. My friends at school mocked me mercilessly for this, but I got 8 free rentals so they quickly shut up, especially when I used one of them to procure a copy of Three Men and a Baby so we could see if the rumour that there was a visible ghost of a small Victorian boy in the film was true. It was. Although, eventually it was explained that it was a piece of set dressing – a small cardboard cut-out of Ted Danson in a top hat, partially obscured by curtains.

I wouldn't say that at this point in my life my tastes were completely mainstream, I'd say that they were completely egalitarian. If it was a film, I liked it. There were films that bored me or didn't interest me but I still had a certain respect for them regardless. I can't remember actively disliking any film until I was 16. By this point, my friend Tom and I were going to the cinema two or three times a week, seeing pretty much anything that came out. That summer, we went to see Universal Soldier which sounded like a dream come true – Van Damme and Ivan Drago/He-Man in an action film together. It was as confusing and unexpected as anything that had passed before in puberty.

It came on very suddenly and I really didn't understand this emotion. I was in the cinema – good. I had my enormous bag of Butterkist – good. Massive cup of Tango – good. There was a film showing – Good. So, what was this creeping feeling, this new inexplicable emotion that was infiltrating every fibre of my being. It was a rush to the head and an explosion in my brain. I suddenly realised that this film was PANTS. The realisation was amazingly freeing and I felt giddy with the excitement of my distaste for this film. I started laughing loudly at how awful it was. I was like Robert De Niro in that scene in Cape Fear, but more precocious and less sinister. This did not impress Tom who was already starting to realise what an arrogant and obnoxious young man I was turning into thanks to an incident the week prior in which I scathingly analysed his CD collection. He'd thrown me out of his house. As he would go on to make a habit of once his zero tolerance campaign to my brattishness was launched. Now he warned me that he wouldn't be giving me a lift home if I didn't immediately shut up.

I would never see Van Damme or Lundgren on a cinema screen again. I had developed taste.

This process had actually started stealthily a couple of years earlier. The corporate glitz of

Ritz didn't last long for me as I became increasingly aware that there weren't many films there that I was clamouring for. They had all of the new stuff but not the films I was reading about or the back catalogue of the film-makers I was growing to love. For those films, I was going to Oxford Video.

Mum had long abandoned her plan to use school holidays for Janis and I to do extra education. She had pretty much realised that the only way to get me, in particular, out of her hair was to rent me a stack of videos and let me work through them, face pressed to the screen. The one stipulation she put down was that if I was going to be watching films all day, they were going to be classics. I worked through all of the Hitchcock films, Chaplin, The Marx Brothers, some Orson Welles, some Hammer films and Universal monster movies. It was all good to me. The sour-faced old girl behind the counter even seemed to be warming to me and my enthusiasm. The films I had enthused about up to this point in her shop must have made her despise me. I still had a palpable taste for crap, though.

Oxford Video had moved from across the road. The guy who had owned the Moulin Rouge cinema had stuck a thirty foot fibreglass shark into the roof of his house on the same street. The council had demanded he remove it but he refused. In a seemingly revenge attack, the council tore his cinema down along with all of the other buildings on that corner and left it an unused wasteland for the best part of a decade. The only similarly sized unit in Headington for Oxford Video to relocate to was the one next to Ritz. Actually, literally, next door to it. A quarter of the size. It was like a little annexe, with more films, but far less actual tapes. They couldn't beat Ritz on multiple copies of new releases but offered a far wider selection, crammed into a far, far narrower space. It was essentially a corridor, with a couple of ante chambers which one would get trapped in if more than 5 people were in the shop. On a Friday or Saturday night, the journey from the counter to the front door was like being born.

When I turned 13, I was finally allowed a TV in my room, swiftly followed by the trusty Ferguson Videostar, once my parents upgraded to one of a long line of VCRs that would last about a year and a half before dying with a whimper. Budget-priced sell-thru (why they opted for this spelling of 'through', I will never understand) videos had arrived a couple of years earlier. A company called CIC was releasing classic movies from Universal and Paramount in smaller-sized stripy patterned boxes for the affordable price of £9.99 which, unfathomably, is still basically the price for a new-release DVD, thirty years later. That weekend, I bought my first three videos. Ferris Bueller's Day Off, The Lost Boys and Bigfoot and the Hendersons. This pretty much shows you where my mind was. Taking tentative steps towards the cool and scary but with a solid foot back in childish pleasures. That said, what a film. Bigfoot and the Hendersons. Beautifully acted – Lithgow and Suchet are amazing in it – and the creature himself. Rick Baker, the make-up maestro behind American Werewolf (they created an Oscar specifically for his work on that) just excelled himself in creating an animatronic creature which incorporated the actor Kevin Peter Hall's own eyes... I'm geeking, excuse me. These were the first films I owned and their bright, colourful cases put my stacks of scrappy E-180s to shame. I liked the look of a video spine on a shelf and resolved to fill a few shelves this way. Another obsession was being born.

I look back at this as a golden age of video shops. You could see the divide all around the country with the Ritz's and other smaller chains cropping up pimping the new releases whilst the smaller indie stores prided themselves on their back catalogue. By about 1990, it felt that most back catalogue films that were going to ever make it out had done. Most tapes wore out or got stolen eventually and weren't often replaced, so it felt to me like it was really just those few years where you really could get any film from a video shop. There was a vast selection but in these pre-internet days, little curation. There was no IMDB, there was no way to find out about a film or get great recommendations apart from the all-too-perfunctory film guide books and Empire Magazine which, along with current reviews, sometimes published great retrospective articles. If you were lucky, someone behind the counter knew their films and could advise you but Oxford Video wasn't really that type of place. Me and my friends were on our own, but that was fine. That made my film education all the more rounded. Along with the classic touchstone films like the John Carpenters, Cronenbergs and Woody Allens, I was seeing odd little classics that nobody talks about but taught me so much. The film Audrey Rose, which I haven't ever seen since but left a massive impression, felt like a horror movie but was intelligent and free of any convention of the genre. Midnight Run, a De Niro film which rarely gets discussed but was incredibly funny whilst not having any of the trappings of any comedy film I'd ever seen. An American Werewolf in London – which has unexpectedly but hearteningly had a huge critical resurgence in the last few years – managed to be both a true horror film and a true comedy. That film still blows my mind in the absolute perfection of its craft.

There's a golden moment in any alert teenager's life where the world suddenly opens up for them. The floodgates of music, literature, art and history past just present themselves for the taking. For me, it was a pop culture landslide. The Clash, The Cure, The Ramones, Elvis Costello, The Stones, The Pistols, Springsteen all flooded through my stereo along with the indie-schmindie crap of the moment which would prove far more transitory.

The breadth of film seemed like an ever expanding universe. On TV, director Alex Cox was hosting Moviedrome – a weekly double bill of cult films which he talked about in a fascinating and intelligent manner. The door was thrown open and I realised that film didn't have to divide into classic cinema or popcorn blockbusters, there were strange little independent films and zany arthouse stuff and films from countries other than North America. In one weekend, my friends and I watched The Shining and Withnail & I.

I didn't even believe films like this existed. The Shining *seemed* like a horror film but... where was the baddie? Only one person even really died. Withnail & I was the first time I really clocked that a film didn't have to be American and star ex-members of the Saturday Night Live cast to make me cry with laughter. Late night on TV, I saw a film called Mother, Jugs & Speed starring Bill Cosby – America's favourite middle class, middle aged dad (back then), and he was beating the shit out of Larry Hagman – J.R. From Dallas. I loved that this existed. I wanted to know all of these seedy weird little films that famous people had made decades ago. Again, this is before IMDB, this information wasn't collected and collated or in any way reference-able. You had to dig for this stuff, you had to search it out. My dad pulled a box out of the attic. It was full of an entire run of 'Films and Filming' magazine which he'd collected in the 70's. So many films I'd never heard of, all with tantalizing black and white stills. I was rabid, I just wanted to see them all.

I wouldn't say my film geekery stunted my social life, but I crammed film watching into every spare minute of the day. In the back of Film Review magazine, a company advertised a device which turned your humble TV into a projector. Dad tried to explain the concept of a scam to me but I

sent off my money and received a piece of
clear plastic and a sheet of instructions about
how to build a unit out of wood which
would house the TV and the sheet of plastic.
I built it out of cardboard and, to my
surprise, it actually worked. Except it
projected the image upside down. On closer
reading of the instructions, it stated that to
get the picture the right way up, you'd have
to buy some hugely expensive device from
them and then get it fitted by a professional
TV repair man. I came up with my own
solution. I rested the TV on its back in the
middle of my bedroom floor and watched
films on the ceiling. My friends would come
over and we'd all lie on the floor to watch
our flicks. The TV went a bit odd and the
only colours it would show were shades of
purple and green but we were fine with that.
Then it died.

My teenage years rolled on.

I had made two conscious decisions at
around 15. The first was that I was not going
to be the geeky type of film geek. I was
keenly aware that surrounding myself with
Star Wars toys was an indication of stunted
growth at this point. I had no intention of
using my passion for film as a way to keep
me in a state of suspended animation and
stay in a childish bubble rather than embrace
the scary pressures of young adulthood.

I used film in a keenly auto-didactic fashion. I used it to learn, I used it to challenge myself, I really used it to open up my mind. To this day, I worry that much of my wisdom and perceived intelligence might come from a rickety old E-180 rather than actual life experience but then, that's kind of the purpose of film. Films are the modern extension of storytelling and storytelling is the craft of subtly passing on knowledge, wisdom and a moral structure through entertainment. As exemplified through the films of Michael Winner. Hmm. I think I only embraced the idea of being a film geek many years later. Certainly until I was out of my teenage, I wasn't quite prepared to engage with the fun of it all without retaining quite a harsh analytical distance.

The other decision I made was that I was going to be a filmMAKER and not a film fan. This turning point came at a very specific moment in my life. In the fifth year at my upper school, pupils had to do a week of 'work experience'. This meant working out your future career, contacting someone in that industry and spending a week in their workplace, shadowing them. I had no idea that nobody else in my year – including the teachers – took this seriously. So whilst pretty much everyone else just went along to sit forlornly in the workplaces of their parents or parents' friends, I set to work breaking into Hollywood.

Since I was 5 years old, I had always intended to be a film director. My sister later told me that I had no idea how lucky I was to have had a clear unshakable goal my whole life, and I can totally see that. The only time my resolve wavered was in my mid-teens. This wasn't the result of a wobble in confidence or passion, but I had developed an obsession with the craft of special effects. I think this had been inspired by my first viewing of An American Werewolf In London which features effects which, almost 40 years later, still look fresh and photo-realistic and have never been rivalled. Part of the joy of cinema is the sleight-of-hand. The craft of the artifice and, in those years before CGI came and robbed the silver screen of any notion of magic, the FX guys were the Houdinis. My hero was Rick Baker, the genius of prosthetic make-up and animatronics. The word animatronic still gets me excited. An animatronic is probably the greatest toy ever made – a monster puppeted through cable pneumatics and radio-controlled servers. Baker was the king but right behind him you had Stan Winston, Rob Bottin, Bob Keen, Nick Dudman (whose subtle yet extreme prosthetic work on Jack Nicholson in Batman still remains one of my favourite iconic jobs). These guys were the ones who actually made the magic.

My folks never patronised me when I talked about my future. They only ever took me seriously and encouraged me in any direction I showed interest. Mum was keenly practical and as soon as I started talking seriously about make-up effects, she bought me a subscription to the trade publication – Cinefex. This was a magazine that wasn't available in any newsagents. It wasn't even really a magazine, once a quarter, a thick envelope from America would arrive on the doormat containing what was essentially a soft bound book. Each issue would look at three recent films and take the reader (who was expected to be within the profession, so there was no hand-holding) through the entire special effects process for the whole film. Everything. Matte Paintings and optical printing, cloud tanks, physical effects, prosthetics and animatronics, everything from conception to post-production, all incredibly illustrated with behind-the-scenes photos that simply didn't appear anywhere else and, until the age of special-edition DVDs, stories that hadn't surfaced. In the Alien 3 issue, they detailed at length an abandoned attempt at putting a dog in an Alien costume. This was like catnip to me. I yearned to be on those sets, in those teams, solving those problems.

So, when work experience came around, it was obvious what I was going to do. Again, there was no internet back then but, much to my mother's amusement, I grabbed the yellow pages and looked up 'animatronics' and struck gold. There was an animatronics company in Oxfordshire. They were called Crawley Creatures and that's all I needed to know. I phoned them up and put my garbled case to them, finishing with the clincher line 'I'm happy to do anything!' and they were really welcoming.

They were located in one of those odd little rural industrial estates, right next to a river. I had to take two buses from Headington to get anywhere close to them, it took over an hour each way. Once I got to the nearest village, I'd have to sit on a bench and wait until someone was free to pick me up and take me back to the workshop. The workshop was like heaven.

The company was run by two guys – Nigel and Jez, who'd been in the industry for a good few years. They were lovely, obliging blokes who were happy to answer my stupid questions and explain any little thing to me. Jez turned up one day in a Revenge of the Jedi jumper. Revenge. REVENGE. That had been the working title of the film. It was a real crew jumper.

"Where did you get that?" I gasped.

"Oh, I was on it" he smiled, before flippantly adding "I did Jabba The Hutt's eyes" and sauntering off.

I was gobsmacked. That night, I went home and stuck on my 'Classic Creatures' VHS – a film about the making of Jedi. There he was! Operating Jabba The Hutt's eyes! For the rest of the week I could barely talk to Jez, I was completely, overwhelmingly starstruck.

The workshop was where magic met industry. It was a dirty, smelly, messy place. Full of clay and wire and chemicals and paints. The office upstairs was incredible, rammed with trophies from their past work. Both guys had worked under Rick Baker on Greystoke and they had some ape heads from that film, Nigel showed me how they worked. They also had the full back catalogue of Cinefex, which I would pore over each day whilst I ate my sandwiches.

My first day there, they were fashioning massive foam rubber phone costumes for a TV commercial. The first stage of this process was to take huge blocks of polystyrene and sculpt them into shape with wire brushes. This would have been fun to do. My job was picking up handfuls of polystyrene brushings and bin bag them up. I had grown my hair long and it was full of these things, thanks to static energy, they clung to every inch of me and for each handful I'd dump into the bin bag, at least 30% would remain stuck to my hand. For 8 backbreaking hours, I shadowed the sculptors and shovelled bags full of tiny balls. At the end of the day, Nigel stuck his head round the door and said "wouldn't it be easier to just use the hoover?". Everybody laughed but me. It hadn't been a prank, I just hadn't come up with a practical, or even obvious, way of doing the job and the sculptors had been too busy or distracted to question my method.

The rest of my time there was far better. Each day a member of the team would take the time to show me an aspect of their job. A guy called Mike really took me under his wing and spent a day giving me an elaborate chemistry lesson in which he showed me how latex and foam rubber worked, how to make a mould and how to take a casting from it. My lungs were full of ammonia but there was great joy in getting my hands dirty and learning the craft.

Another guy, Sean, showed me how to construct a wire armature for a sculpture, then build it up with chicken wire and plaster bandage and sculpt clay over it. He was working on dinosaurs for a TV movie of Conan Doyle's The Lost World, I got to see every step of that process from the initial sculpt through to animatronic tests. Crawley Creatures would, years later, go on to great acclaim for their creature work on the BBC's Walking With Dinosaurs.

Over the week, they set me the task of creating my own monster and building a full maquette of it. Starting with sketching, then building an armature and a frame, then sculpting it. I learned one of the most valuable lessons of my life that week – that I simply wasn't cut out for that career. I didn't take this as a defeatist thing at all, but the simple truth was that to work in that field you had to either be mechanically minded, with a passion for engineering and electronics or you had to be artistically gifted – a painter or a sculptor. I'd had a huge amount of fun and hadn't left disheartened, but I'd realised that my skills were always going to rest in the writing and the photography side of film-making. Those were my natural skills and the ones I would best pursue. So, that's when I got serious about being a writer-director.

For a long time, I refused to acknowledge that being a filmmaker and a film fan were mutually exclusive, despite the fact that you certainly couldn't be the former without being the latter. To me, film fans were passive, they were spectators. A filmmaker could still enjoy a film but he had to be able to articulate why, he had to be able to deconstruct and relate what he saw on the screen to his own work.

I commandeered the family camcorder and I started making films. I looked at a lot of video art and experimental techniques, I shot little short films with my friends. The camcorder was often to hand, just playing about with framing and lighting choices. It was generally more technical than creative. I didn't really have an interest in producing a finished film then, I was very conscious of running before I could walk and being in a pretty rough state school, I had no interest in the beatings that would ensue for appearing as precocious as I undeniably was.

I started taking courses at Oxford Film & Video Makers, at first with video, which by then seemed a bit remedial to me and at 16 I finally got my hands on a film camera. They taught me all disciplines of 16mm film-making. I could load a magazine (I can't anymore. I tried recently. It's a digital world), operate, focus and then edit on a big flatbed Steenbeck machine. Editing on a Steenbeck was the most gloriously tactile experience any film lover could have. A huge machine which made incredibly satisfying clunks and whirs and whizzes. You'd sit at it with a pair of white cotton gloves and a white grease pencil and plough through reels of film. Winding, unwinding, cutting, splicing, watching back. I could see a happy future sat at a Steenbeck.

When I was 18 years old, I got accepted to film school in Edinburgh, which seemed a long way away. A few days before I was due to start, the university told me that they'd screwed up the accommodation procedure and that I had nowhere to live. I figured I would head up there, rucksack on my back, and spend a few days enjoying the adventure of finding digs.

The night before I was due to set off, I stopped into Blockbuster and rented a film. Oxford Video had quietly vanished some months earlier, a victim of the industry's tilt towards New Releases and lots of them. With Blockbuster UK buying centrally and funded by the success of its American patriarch, it had become a war of attrition with the original indie video stores. Blockbuster's model was a bold one – they stocked huge amounts of copies of each new release and quickly transferred them to ex-rental sales. Since, at that time, there was a window of at least 6 months between a video being available to rent and being released to retail, Blockbuster was pre-empting the home sales market. This meant, as an example, they could buy a tape in at say £20 per unit, rent it as many as 21 times in it's first 3 weeks of release, then sell it ex-rental at around £15. The gross profit on each tape could be around £70. Meanwhile, the indie stores were still having to pay around £60 a tape initially and were lucky to break even on that investment in the first month or so of release. It was punishing. The disparity between those business models is too big. No indie store could have bolstered its buying to compete as Blockbuster had seemingly unlimited resources.

Blockbuster was now Headington's only video shop. I don't remember what film I rented but I bought a box of jelly babies to enjoy with it. As I started eating them, I distinctly remember the thought 'oh, these are a bit sweaty' but in a young mind, untainted by the experience of food poisoning, it passed as an observation rather than a warning sign. I dozed off and woke up vomiting. Projectile vomiting.

As with any teenage boy's bedroom, mine was a post-apocalyptic landscape of mountains and valleys of detritus. The one good thing to come out of this experience was the removal of the decision as to what would accompany me to Edinburgh, what would remain in the house and what would be thrown away. Everything would be thrown away because everything. Everything. Was covered – COVERED – in sick. I puked all over the bed, all over the walls, all over the desk, all over everything on the floor – I have distinct memories of trying to avoid puking on a Cure vinyl bootleg which a friend had lent me only to vomit all over my Bill Hicks cassettes. And then the Cure vinyl bootleg. I crawled down the landing and yelped towards my parents bedroom. My dad emerged just in time to watch me puke, through the balustrade over the stairs and wall. He got me downstairs (my bedroom, he observed, would have to be incinerated) and puking into buckets in the shower room until I was heaving up only air. I was unwell for days and my mum correctly forced the decision that instead of going up there late, with nowhere to live and missing those first few days of bonding with classmates, that I should take a year off. That was the first time that Blockbuster would make me sick. But not the last.

CHAPTER 4

BUSTING BLOCKS WITH MICHAEL IRONSIDE

1996

The drive home from Edinburgh to Oxford was like a big 360 mile sigh of relief. Which is in no way to say I hadn't loved my first year of film school, I had had an incredible time, met some amazing people, done some great work, finally made a group of friends who were as obsessed with film as I was – conversation was an endless joy, I'd done more living in that academic year than any other year of my life and I was exhausted.

I was glad to finally get out of that battery hen university flat. I'd bid my two psychopathic flatmates goodbye with the vengeful gesture of snapping most of their CDs in half. They deserved it, having dominated the place with a reign of random room-trashing terror in the way only nocturnal agoraphobic video-gaming stoner rave-heads could. My weirdo reclusive flatmate had vanished months earlier, there was a chance he was still in his room, of course, but I didn't bother to knock. The one flatmate I was friends with had thrown himself full force into his new band and, unbeknownst to all of us, was just months away from appearing on the covers of the NME and Melody Maker so we weren't destined to spend the next 3 years of film school together as we'd assumed. It was the end of a monumental year and it felt good to know that I was going home to a fully stocked fridge, not having to keep my own stash of toilet paper and the near-certainty that my parents wouldn't stay up all night playing video games whilst listening to George Michael CDs at full volume or decide to shave their heads in the living room, leaving the hair scattered there for months. Most importantly, I had the whole summer of 1996 to earn some money. I was not popular with the Bank of Scotland. I wasn't looking for sympathy, the allowance I got from my parents was perfectly generous, I was just crap with it. I'd even taken out a full student loan of £1,300 and got through it in weeks (I applied for it as it seemed to be the only way

I could afford to buy the limited edition £70 Star Wars trilogy video box set in a tin on its day of release).

My plan was to spend the best part of the summer working at a job I'd lined up for myself at the exam board, which basically involved double-checking exam papers to make sure the scores had been added up correctly. I started work there the first Monday I was back in Oxford. It was stupidly easy and ridiculously overpaid but it was like being in prison. And, no I'm not making the hippie similes of so many who live the slacker life and hate 'the suits' and their real jobs in boring places. It was literally like prison, we were sat in groups of 8 around tables, we were supervised by old crotchety looking people on a mezzanine level above us. Silence was enforced, tables that talked had people swapped out of them. Your breaks were closely monitored and to use the toilet was to walk across a completely silent room full of hundreds of people who knew where you were going, many of whom were probably mentally timing you to see if you had done a number one or number two. I was going out of my mind. On the fourth day, I drove home through Headington and decided, on the off chance, to stop into Blockbuster, see if they had any work – even if it sucked, at least I'd get a summer of free videos. I got talking to the guy behind the counter, who seemed friendly enough and said there definitely was work going and to leave a note for the manager. I scribbled something about being totally available and having gone to film school, so very knowledgeable about films, thanked the guy and went home.

The phone rang an hour later and I answered it to be greeted with a strange, gurgling, high pitched voice.

"Zat Jon?"

"yeah."

"Hello Jon, it's Caaaaaaaarl, from Block-busters"

Surely it was called Blockbuster? Why did he pluralise it? Was this actually the manager?

"I'm the manager"

Guess so.

"Yeah, I got your note, do you want a job?"

"No interview?"

"It's a phone interview"

"This is the interview?"

"Yeah. Do you want it?"

"The job or the interview?"

"The job"

"Yeah… please"

"OK, can you come in on Monday?"

"Sure."

"Ten o' clock"

"OK!"

I had never got a job so quickly, I felt rather proud of my credentials. He must have read the note and thought 'Now THIS is the kind of guy we want here!' It gave me a little swagger. Of course, at the time I didn't realise that the note really could have said anything and I would have got an identical call. I would find Blockbuster to be a big inefficient lumbering beast of a corporation with badly thought out practices and, consequently, completely apathetic staff from the bottom to the top. Those at the bottom, on minimum wage, didn't really stick around too long so there seemed to be a very high turnover of them, they appeared to be constantly short-staffed and desperate for new recruits. This institutionalised apathy became transparently obvious the following Monday, when I actually met Carl.

I don't know how to describe him without sounding mean, so if you'll excuse me and understand that I have no ill will left against the guy, there's just no way of putting a positive spin on it, it's better just to embrace the truth and do justice to his wretchedness. Carl was what could be described as the runt of the litter. From a distance, as I walked in to the shop, he just looked small. Not short, but small. Narrow shoulders, sloping into limpness. A very slight frame, his clothes hung off him and his use of a belt accentuated their bagginess and his tininess of stature. Like a little boy in a school uniform two sizes too big which his mum had bought so he could 'grow into'. As I got closer, the image became worse. He looked ill. His eyes were sunken and bloodshot, the skin around them dark and sweaty. His skin had a bizarre green pallor which, at first, I assumed must be to do with either the lighting or my eyes adjusting to it, but when I glanced at my own arm for a frame of reference, it looked healthy and pink. He just looked diseased. His head hung forwards off his neck as if he'd given up supporting it years ago, his teeth were crooked and kind of somewhere between translucent and buttery. It was impossible to assign an age to him, he could have been 25 or 50. He looked like he hadn't seen sunlight, or soap, for a very long time. I certainly didn't assume it to be the manager. I approached him with a smile and asked to see the manager,

"Tha's me!" he gurgled.

He actually did gurgle. Carl had a strange way of talking, there was no enunciating from the diaphragm, he spoke from the mouth, with an added gargle if he got louder or added emotion. Phlegmy, spitty gargle. His voice was a dragged out high pitched, whiny attempt at sounding professional.

"Are you Jon, are you?"

His tone was kind of camp and unimpressed and in a bizarrely over-zealous way. I instinctively offered him my hand to shake, knowing I'd regret it, which I did instantly as he dropped his cold wet flounder of a hand into mine and allowed me to move his arm up and down with it. The only thought in my head was how quickly I could get to a sink and would there be soap there?

"Why don't you come round and we'll see if we can find a shirt to fit you"

An hour later, barely contained by an itchy, new Blockbuster short sleeved waffle shirt with highly starched collar, I found myself 'moving the wall'. Blockbuster had more redundant lingo than any other company in the world. What normal people call 'staff', Blockbuster refers to as 'CSR's' – admittedly a welcome abbreviation to Customer Service Representatives, but still a full two redundant syllables over 'staff' – which is a word everybody understands. What the world calls 'ex-rentals' – videos that have been rented out before but are now surplus, so being sold cheap, Blockbuster called 'PVT'. Previously Viewed Tape. Totally pointless and somewhat baffling in that whilst the plural of a CSR is CSR's, the plural of PVT is PVT – as in 'Jon can you sort out the PVT?' 'You mean PVT's?' 'Would you rather move the wall?'

So, back to moving the wall. Moving the wall is one of those things that was clearly invented by someone with an undefinable job title deep in Blockbuster's international HQ who was paid a lot of money but even he didn't know why, so a couple of times a year, he'd invent a new method of doing something which worked fine before, and he knew that, and in 2 years time when all the staff in the entire company have changed, he'd change it back to the way it was and that would be his genius new working method until the cycle dictated he change it back.

Moving the wall meant every single Monday, you'd move ALL of the stock in the ENTIRE shop. Oh, maybe not always the older stuff, but the New Release wall, which in this branch was 3 huge long walls representing thousands of videos. The newest releases had to fill the first unit, everything else moved down, some came off new release and became PVT (not PVT's). Now, I understand the principle of stock rotation, although it makes slightly more sense with food and product with a short lifespan. I even understand the advantage of customers knowing where the new product will be. My point is, if a whole wall is labelled 'New Releases' and you're stocking 60 copies, box facing out, of each title – people aren't going to miss it. You can pretty much put an entire wall of copies of a single film anywhere in the shop and people will find it. But no, policy dictated that Monday was spent moving the entire wall (Sunday had been spent opening hundreds of videos, making up 'rental cases' to put the tapes in, then inserting the pricing slip into the original cover ready to be moved on to the wall). I later found out that until I had turned up, Carl used to come in at 6 or 7 o'clock each Monday morning and work for four hours, UNPAID, to move the wall in time for opening because everyone else refused to do it. Within a couple of hours of me learning this, he was to be doing it again.

So that first day was crappy, I moved the entire wall by myself, wearing that stupid horrible shirt and, bizarrely, a Blockbuster name badge that said 'ALEX' on it because, as Carl explained, it'd take a few days for my badge to arrive. It says a lot about a company and their attitude towards their staff and customers that it's of far more importance for an employee to be wearing a name badge than for that badge to have their actual name on it. I spent a while deciding whether I'd refuse to acknowledge anybody who addressed me as Alex or if I'd refuse to acknowledge anybody *unless* they addressed me that way. I've never understood the need to display the name of a low-level employee on a badge other than to allow nasty asshole customers to patronise them. When you don't wear a name badge, you find out who are the nicest customers as they actually ask you your name, which is a welcome gesture illustrating that they don't just see you as their retail bitch.

The big new release that first day was Ace Ventura 2 – When Nature Calls. The cover art is burned onto my retinas still. I hadn't expected working in a video shop to be like the hell you witnessed on every trip to a corporate fast food place where you saw people actually physically *working* to make minimum wage. For the rest of the day, Carl had me dusting video boxes and hoovering the shop in what felt like standard corporate retail monotony but turned out to actually be him exploiting one of the rare moments in his career when a member of staff didn't ignore, mock or press charges against him.

The next day, getting up and going to work felt like an enormous hassle. I could only imagine what Carl had in store now the shop was clean. When I got there, he wasn't anywhere to be seen. In his place was a taller, ruddy faced guy with a mop of ginger hair and a surprised smile.

"You must be Jon, I'm Kevin!"

I offered him my hand and got a good firm shake, accompanied with a surprised "Oh, very formal!"

"Is Carl not in today?"

"No, no, not today. Did you meet him?"

"I did, yeah"

"Yeah….. what did you think?" he asked conspiratorially with a grin waiting to explode.

"Well, he's…."

"He's quite horrible, isn't he?"

I still didn't know if I should join in or if this was some kind of elaborate test, but I took the bait.

"He seems kind of ill"

"Oh, no, that's him healthy, when he's ill you know it."

Kevin had a soft London accent, which was really warm and inviting. He felt like a friend straight away, he had a way of being brutally direct and cruel whilst sounding more like he was pondering it in an innocent, awestruck way. He was warming up to the idea of a good conversation about Carl.

"One time, me and him were stood right here, nobody was in the shop, it was completely quiet and we weren't talking or anything. Just stood looking out at the shop and he turns his head to face me, so I turn to face him thinking he had something to say but he goes 'Ahhhhhhheh' and coughs right in my face. And I felt it hit me like a mist. I just wanted to puke, I felt sick straight away and then I got ill, I was off for two days."

This had me laughing so hard it was embarrassing, mainly because Kevin's effeminate 'Ahhhhhheh' was exactly what I would imagine one of Carl's coughs would sound like. Kevin started giggling and soon we had set the pattern for the entire summer, Kevin and I just laughing at the absurdity of it all. He was 37, which seemed incredibly old to me at 20, but he was every bit as gloriously immature as me. In fact, maybe even more so. As I got to know him, he just became more and more impressive. He was a trained artist of a fantastic standard, he seemed comfortable in all disciplines of drawing and painting and, whenever bored would just knock some-thing out and hand it to me. Sometimes it would be a sketch of one of the customers, sometimes a caricature of Carl (I wish I still had these) but more often than not, a naked girl. I once pointed out a customer I had a crush on and 20 minutes later Kevin illicitly slipped a piece of paper in my hand. It was a naked drawing of her. That pretty much sums up the combination of warped perspective and utter generosity that made him so much fun. He was stuck in a rut and angry at himself for accepting the job of Deputy Manager (DM), deputy is obviously a stupid word and normal companies would have branded him Assistant Manager, however because the abbreviation AM belonged to the more senior Area Managers, Blockbuster had decided to deputise it's longest serving members of staff in each store. I don't think he knew how to generate an artistic career, he really wanted to draw comics, and often did, but it never seemed to happen for him. He did have a brief period of success in London after finishing art school – the crowning glory of which had been being hired as the Storyboard Artist for Duran Duran's music video for A View To a Kill, which really impressed me. That and the fact that he was friends with a couple of real life screenwriters – the guys who had written the film about Derek Bentley – Let Him Have It (Purvis and Wade, who would go on to revitalise the James Bond franchise) but he couldn't seem to catch a break anymore and I never really understood why he ended up in Oxford which, whilst being close to London, is kind of worlds away.

Over the next couple of weeks, I got to meet the other staff, sorry, CSRs. Phil was a student finishing up his Masters degree. A very dry wit and as cynical as you could get, he had an amazing ability of putting customers down to their faces without them ever realising. A woman once asked him if the Sandra Bullock film 'The Net' was any good and he replied with a sincere smile 'it was made for people like you'. Then there was Mad Bob. Bob was a nice enough bloke, he had kind of a hippie thing going on but he had these terrifying eyes with the gaze of a bird of prey. If you could imagine The Childcatcher from Chitty Chitty Bang Bang having a weekend off at Glastonbury – that was Bob. He was the member of some religious cult who all lived in some commune. Kevin said he'd been to dinner there and found it all suspiciously nice. Bob was a good guy, I mean, he was the most honest and principled of all of us but he was still kind of scary.

Shifts at Blocky were always scheduled strangely – you'd have two people working 10am-6pm, then two more working 3pm-10pm, which meant you had four people working together for three hours during the slowest part of the day. Never made any sense, especially since three of us would undoubtedly just be standing around, shooting the shit, whilst Carl actually did stuff. I mean, all credit to Carl, he worked very hard – inefficiently, sure, but definitely hard. It was a mindset I just couldn't get into. He seemed to live and breathe Blockbuster (which actually probably goes a long way to explaining the wet rattle of his mouth-breathing), he relished any opportunity to use corporate jargon and was forever trying to set a good example to us in the way he dealt with customers and carried out duties. Phil was sly and adept at avoiding being in the wrong place at the wrong time when Carl would hand out tasks, Kevin would politely decline or say something like 'I don't think it's really the kind of thing you or I should be doing, Carl – as management', Bob, well Bob would do whatever he was told with a good attitude. I preferred to play dumb as it would exasperate Carl to levels where he'd either shout or sigh so hard it looked like his body would crumble and never re-oxygenate. One time he wanted me to clean the windows. I told him I didn't know how, could he show me? I watched him give a brief demonstration, and as he left the job to me to finish, I asked:

'So, why do you wring the water out, surely the water is the part that cleans it!'

'Jon, I can't believe you've never cleaned windows!'

'I know, and I'm excited to try, I just don't understand it – show me again!'

'OK, you put the rag in the water, you wring it out, you wipe the window with the soapy water – are you with me'

'I was until the bit where you wring it out, I would just have thought that you'd need water'

'You don't need that much!'

'Oh, there's still some in the rag?'

'Of course there is, it's wet!'

'A lot of water seemed to come out.'

'Well, you only need a little bit, don't you?'

'But you have a whole bucket!'

'YOU DON'T USE THE WHOLE BUCKET'

'But it's full, Carl!'

'YOU DON'T USE IT ALL!'

'Well, don't you think that's a little wasteful?'

'It's water!'

'We're a planet in crisis.'

'Just clean the windows!;

'Well, you've practically done them yourself now, I don't want to come in at the last moment and claim credit for your work.'

At which point Carl would send me away and get on with cleaning the windows himself because he just couldn't bear to be around me. Although greater tragedies were in store for Carl, I think the sorriest I ever felt for him (you could only feel sorry for him when he wasn't around) was when Kevin told us all that Carl, as manager, was salaried for 30 hours per week but worked around 45-50 (often having to cover shifts at other branches and coming in hours earlier to do all the work expected of him). So with him working that many extra unpaid hours and with us as students, getting paid for the hours we worked AND not getting taxed (Kevin only accepted the DM role on the condition he still be paid hourly but at a higher rate) we were actually taking home double the money Carl was. And we really weren't working at all. The most horrific moment that has always stuck in my mind with the most clarity involving Carl was when, during a quiet period one day, I asked him how he came to work for Blockbuster.

'I'd had experience managing a shop before, but I'd been unemployed for a while. I got taken to court by four boys, they accused me of doing something to them that I never done. I got off, but couldn't get work for a while. Blockbuster didn't care about all that.'

He shrugged and walked away. I couldn't even begin to process the information, this completely blasé reference to… badness. I asked Kevin, but he'd never heard anything about it and it seemed unsavoury to delve for more information. We just left it and ignored it. About two years later, I found out there was a chain of newsagents called Forbouys and the whole story thankfully fell into place. Or, at least, I like to think so.

That summer at the Blockbuster in Headington started to gather momentum about a month in when Carl decided we needed more staff. We didn't need more staff. What had happened was that a girl had come in to ask for work and giddy from the experience of having an actual live woman talking to him with a smile, Carl had hired her on the spot. I wasn't actually there that day but when I turned up the next day, Kevin seemed pretty excited about it 'She's very bubbly!' he said. There had been a girl working there the first week I was hired, but she was kind of dowdy and aloof. Blocky was kind of a male environment and we were all intrigued to see how it might change.

The first time I actually met Becky, she was being trained up by Carl and Kevin. As I walked in, Kevin's eyes widened and he surreptitiously motioned towards Becky with his head. Long peroxide hair, short skirt, whatever. I'd seen girls before, Carl's vile conspiratorial nod sickened me. It immediately felt strange to see a woman behind the counter and I could see that it was going to cause problems because Carl was not cut out to be around someone he found attractive. Carl's horrible voice became even more displeasing as it took on a fawning tone when he spoke to her. He seemed to clasp his hands together a lot and to address half of what he said to her face and the other half to her chest. I don't think he'd ever been this close to a woman, let alone one as imposing as Becky. Kevin told me that watching Carl train her was like watching a guy who had just finished reading one of those books about how to hypnotise girls into going out with you. Lots of long periods without blinking and use of strange phrases that sounded somewhat coded. I think, in Becky, Carl saw both someone who would respect him for his power and serve him diligently. A beautiful queen who would sit alongside King Carl and watch lovingly as he ruled the kingdom.

"Oh, he's not nice. He, uh, was actually accused of... interfering... with *four* boys"

"Oh my god!"

Becky's initial misguided non-loathing of Carl lasted about as long as it took to work a shift with us. It turned out that I knew, and had always liked, her brother and we had a whole bunch of mutual friends, so we clicked straight away and she very quickly became the kind of friend that you just have your whole life. Underneath that slightly bimbo-ish exterior was a dirty mind, a crushing wit and a case of flatulence so unbelievable that she would never be attractive in 'that' way to anyone that really got to know her. She was always funny and enthusiastic and her presence really bonded her, myself, Kevin and Phil as a unit and a force that probably kept Carl awake at night crying.

We became like the Bash Street Kids, with Carl as the long-suffering teacher, bewildered at and targeted by our childish japes and scrapes. One of the most fun parts of video shop work is building the standees – the afore-mentioned cardboard cut-outs. We used to fight for the chance to build them, then compete with each other to deface them. Kevin spent several hours making the Michael Flatley – Lord of The Dance standee as offensive as possible with cartoon genitals, various speech balloons and then, in a fit of disaffected pique, he ripped the head off. The decapitated and desecrated Flatley remained a disturbing yet benign presence at the threshold to the Family section for several days until Carl, despite having had it in his eyeline for days, finally noticed.

Kevin's favourite job was what he called 'box jumping' – all of the delivery packaging had to be flattened to go out for the bin men and rather than just take the boxes apart and flatten them, he preferred to put them all in a pile and jump on them until they were dead. One day, Carl asked him to assemble the Toy Story standee. Kevin unpacked it and decided to flatten the packaging before building it. Carl watched in horror as Kevin, unaware that the packaging was actually used as a central part of the structure on this one, jumped up and down, red-faced with a fixed grin of psychotic glee, on the season's most important piece of marketing.

We got to know the regulars and they got to know us. There was Jason the insomniac who would come in every night, right before closing, and choose three films, all of which would be in the drop box the next morning. Dude watched three films a night and didn't even start until 10pm. He told us he'd given up trying to sleep, inevitably at some point he'd pass out for an hour on the sofa and that's what he was running on. There was speedy porn guy, this guy would rent a porno and be back within the hour to return it. I say 'porno' – officially Blocky didn't stock porn as they were signed up to some kind of family-appropriate establishment scheme. They just had an extensive 'DRAMA/THRILLER' section which was kept hilariously separate from both the Drama and Thriller sections. These were softcore pornos with storylines and artistic aspirations. Fascination dictated that we watched the occasional one, they seemed to be either about a woman on an erotic journey of self-discovery or L.A. Based Femme Fatale-lead stories of sub-Mafia dealings, all taking place in an around one house and mainly lit through a slatted blind with an orange light. Anyway, this guy was also our renter with a double life. On weekdays – most weekdays – he'd do his one hour 'drama/thriller' rental, a bit shifty, no eye contact, then on weekends, he'd turn up with his girlfriend and they'd rent romantic comedies and they'd both talk to us and be all friendly, despite the obvious, desperate, pleading fear in his eyes.

If a customer was rude, we'd slip the wrong film into their case, if they were nice, we'd give them free rentals or confectionary. Confectionary at Blockbuster was always a questionable thing anyway and I still hadn't forgiven them for the Jelly Babies incident. The chocolate was OK until the first heatwave of that summer, at which point it all melted and formed weird shaped blobs within the packaging. We told Carl that it probably wasn't ok to sell but he ignored us. Over the summer, it would melt and reform several times. I once opened a bag of revels and found what looked like a bag of sticky chocolate tumours, all hardened with white stuff on them. Carl said 'chocolate goes like that sometimes' and ate some to prove his point. 'See? I'm alright!' 'you really aren't'. I pointed out to him that chocolate isn't supposed to be covered in white stuff. He replied "That's just the milk coming out".

One day, Carl unplugged the ice cream freezer to plug in the hoover and forgot to plug the freezer back in. By the next day, all of the ice cream had melted – we're talking about over a hundred tubs. Kevin was the one who realised. Carl told him to just plug it back in and it'd freeze again. Kevin laughed but then realised Carl was serious. Carl said Head Office would be livid if we cost them that much money. Kevin said that if Carl didn't tell them, he would, and he'd also phone the health department since that freezer would probably become more terrifyingly bacterial than Carl's handker-chief (if he had one, which he didn't, he'd do

these open-mouthed sneezes that just....
Bleurgh!). Carl phoned Head Office and told
them that 'someone' had done it and, rest
assured, that person would be dealt with.
Meanwhile Kevin spent an entire morning
pouring melted ice cream down the sink,
using a biro to push the chunky bits through
the drain.

No sooner was the ice cream freezer stocked
as it was empty again. In one of the single
funniest pieces of CCTV footage I have ever
seen, the shop was laid siege to by a gang of
kids. The Barton estate is just down the road
from Headington and local traders lived in
fear of the Barton kids. What a bunch of
nasty little toerags, they moved in vast
numbers and ransacked the area like a
plague of locusts. One particular Sunday
afternoon, Kevin was working by himself
when a gang of about 15 of these kids came
in. The typical teenage shoplifting routine is
that one kid approaches the counter and
asks inane questions whilst his mates pilfer.
Every generation seems to think they've not
only invented this tactic, but are really good
at it. It was obvious why they were there
and Kevin was quite rightly not about to put
himself on the line for the sake of Blockbuster. So, the silver tongued ambassador of
the group approached the counter and asked
when the next Van Damme film was out and
Kevin replied 'Just get on with it'. At which

point, they just took the place apart. The footage was hilarious, young lads carrying stacks of ice cream tubs as tall as themselves and as many bags of popcorn as they could carry whilst Kevin just stood at the counter and watched with a bemused smile. The following Sunday, due to a genuine error in communication, nobody came in to work, the shop stayed locked until 3pm when a couple of us non-key-holders turned up to find that not only could we not get in because Kevin wasn't answering his phone (nobody bothered to take down Carl's personal number), but the drop box was so full, customers were just leaving their returns on the ground outside the shop. This might have been the biggest act of mass stupidity that I have ever seen. Unable to get in to work, we went home. The next morning, surprisingly, any videos that hadn't made it into the drop box were just a distant memory and Carl was in trouble.

If Carl was in trouble, we were all in trouble. Apparently when asked for an explanation as to why his store was going to shit, Carl's response was that his staff were awful. Which we absolutely were, but still. The first I knew about it was my next shift, I walked in to work and found myself facing our area manager Russ. Russ was ex-military and looked just like Michael Ironside. He had tattoos on his arms and was probably terrifying in a military situation but it's hard to command much respect in retail when you're unarmed, at the mercy of civilian law, your staff are smarter than you and only getting minimum wage. I don't want to paint him as a pathetic figure, because he wasn't, he was a perfectly respectable guy, it's just that nobody really cared about their jobs enough to take any shit (except Carl) and it's not like he would have courtmartialed us or resorted to violence.

"Why aren't you in uniform, Jon?"

"Because my shift hasn't started yet"

"According to my watch, Jon, your shift started 2 minutes ago"

I check my watch.

"No, I've got like a minute and a half to go"

"Not according to my watch, Jon"

"Well, I set mine by the GMTV clock and, you know, that must be the official time"

"It's not good enough, Jon."

He was overusing my name and I couldn't work out why, I thought it must have been one of those military psychological tactics where they throw you off-balance by creating confusion then your mind is theirs for the taking. Since I had no such strategy up my sleeve, I just used his.

"What's not good enough, Russ?"

"Jon, you should be here, in uniform ten minutes before your shift starts"

"Russ, why should I do that?"

"Because it's good practice, Jon"

"Russ…"

"HEY! Don't get smart with me, Jon"

"I wasn't trying to, Russ"

"Now, you've wasted two minutes of both of our time. Go and get into your uniform, Jon"

"OK, Russ"

What followed was a day of training the Russ way. It was frustrating and idiotic but I could easily see how people of lesser will could be brainwashed and indoctrinated into becoming horrible little corporate puppets. The most insulting part of it was that he genuinely seemed to think that if I did a job properly and well, I would actually get some kind of sense of satisfaction out of it.

At one point, Russ had gone off to make some phone calls and I was stood at the counter seriously considering a dramatic resignation ("Russ, I'm leaving, Russ. You see, Russ, Russ, I just Russ can't put Russ up Russ with Russ this Russ shit Russ any Russ more, Russ!"). Russ appeared behind me, seemingly out of nowhere. Stealth like.

"What did you just do wrong, Jon?"

"Russ, I just don't know"

"Jon, think about it"

"...... no, Russ, nothing springs to mind."

"Think, Jon. I want you to think."

"Russ, are you reading my mind?"

"Jon, what's the magic number?"

Woah. Was this fucker programming me? I had nightmare visions of Carl croaking "Jon, 26!" and me having some Pavlovian response like cleaning the windows or dusting the back shelves.

"Russ, is it a hundred and two?"

"Jon, I told you the magic number!"

"In my mind, Russ?"

"An hour ago! THREE! THREE IS THE MAGIC NUMBER! Weren't you listening?

Of course I wasn't. The only way I'd got through his training was by picking out key jingoistic sentences and setting them to music in my mind ("Oh, the company is a pyramid and you are at the top and all our work is squandered if the tiles you do not mop!", "Respect for your job, means respect for yourself, the feeling of a job well done, a perfectly stocked shelf!" yes, Blockbuster The Musical was shaping up nicely).

"The Rule of Three, Jon. If a customer is either three feet into the shop or has been in the shop for more than three seconds and you haven't greeted him, you're letting the side down."

"OK, Russ"

"Here comes one, Jon"

A guy walked into the shop, we made eye contact, I smiled and nodded, he smiled back and went to look for 'drama/thriller'. That actually was kind of nice, it's nice to get a smile! Maybe Russ was right!

"Jon, what was that?"

"I greeted him, Russ"

"Jon, that was not greeting"

"Really, Russ? I mean, he seemed adequately greeted"

Another guy walks through the door and heads for the New Release section.

"GOOD MORNING, SIR, HOW ARE YOU?" Russ roared at him. Both the customer and I jumped in shock. The customer stopped and stared at Russ. "GOOD MORNING!" Russ continued. The guy offered a confused smile and a nod.

"You see, Jon"

"Russ, you terrified him. People like being acknowledged, I'll give you that, but nobody wants that Disney Store crap where they stand outside and patronise you in."

"I think Disney are fantastic, you always feel welcome there, Jon. That's EXACTLY what we should be doing!"

Another guy walks in and I scream "HEELLLLLLLLOOOOOOOOOOOO!!!!!" at him, The first guy, having overheard the conversation, giggles. The greeted stares at me for a minute as if he wants to see me bleed then stomps off towards the horror section. I turn to Russ for a reaction. He pats me on the back with something between pride and murderous disgust. "Well done, Jon".

As Carl stood and waved Russ off with a smug sense of satisfaction at having seen me be disciplined, I tried to think of a brilliant revenge. My mind too exhausted, I simply picked up a broomstick and brutalised him from behind. Kevin, who had arrived by this point, thought he seemed to rather enjoy it.

The summer pressed on and we all fell into a comfy routine of working, hanging out and then gathering at the shop at closing time to walk round the corner to the one bedroom flat Kevin shared with his girlfriend to watch films, shoot the shit, eat and drink and laugh. We did a lot of laughing. In my last couple of days there, me and Kevin were sorting some stuff out in the stock room when we found, wedged on a high shelf, a huge heavy old box. We managed to wrestle it down and realised we'd hit the motherload. A genuine haul of booty. There had been a time, not long after Blockbuster had taken over Ritz and they were looking to move or sell off the older stock to make room for vast quantities of New Releases. At this time, that guy at Head Office who invented 'moving the wall' hatched the single worst promotion any video shop has ever offered at any time. Blockbuster's Mystery Video promotion. Yep, they hid all of the back catalogue covers and replaced them with a wall of video boxes with question marks on the front. The customer was to select one randomly and whatever movie they got was whatever movie they got. I don't think a single customer was dumb enough to do this even once. So after a few weeks, they just took all of the videos off the system, stuck them in a box and forgot about them.

Carl confirmed that they weren't on the computer and there was no way – or point – to put them on, so we might as well have them. As we piled through the box, greedily staking our claim to the big rental box classics that appeared, I was amazed to find the original John Hughes films – the actual tapes – that my sister and I had rented out all those years ago. The satisfaction of owning them was huge and I made it my mission on returning to Scotland to track down the big box rental versions of all of my favourite films.

As the last week of my summer rolled around, I was actually rather sad at the prospect of leaving. It wouldn't have lasted, though. Becky was off to uni in Sheffield, Phil had finished his course and was heading to Japan to teach English to kids. I could see that Kevin was dreading being left alone with Carl and Mad Bob, but a bunch of new recruits were interviewed and they seemed like fun people. Besides, I had new adventures to pursue, not least a year living with a Bi-polar James Bond obsessive.

CHAPTER 5

PRIDE, PREJUDICE, FEAR AND LOATHING

1996 – 1997

I returned to Edinburgh basically debt-free (every good student knows that Student Loans aren't *real* debts and debts to parents ebb away with the tides of time and decency) but without any actual money. Not being overdrawn felt like an achievement, regardless of the fact that I was only hours away from being back in the red. Carl, in a display of suspicious decency, had arranged to have me transferred to a blockbuster in Edinburgh, where I could work 3 nights a week and thereby, supposedly, stay out of debt. True to form, Carl's apparent act of kindness would lead to nothing more than frustration and recrimination. As with any city, there were a load of Blockbusters in and around Edinburgh. That year, I was living just off the Royal Mile – about as central as it's possible to be in Edinburgh. The store that Carl got me a job at was in Gorgie.

This sucked on a number of levels. To begin with, Gorgie was two separate bus rides away. Which was annoying on my way to work – stuck in rush hour traffic – and rage-inducing on my way home as buses were only once an hour and very very rarely did those two timetables align. So, it was hell to get to, and once you were there… it was hell. Gorgie was the armpit of Edinburgh. I'm sure you've seen Trainspotting and would assume that Leith was the armpit. Leith is the arsehole of Edinburgh(or it was, it's almost completely gentrified now), you know what you're getting there. You know it's shitty and awful and there's a glory to that. There's no glory to an armpit, it's just unpleasant. It felt a bit Film Noirish at night – row after row of huge ugly tenement buildings, each window a pinhole view into some story of desperation or degradation. I hated the place. There weren't even really any other shops about, a few boarded up long-gone-bust businesses, a pokey little Scotmid (Scotland's answer to the super-market). The Blockbuster was the brightest light on that whole long street. Maybe the brightest light in Gorgie. The shop itself was tiny. There was only ever one member of staff on because only one member of staff could really fit behind the counter. I don't think I ever found out the names of anyone else who worked there apart from the manager.

Scott was a good guy, a strange balance, though. He was clearly a rock dude, mentioned being in a band, although I forget which, young, energetic and decent. He had longish shaggy black hair, pierced ears and a tattoo. Yet he was a company man through and through. A stickler for the rules and far more efficient than anything I'd ever seen in Oxford. Russ would have loved this guy. On my first shift, he talked me through the shop, showed me the safe and the keys I'd need, the software was the same throughout the company (horribly dated even then, DOS based software running off, I believe 186k PCs with all printouts coming on that computer paper from the 70s with the holes in both sides and thin green stripes going across it. At one point there was panic in the company when their supplier stopped making it. I remember Carl coming back, having found two boxes of it in Oxfam and holding it aloft as if it were Excalibur. That's probably a false memory, I doubt he had that kind of strength). As Scott was leaving, I asked him where the chair was 'we don't have one, it'd just get in the way back there, besides, there's always something you could be doing, no need to be sitting around!' he waved me a cheery goodbye and I cursed his chipperness as soon as his back was turned. No fucking chairs? I found a fold-out ladder in the bathroom, set it up behind the counter and sat on the top of it, four feet above the counter. This is the position I would spend most of my weekday evenings in for the next few months. When customers would come in, I'd have to fold away the ladder and stow it in the bathroom or else the videos were inaccessible. Not that many customers would ever come in. I imagined that Gorgie was the kind of place most people got their videos on a Sunday afternoon from a bloke in the pub with photocopied covers.

I was told that all of the ordering for Blockbuster was done centrally and I could well believe it when faced with this store. In an area where the only things that rented out were (in this order) Horror, Porn (Drama/Thriller) and Action films, there was an insane amount of chick flicks and real-life drama (the rightfully much-maligned Odyssesy label seemed to release only 'Real Life' dramas called things like 'Don't You Rape My Daddy!' and 'The Miscarriage of Martha Jane'). I doubt anyone at Blockbuster HQ had actually heard of Gorgie, much less ever visited it. The New

Release delivery each week was often amusing. One week we got in about 20 copies of Sense and Sensibility, but just one of Jean Claude Van-Damme's Sudden Death ('Terror goes into over-time!'). 19 copies of the period drama remained shrinkwrapped in their cases throughout my tenure there whilst the other, I was assured remained unwatched by the guy who'd rented it for his daughter to 'teach her something'. The demand for Sudden Death, however, was rabid and the renting population of Gorgie were livid to discover that it actually got stolen on it's third rent.

On my second night, a gang of kids came in to cause trouble. They stole some sweets and knocked some boxes off shelves and I tried to ignore them. Fortunately, a car backfired outside and they all ran out in the vain hope that it was in fact the sound of somebody getting shot. I ran and locked the door behind them. They realised within a few seconds and angrily banged on the window. There was no back door and they showed no signs of leaving, even when I turned the lights out, hoping to give the impression I had left out the fictional back. I sat alone in a dark Blockbuster atop my metal ladder for two hours. When the gang eventually dissipated, so had any hope of a bus home, so I spent my nights wages on a Taxi.

There were no normal customers in Gorgie, just varying degrees of freak, and by freak I suppose I mean Scotland's terrifying underclass. People with fucking big dogs, people who liked to shout, people who liked to steal – just like any disenfranchised, impoverished ne'er-do-wells but with the added bonus of an absolutely incomprehensible accent and dialect. Now, I love Scotland, and the accent is great when understandable, the only thing that drives me nuts is their use of vowels. To sound Scottish, all you have to do is swap the vowel sounds around randomly. So 'Do you not want to do that?' becomes 'Dae yuh know waanner Dee thut?' It's mindblowing and, I'm convinced, completely affected and staged to confuse English people. One customer came in and said 'ohlright, pul? Hoo Motch uz yuh jizz?' How much is my jizz???

'Yuh Juhss'

'my juhss….'

'YOUR JOOOOOOOOOOOOOSE'.

'juice?'

'aye'

'we don't have any juice, I'm afraid'

'AYE YUH DAE! YUH GOHT UH HAIL FRUDGE UFF UT!'

I fuhgured, sorry, *figured,* the guy had been sniffing glue or something.

'We don't stock juice, man, sorry'

'DUHNNEE FUCK WUTH MAE, PUL! HOO MOTCH UZ YUH JIZZ?'

'juice?'

'JOOS! JOOS! JOOS!'

He grabbed a can of Coke out of the fridge and holds it up and points to it.

'HOO MOTCH US THUS CUN UF JUHSS?'

'Coke? 65p'

'Uh gut fufty!'

He slammed fifty pence down on the counter and stormed off with his can of drink. Which I learned that day is referred to as 'juice' in Scotland. Might explain that whole 'unhealthiest nation in Europe' thing. As soon as he'd gone, I locked the door and sat up the top of my ladder, reading a book. I spent a lot of time over the next few months up that ladder with the door locked. It just seemed easier. Especially when I started doing weekend shifts and realised that Tynecastle Stadium – the home of Hearts football club was just down the road. Traditionally, if there had been a game on, the little Blockbuster on Gorgie Road would have hugely swollen takings by the end of the day on 'juice' and confectionary sales.

Not when I was on, though. I would lock the door and sit at the top of my ladder, listening to the frustrated would-be customers banging at the front door.

On the rare occasions when the door was unlocked, I got a horrible perspective on the whole home video thing and for the first time in my life, realised I might potentially agree with the Daily Mail about something. The video nasty scandal was over 10 years gone but I was suddenly faced with the reality behind it. Fathers, barely out of teenage themselves, would come in with their infant kids and tell them to choose a film. Without fail, the five or six year old would select some particularly gruesome looking horror film and the father would bring it up to the counter. It's a deeply horrible feeling to supply someone with a nasty film in the full knowledge that it's going to be watched by a very young child. I think censorship is really dangerous but exposing young kids to certain things under the guise of entertainment can't be much better. Sometimes I'd switch their choice for some cartoon or apologise and say the film they wanted doesn't seem to actually be in stock. Most of the time, I'd just lock the door and sit up on my ladder. It made it easier for everyone.

For a while, there was talk of moving me to the soon-to-open Blockbuster superstore on

South Clerk Street, just a five minute walk from my flat. At first I was elated, but then I realised that working in a flagship brand new store would involve... well, working. There's be no leniency on uniform, no watching films in the shop (just an endless loop of Ulrika Jonsson hosting 'BTV'), no sneaking the occasional can of Irn Bru or bag of Revels and I seriously doubted I'd get away with locking the shop and sitting up the top of a ladder for hours at a time, so I put the kibosh on it myself.

One winter night, I got in from work (an hour and a bit after leaving work) to find that the electricity meter had run out of power cards and my flatmate had used his good sense and gone to stay at his girl-friend's house rather than buy new ones. A pattern it took me a long time to detect. Sleeping with no heat in a draughty old flat in Edinburgh in January is really not an option unless you enjoy death. The only place open at midnight that sold power cards was an all night garage. In Gorgie. So, an hour and a half later, there I was in Gorgie, power cards in hand and waiting for the first of my two buses back to an icy cold flat that, despite my nocturnal voyage, wouldn't be warm until 7 o clock in the morning. I took a good long look down Gorgie Road and realised I never ever wanted to be there again. And I never have been.

CHAPTER 6

ULRIKA JONSONN VS POOZILLA

1997 – 1998

My return to the Headington branch of Blockbuster in the Xmas holidays was reminiscent of Luke Skywalker returning to his homestead after first meeting Ben Kenobi. It was in ruins. Carl, in what was to become a career pattern, had been demoted and sent off to run the much-smaller Summertown branch. This had, for a while, left the shop without a manager. Which was funny to think that the powers that be would rather have anarchy than Carl running things. These few lawless weeks had become the stuff of legend. Only Kevin remained from the previous bunch and he was eager to tell me all of the news. One of the girls they'd hired had a coke habit and would powder her nose several times a shift, another was a heroin addict fresh from rehab. They were stealing and brawling and slipping into comas in the toilet. He painted a picture of utter chaos. At the time, Blockbuster was doing a promotion with a breakfast cereal in which you got a free rental when you bought a box. Certain staff members carried one of these vouchers at all times and would scan it and pocket the customer's cash on a huge percentage of rentals. People had been making hundreds of pounds a day in cash.

A couple of weeks before I got there, a new manager had been installed. A beast of a woman. A candy-floss haired monstrosity from America called Mindy. She strutted about like a loud, bitchy, irrational old turkey. I didn't like her so much and she didn't like me from the moment we met. I guess I was the first member of staff to arrive after her so she ignored the problems of the past and concentrated on building a future workforce that would do her proud. Actually, that gives her some kind of rationale. She was a nasty old woman who ignored the anarchy going on around her, yet picked on me before I even had a chance to misbehave. It was as if she'd been tipped-off that I was trouble or something.

I didn't like the new people who were working there either, they were a bunch of thieving burnouts who didn't know or care about film at all. They say you pay peanuts, you get monkeys. They'd got slugs. Nasty, rude, uninteresting, hollow-eyed slugs. They made me genuinely miss Mad Bob. God, I even missed Carl. At least you could have fun with Carl, well, not with him maybe, but certainly at his expense. There was no fun to be had anymore. It was still great to be around Kevin, but with Mindy around, we didn't get to be ourselves.

My first evening shift was with a guy called Billy. I knew Billy, or at least of him, through school. He was kind of notorious, everyone loved him but he was wild. He was definitely a nice guy but anyone would be a fool to trust him. I trusted him. It was actually a pretty pleasant night working with him, we talked about the people we knew and friends we had in common and bitched about Mindy a bit. He was pretty funny, good company. It came to ten o clock and time to close up. "You can go, if you want, mate!" "Nah, it's OK."

The atmosphere suddenly turned frosty, but Billy stayed polite and chipper.

"There's only the cashing up and locking up left to do and it only takes one person to do them, go home, it's OK"

"I should just hang around, we're not supposed to…"

"Do you think I'm going to steal or something?"

"No!"

"So what's the difference? I mean, if you don't trust me, then, whatever"

He stared me down.

"No, I trust you. OK, I'll see you soon"

So, I left.

Of course, when I came in the next day, Mindy was waiting for me.

"Jon, is there a reason the take is down £100?"

Ugh.

"I don't know, Billy cashed up"

"He said you double checked it"

"Well… I did. Yeah. It all seemed to be OK"

"Did you double check it?"

"….yeah"

"Were you there when Billy cashed up?"

"….yeah"

"He didn't send you home early?"

"….no"

"and you counted that money?"

"…..yeah"

"How much was there?"

"I don't remember the exact amount"

"Roughly"

"….I don't remember. I've done a lot of maths since then"

She knew, of course she knew, after I left I remembered that Billy had forgotten to turn off the CCTV cameras (the traditional and essential cue for any kind of wrongdoing in that store), so she would have seen me leaving before the till was even opened and, more than likely, had footage of him doing some kind of exaggerated jump for joy. There was no punishment or follow up for Billy but she went on to treat me even harsher for the lie.

Not that I lasted long, at the end of my first week she did an unannounced bag search and found a video that I was returning, but hadn't checked out on the system. Why hadn't I checked it out? Because Blockbuster employees were not allowed to take home New Releases. We were allowed 3 free rentals a week and they had to be old films.

There are fifty copies of the newest films just sat on the shelves all week, not really renting out until the weekend, but there they must stay. You'd think it would be good practice for the staff to have actually seen the films, so if a customer said 'is this any good?' or 'can you recommend me something?' we'd be able to actually answer them. But opinions were discouraged in Blockbuster. Not even discouraged, banned. Russ told me on several occasions that there was no such thing as a bad film, just a film inappropriate to certain customers. He'd clearly never seen many Michael Winner films. Actually, what he said is frustratingly astute, but badly phrased. I'd rephrase it this way: For every dumb film, there is a queue of dumbasses who will love it. Of course there is such a thing as a bad film, some weeks when I'd check the delivery of new releases, I'd actually question whether there was such a thing as a good one anymore.

So we weren't allowed opinions. Only one person was allowed an opinion in the company and her view was sacred. That woman was Ulrika Jonsson. Host of the in-store programming BTV or Channel B, one of those, maybe both, I forget. I had to force myself to forget. That fucking in-store show was looped and, if Mindy was around, we'd be subjected to the same 30 minute show 16 times a day. It was like Chinese water torture or the death of a thousand cuts. It had 'reviews' of new films. These weren't reviews, although Ulrika put on a professional voice and assumed a tone of intellectual pondering ("Batman Forever is probably the greatest superhero film ever made. How could it not be with a cast featuring Jim Carrey?"), she found only good things to say about the dross we were 'moving the wall' for each week. And between her considered, weighty reviews, she would suddenly become light and bubbly again and pose questions such as 'Do you LOVE movies? Why not make it a BLOCKBUSTER night? For just £10, you can take TWO New Release movies and THRILL the whole family with a large bottle of Coke, two bags of Blockbuster popcorn and a bag of sweets! WHY NOT MAKE IT A BLOCK-BUSTER NIGHT?' It was transfixing to watch, almost hypnotic. And people went for that shit. People came in to spend £3.50 and happily spent a tenner to walk away with more food than they ever planned on eating, that they could have gotten cheaper in any other shop in the area. Credit where it's due, it takes talent to convince someone to spend three times the amount they intended to on things they didn't want and make them feel like they got a bargain.

Anyway, so, Mindy found this video in my bag, which even if I hadn't been returning, hadn't been stolen – since it was still on the premises. She hit the roof, I hit it too because it's totally illegal to search someone's bag without them being present. She told me I was fired and I told her I refused to be fired. She told me to leave the premises, I refused and instead went and phoned Russ. I used all of the words that terrify middle management – 'tribunal', 'code of practices', 'prepared to go over your head on this'. He told me to go home and that I would be paid for this shift and he'd phone me later with a solution. The solution was a transfer to Summertown, I could practically hear Carl sobbing.

Summertown is the poshest part of Oxford, which isn't to say it's trouble-free – Blockbuster being somewhat of a magnet for your undesirables of an area – but I knew the clientele would generally be of a higher calibre. I'll be honest, it was heaven. Carl was, it turned out, also managing the tiny branch in Rose Hill, so he was hardly ever even there. His assistant manager was a guy called Nick.

The first time I saw Nick, I was struck by how much he looked like a kids TV presenter, huge toothy smile, longish curly blonde hair and bright colourful jumpers, which he made a point of telling me he'd found in Oxfam. That probably makes him sound like a bit of a wimp but Nick was built like a brick shithouse. He did body-building for two hours a day, was proudly working class and had a temper on him unlike anything I had ever witnessed. He was biding his time, waiting until the following September when he had a place studying Sports Science at Chichester University. We bonded instantly over our love of Kevin Smith's films. Nick was funny both in the things he said and his general attitude, which was an impressive belief in the level of respect he was entitled to. If you were his friend, you could bust his balls all you wanted, but if you weren't, he tolerated nothing.

Where I always felt the need to rebuff Carl's attempts to get me to work with some kind of protracted witty excuse, Nick could do so with a simple, curt 'no'. Which probably made him just as frustrating but far less annoying than me. It was kind of like Carl didn't exist to Nick, that's how ineffectual he was. Even if they were stood next to each other, Nick thought him beneath even contempt. He just ignored Carl's presence completely unless absolutely necessary. Even then, he seemed to refuse to make eye contact or sustain an actual conversation. Although he would never admit it, nothing gave him more joy than throwing people out of the shop. He was so good at it. If ejection was an art-form, Nick was its greatest practitioner. He was the Rembrandt of chucking-out.

One time, a couple came in to dispute a late fee, Nick was perfectly professional with them and checked their account and realised that not only was the late fee valid, but there was a note saying they always try to contest their fines. I could see the change fall over him as he read the message and he looked back up at them with hollow eyes.

"You have to pay it."

"Fuck you!" the woman snapped.

I instinctively winced.

"What was that?" roared Nick "You don't fucking come into my shop and fucking swear at me!"

"I was swearing at my husband!" she shouted back.

"Right."

Nick was over the counter in a heartbeat and grabbed each of them by the scruff of the neck, marched them out of the shop, the guy stumbled so Nick actually *dragged* him out and threw both of them onto the pavement. The door closed behind them, so I couldn't make out what he shouted at them, but he turned around, marched back through the doors, grinned at me and rubbed his hands together gleefully. He absolutely lived for moments like that.

Then there was Dave. Dave was a strange one. A perfectly nice guy, kind of confused by the world. Whenever someone spoke to him, you could see a look of mild panic on his face as his eyes betrayed his mind processing and re-processing what he had just heard. Once in a while, he'd malfunction and something said to him quite innocently would result in a terrifying reaction. One time, the following summer, everyone who worked at the Summertown branch went out for a meal, we were happily all chatting away, Dave told us a story about his mate Kelvin, I asked if they lived together – a question which was pertinent to the story – and Dave paused, picked up a fork and lunged for me. Luckily, Nick was there to block the attack and calm him down. Turned out, he'd thought I was insinuating he was gay – which I honestly wasn't and made a mental note never to do under any circumstances. Dave was obsessed with Sylvester Stallone and actually looked a bit like him, but I think that was by design, not coincidence. His hair was slightly bouffant – just like Sly's in Rocky 3, and he held himself in a similar way. I mean, he even did the lip curl and slightly slurred speech if a girl was present. It was all quite subtle, but it was there. He had a fake tan, some big jewellery and would often quote Stallone's biography or just generally steer the conversation that way. His other obsession was Eddie Murphy, whose horrible trademark laugh he had shamelessly stolen. His favourite Eddie Murphy film was Boomerang and he would happily quote entire chunks of dialogue from it. Nick used to love to get Dave all worked up to the point where he'd be shouting Murphy or Stallone impersonations into the night. I was way too scared to try.

Dayshifts at the Summertown Blockbuster were heaven. You know how sometimes in life you just stop and go 'I'm really happy'? That was one of those periods for me. I'd wake up at 9, shower, get in my car and cruise over to Summertown, park behind the shop and open the shop up. I didn't wear uniform because nobody cared and I was alone until 3pm everyday anyway. Once the shop was open, the guy who ran the coffee stand outside would come in to fill his urn with water. In return, I'd quickly be given a huge yummy hot chocolate – the perfect start to a winter morning. Then I'd choose a film, stick it on and relax into the comfy chair to watch it. Sometimes with a half-inched bag of tortilla chips. My dad owned and ran a linen shop around the corner. At lunchtime, I'd lock up and go spend some time with him, which was always fun. Blockbuster didn't actually give breaks or lunch hours, so I gave myself an unofficial hour off each day. On my way back to the shop, I'd pick up a baked potato from the little baked potato van on Banbury Road and get back into the warm to eat and watch my second film of the day. Sometimes I'd have a little snooze behind the counter. I really loved it. Around three, Nick or Dave would turn up, we'd hang out for a few hours and I'd go home. I got paid for that.

You see, that's when working in a video shop was at its best. When the weather outside was horrible, no customers were coming in to bother you, you got yourself comfortable, something good to eat or drink and enjoying a good film. Those were the golden moments. Knowing that other people were busting their humps in offices or doing manual labour, getting stressed out, exhausting themselves, being generally miserable and you're getting paid to chill out and watch films. I still can't think of a job I'd rather do.

I phoned up the Summertown Blockbuster to make sure I had a job for the summer of '97. I was told that Carl was now only managing the Rose Hill branch.

My blood ran cold. I was not going to work in Rose Hill.

Rose Hill was, without doubt, the crappiest Blockbuster in town. In fact, the crappiest one I'd ever seen. It was worse than Gorgie. Although I'm sure it sounds quite charming, there are no roses in Rose Hill. No hills either. Rose Hill is a housing estate whose main export at the time seemed to be stabbings. The store itself was tiny and could only really accommodate one person working at a time. I had worked one shift there the previous winter. It was the only branch in Oxford with metal shutters. Even with them rolled up, the shop was shrouded in darkness. They kept a baseball bat under the counter, which is never a good sign. Within ten minutes of opening, a terrifying man with a big moustache (that on any other face would be highly comical but on this one merely acted as a confusing method to ratchet the terror up another notch or three) and a HUGE Alsation was shouting at me about the fines on his account. I deleted them and gave him a £20 credit by way of an apology. There was no way on earth I was putting up any kind of fight on behalf of Blockbuster. As soon as he was gone, a teenage girl came in trying to rent a horror film. This is a slightly different situation, if an underage person is served an 18-rated film, the company is not at fault at all, the employee is. Which, I suppose, makes sense but it certainly keeps you vigilant, especially since all the training materials when you start working at Blockbuster make it very clear that the government are employing a crack squad of undercover underagers, desperate for a bust. So I refused to serve her. I watched her leave and realised she was returning to a huge gaggle of rowdy looking teenagers to tell them that I, specifically, had denied them their after-noon's entertainment. My Gorgie training immediately took control, I locked the door before the information could disperse and the ramifications sink in. So, again, I found myself locked, cowering, in a Blockbuster in a depressed area. I phoned Carl and told him I was going home. He asked why and I told him because I didn't like it. He said the only time it was acceptable to close the shop was if there was a computer error. I hung up, removed the fuse from the computer's plug, phoned Carl back and told him the computer had gone down and I was going home. Which I did, once the crowd had dissipated.

I didn't want to spend a summer working at Rose Hill. I wouldn't. I took a moment to marvel at Carl's career trajectory. There was really no place farther he could fall than to end up managing Rose Hill (actually, it turned out there was – 2 years later, he'd be the assistant manager there). I called him, didn't insult him, played nice and he told me he could get me a job in the Summertown branch again. Thank God. He told me that the new manager there was a French woman called Matilda – a Gallic beauty by all accounts. He also warned me to look out for someone called Gina – "You'll see her ten minutes before she walks in the shop!" he told me. "I don't know what that means" I replied. "You know!" he continued "TITS!". "tits?" "She's got big tits!" "….ok."

It's a shame that's all Carl found to focus on because she was also a very clever, very funny, very nice person. Her most generous assets were certainly not the ones that Carl visibly fixated upon. Matilda was less well endowed in every sense. She was odd. And not in the good way. Not in the traditional video shop way. She was just… odd.

Nick, who was still working there, summed her up thusly:

"She's alright but she doesn't really know what the fuck's going on. Hasn't got a clue. And she just goes away for most of the day, dunno where. And she's a liar. She told me she has one brother and he's like a millionaire, but he isn't, he works in the Co-op. And I think she's sleeping with him. Oh, and she fucking stinks"

Nick was never one prone to exaggeration or lying, he summed her up pretty well. She was perfectly affable but very odd and, well, yes, pungent.

Blockbuster, at the best of times, didn't smell good. I worked in 5 or 6 separate branches over the years, and visited countless more and they all smelled the same. That Blockbuster smell. It was a mixture of must, dust and the death of many aerosol air fresheners. There were no openable windows in any of the Blockbusters I'd ever been in and, as apparent corporate policy, all branches had those suspended ceilings with polystyrene tiles. So it was like every bad smell that got released in those shops was contained within them for all time. A community fart archive, endlessly heated and re-heated by the light coming in the big front window. If you did a single shift in a Blocky, your clothes took that smell away with them. Although we rarely wore uniforms, we all had our separate set of 'work clothes' because we didn't like our normal clothes getting all stanked up.

Gina briefly considered talking to Matilda about the subject of hygiene, but her subtle attempts went unnoticed and she wasn't the type to be rude. Becky, who was now also working at Summertown, was far more brash in her attempts to inform Matilda, but was also unsuccessful. We basically had to grin and bear it, which became increasingly difficult as the summer got hotter and the shop became one big box of stink. There was only one fan in the whole shop and it was anchored to the ceiling, facing the customers. All it really did was waft the fetid warm air about a bit but even as a token gesture, it would have been nice to have one facing those of us dying behind the counter. To cool down, we'd open the deep-chest freezer in the back and climb in, sit on or just breathe in the coolness.

One morning I came to work and got on with stuff as normal. Matilda was there, doing whatever it was she did with the paperwork and I happily served the customers as they trickled in. Just after lunchtime, Matilda announced she had to go and do something and wouldn't be back until tomorrow. Happy to have the place to myself, I waved her off cheerily. In need of relief, I headed to the loo only to be greeted with what can only be described as a wall of methane. as I opened the bathroom door. The air was so thick with the smell of faeces, I felt my lungs turn brown. I ran away, grabbed a can of air freshener and sprayed the entire can out into the room as I clasped my other hand over my mouth. You could almost see the air freshener fizzle and evaporate as it hit the pungent cloud. I opened the back door of the shop and held in my wee until I thought the smell might have diminished sufficiently.

An hour later, I braved the room once more. It still STANK but was marginally more bearable. I flipped open the toilet to be faced with what would shortly become known as 'Poozilla'. The biggest single turd I have ever seen in my life. It looked like a boa constrictor. I still to this day can not believe that a lady as small as Matilda was capable of giving anal birth to such a monster. It wasn't even floating, it was too big! It was resting on the sides of the pan, half out of the water. As my respect of the magnitude of the beast faded and I realised what it was, I instinctively gagged. I thought I was going to puke, I ran out, closed the door behind me and went out the backdoor and took a piss against the shed out there. With the bathroom door closed, my repulsion turned into amusement.

At three o clock, Nick showed up for work without a care in the world. He greeted me merrily as he rounded the counter.

"Check out what Matilda's put in the bathroom!"

Now, this was an innocent statement to him as our bathroom there was so large, it was often used for storage, indeed at that time, it was full of unsold life-sized cardboard cut-outs of the Spice Girls.

"Oooh" he grinned, heading straight for the crime scene, expecting some kind of fantastic and exciting treat.

It took him a few seconds, then the squeals of disgust and giggly delight filed the shop. He came running out of there guffawing and retching.

"I THOUGHT IT WAS A MONSTER!!!!!"

We rolled about giggling for ages, but our hysteria was interrupted by a phone call. It was the manager of the Cowley Road Blockbuster, who was speaking in hushed and desperate tones she said simply "It's Cowley! PETER LUSH IS HERE! Full inspection! All branches! Phone the others!"

Peter Lush was the most senior executive of Blockbuster UK that any of us ever came into contact with. Unlike Russ and his middle-management cronies, Lush had a brain in his head and knew instantly if you were pulling any crap. The only way I can compare it is how at school you could gleefully be mocking a supply teacher and then the head teacher would walk in and you knew you were in shit. Lush was like a head teacher, you instantly respected him for his authority and distance. Full inspection meant FULL inspection. He would do a tour of the shop and demand answers as to why things weren't exactly as they were supposed to be.

We panicked as we realised that we had intentionally destroyed and discarded the damn Ulrika Jonsson video that was meant to be playing on a loop. Nick ran out into the shop and started tidying as I tried to put straight everything behind the counter. We worked fast and maniacally and, fairly quickly, we were done. The store looked as good as it could. We'd even restocked the fridges in accordance to the 'plan-o-gram' head office routinely sent and we routinely ignored.

We breathed a sigh of relief. Then stopped.

"The shit!" Nick gasped.

"Maybe he won't inspect the bathroom?" I tried to convince myself as much as Nick.

We just knew he would. And he wouldn't miss the smell or the tree trunk poking out of the bowl. Worse still, there was no sign of Matilda, so he'd think it was one of us. Nick ran in and flushed the toilet. A futile action. Water merely cascaded off the mighty jobbie. I dumped some toilet paper on top, hoping that it might dislodge the turd as it was pulled down. No such luck. The turd sat, proudly unmoved and glistening wet as the paper vanished down the U-bend.

"Get a stick and knock it off the sides, get it vertical so it can flush!"

"You get a stick! I'm not touching that fucking thing!"

Nick put his foot on the head of the broom and yanked the handle off it. He advanced towards the toilet then stopped. "Toss a coin" "Nah, it's alright, you're halfway there" "TOSS A COIN!"

I tossed a coin. Nick called Heads. It was Tails. He roared in frustration, marched towards the bowl and attacked the beast that awaited within. "Got it!" he cried and flushed. The poo was now vertical but far too enormous to flush. It was kind of jammed into the outlet now, swaying slightly as the water passed over it.

"You should break it up – into smaller pieces" I ventured.

"No, you should!" he countered

"COIN TOSS!" I cried

"No." he responded, handing me the broom handle.

I tried a couple of jabs. The poo was wily. It seemed to rotate in the water to deflect my strikes. I tried to push it up against the side of the pan to squeeze the stick through it, but it slipped out of grasp. I rained blows down upon it hoping that just one might connect and cause a breach. I was Captain Ahab, consumed by my mission, but nothing worked.

"One of us needs to hold it down while the other chops bits off it!" I reasoned. Nick found a mop and unscrewed the handle from the head. We both stood there trying to figure out in our heads which was the least disgusting job.

"I'll hold it down!" we both declared. "You hold it down" he sighed.

I got the little bugger up against the side of the bowl and wedged it there with the side of the broom handle. Nick started the attack. He noted, as the first chunk achieved separation that it was a different colour inside the poo from the outside. It seemed to be a sticky light brown confection wrapped in a thick rubbery green-brown coat. Eventually, we'd got the turd into 4 or 5 large but manageable chunks. Nick triumphantly flushed the toilet. Not one of them disappeared. They were completely buoyant. They just sat there bobbing away at us mockingly.

"PAPER!" We dumped toilet paper on the nuggets and flushed again. Victory! One had gone! It took another 15 minutes to finally flush all of those little bastards.

Peter Lush did not show up.

CHAPTER 7

SCOTTISH INDEPENDENTS

1998 – 1999

I was always somewhat confused by the business minds behind Edinburgh's video shops. For a fairly small city, there were an awful lot of them. Blockbuster, obviously, was well represented with six or seven branches. Global Video was a successful Scottish chain and had almost as many. Fast Forward was a chain just in Edinburgh with, I think 4 or 5 branches. Then you had the independents – C&A Video with it's bizarre mock-Roman interior design. Planet Video – hand-painted and unambitious – tucked away down a seedy side street. Vogue Video – flashing lights and dated Hollywood aesthetic, garish and pokey. Finally, the mighty Alphabet Video.

Alphabet was a revelation to me, I'd been in independent video shops before but I'd never realised how far you could push your independence. They didn't look like a video shop, to start with. No plastic walling or desperate promotions. The building itself was bizarre, it was like a normal house, but someone had taken a sledgehammer to it. The upstairs had been smashed out and what remained formed a rickety wooden mezzanine level which creaked ominously and looked like it could collapse at any moment. The walls were plastered with pictures torn out of film magazines. It was dark and cosy. There were films EVERY-WHERE, thousands of them, stacked with their spines showing in a multitude of ramshackle bookcases. They were organised the way someone who loves films would organise their collection – split into genres, then sub-sectioned into important directors and stars, then alphabetised. The guys who worked there were friendly but not intrusive, they didn't sell food or mess about in any way. Their sole deal was three films for a fiver. In the middle of the shop was a huge fish tank and the atmosphere there was unlike anywhere I'd ever been. It was like being in the world's biggest movie geek's living room. The shop could be full, but there was a respectful excited silence as people discovered films they hadn't seen for years or had always wanted to see. It was the best video shop I'd ever been in.

Anyway, Alphabet was on Marchmont Road, one of the nicer, more studenty, parts of town. A two minute walk from it was a Fast Forward and literally across the road from that was a Global. I never understood how all three managed to stay in business. Was there that much video money being thrown around? I assume it was a hangover from the 80s, where the video retail market had yet to blossom and rental was still a regular and dependable part of most family's weeks. Even before the advent of DVD, rental had taken a huge hammering from satellite TV and reasonably priced retail videos, also, it had been a boom industry and whereas there may well have been a point where three video shops could prosper within minutes of each other (like wanky coffee places and mobile phone shops do these days) there was clearly at least one video shop too many on Marchmont Road. But which one was it?

Alphabet was an amazing independent shop in an affluent student area, they were probably the healthiest of the bunch financially. Global had the power of a national head office behind it, they were heavy on promotions and had a management structure which ensured their shops were well stocked and well looked after. They were certainly less horrible than Blockbuster whilst still successfully emanating that corporate 'why not give us all of your money?' thing. So, who was the odd one out? Who was the video shop chaff?

Poor old Fast Forward. I kind of liked them. They were a genuine relic from the 80s. The logo was all written in a red and yellow dynamic electro-looking font. I don't know who named the company, but I suppose they did choose the most dynamic (whilst utterly meaningless in it's new context) sounding feature of a video recorder. The Marchmont Road branch was small and narrow – essentially a corridor with red plastic walling on each side, inefficiently, for such a small shop, displaying all the films with the covers facing outwards. If memory serves, the carpet was even red and yellow. Suspended polystyrene ceiling, of course. It kind of had that Blockbuster smell but not as 'corporatey'. The smell probably aspired to be like Blockbuster's but never quite achieved the same level of depravity.

I was looking for work, living just off Marchmont Road, so applied to all three shops. Which do you think hired me? Yeah.

Fast Forward was owned by a plump friendly woman in her early forties called

Sandra and her husband Eddie – who I never actually met. As I understood it, they belonged to one of the big business dynasties of Scotland. Eddie's father had apparently made a lot of money in business and some of his acumen and, well, most of his money seemed to have passed on to Eddie and his brother Ron, who owned a factory on the other side of town producing corporate gifts and clothing or something like that.

Most video shops that opened in that initial boom were like Fast Forward. These were not labours of love, but sound investments for keen young entrepreneurs. Indeed, the undoing of most of these small chains came in the nineties when Blockbuster appeared to target the more successful ones and open up stores within spitting distance utilising a far better business model (and, if we're to believe rumour, since Blockbuster was only in the UK to keep the corporate flag flying, not to make money, they really had nothing to lose and could undercut forever) and took all of their business away. Not able to out-Blockbuster Blockbuster, the owners of these chains didn't have a clue about creating a sustainable alternative or even how to stock their own shelves efficiently. Many tried to fight back by matching Blockbuster on 'copy depth' (horrible jargon, just means how many of each title you buy) and trying to beat their prices – which meant they were spending big (bigger then Blocky, who bought centrally for the whole of the UK operation, presumably paying very little per video) and charging too low to ever maintain a profit.

I have no idea how Fast Forward survived into the late nineties. They certainly weren't taking much money. Nobody seemed to ever come in except the perpetually confused. I got quite depressed during my shifts there. The shop felt too red, to begin with. It felt like I was stuck in a big wound. At the other end of the shop, the tiny window gave me a glimpse at the normal non-red world outside, which I pined for. On the wall was a promotional clock from Columbia Tri-star from 1985, announcing some of their new releases including Ghostbusters. The cheap cardboard print inside had faded from over a decade of the barest glimpse of sunlight.

Sandra knew nothing about films. She almost proudly admitted this. She was also strictly hands-off – she owned the shop, did the hiring and firing and paperwork but she very rarely visited. She totally trusted her manager Adrien. Adrien was a very nice guy but I have no idea why she hired him. I think he was Greek, but he could have been Middle Eastern or maybe Italian. He had a permanent smile plastered on his face and incredibly vacant eyes. He knew nothing whatsoever about film and had no interest in it at all. I wasn't aware of him ever taking films home or ever wanting to discuss them. I'm not entirely convinced he actually understood what a video was or did. He wore lots of aftershave, which meant even after he went home for the day, he left a tangible sense-memory of his presence right through to closing time.

The place was just so desolate. It was like a little black hole in the middle of a vibrant area. The stock was shameful, there was a small and rubbish selection of new releases – padded out horribly with cheap TV movies and there was a baffling selection of older films which seemed to cover only a six year period and really none of the highlights of those six years.

The most poignant moment I have from that shop was the day a delivery came in that contained the first ever DVD released in this country – Armageddon. It was like a 150 year old man being handed his great great great great grandson to hold. Mind boggling to think that these two things could share the same moment in time. It seemed confusingly progressive that Sandra had actually ordered it at all – it never once rented in the time I worked there. Nobody actually had DVD players at that point, it'd be another year before I even got one. Adrien was characteristically befuddled.

"We are renting CDs!" He proclaimed.

"No, it's a DVD, Adrien"

"Is CD! Is music from film!"

"No, that's the film, man."

"Yes, music from film"

"The film is on the disc!"

"No, is CD! Is music!"

"They've put a film on there!"

"Noooooooooooooooo! How you watch it?"

"On a special DVD player"

"On TV?"

"Yeah, it plugs in like a video recorder"

"Noooooooooooooooo!"

and he held the DVD up to the light, trying to see the individual frames of footage. When I came in the next day, he'd put the dvd on a small shelf above the counter with a little cardboard sign that said 'RENT THE CD!'

I don't have many memories from my time at Fast Forward because, honestly, nothing ever once happened there. My friends wouldn't even visit me there because it depressed them. I actually managed to get fired for the first time in my life because despite booking 3 weeks off through Adrien so I could go and film my graduation film, he forgot to tell Sandra. So she sacked me and he never fessed up to her that I hadn't in fact been skiving. When I went in to confront him about it, he started sobbing uncontrollably. I couldn't be bothered to fight for that job – especially with graduation in sight and the possibility that I could feasibly spend the rest of my life stuck behind that very counter in lieu of something else ever coming along.

CHAPTER 8

BOX OFFICE SMASHES

1999

Part of me thought I'd never work in a video shop again. Although it'd always been my dream to own one, I was a graduate now. My graduation film was going into film festivals, I had production companies courting me. I had absolute confidence that my path from film vendor to film-maker was clear. But I didn't have any money. Lots of people were saying lots of nice things to me but nobody was actually paying. I was living in a one bedroom flat with one other guy and a menagerie of mice and flies.

I hit my overdraft limit and realised that I was essentially screwed. Not only that, the only thing I was really qualified for now was working in video shops so I decided to swallow my pride and apply back at Blockbuster. The great thing about Blocky was that you could get fired for gross misconduct – not, confusingly, that I ever did – and then rehired at the same branch within a year because the turnover of staff – including management – was so high nobody would know who you were. I would rather have starved than gone back to Gorgie, so I decided to apply to the Tollcross branch. It wasn't so small that I'd be alone and bored, it was fairly close to my flat and Tollcross wasn't too dodgy of an area. As I walked up Lothian Road, CV in hand, I noticed a new shop being fitted. A new video shop. It seemed too bizarrely serendipitous to ignore, so I knocked on the door and asked if anyone in charge was about. One of the guys stocking shelves told me they were hiring and that the boss wasn't there right now but he'd pass my CV on to her. I decided not to go into Blockbuster until I'd heard back. I got a phone call that afternoon from the new shop's owner Diane. She said it was an excellent CV and could I come in for an interview the following day. I told her I'd be happy to.

Diane was exactly the kind of person who could take on Blockbuster and win. She was opening a video store practically opposite an established Blocky and seemed pragmatic enough to beat them at their own game. As soon as we started talking about it, I got excited. She had actually worked undercover at that Blockbuster for a couple of months to get the inside scoop and we both traded stories about their inefficient and ridiculous practises. We agreed that the way to beat them was to offer good but brief and ever-changing promotions as it would take weeks for Blocky head office to approve stuff like price changes or special promotions to beat or match ours and by the time they had, we'd have a new and more exciting promo. It was exhilarating to hear her talk about this stuff and I felt like I might be joining the Rebellion, preparing to destroy the evil blue Empire. Diane was in her late thirties or early forties and seemed very keen and motivated to make a genuine success of this. It was the first time I'd ever seen anybody in the industry give even the slightest shit about anything.

Our conversation came to a natural break and she glanced over my CV again.

"Well, you certainly seem qualified! You clearly know what you're doing. Tell me, why did you leave Fast Forward?"

"Oh, I was finishing off my degree, I was too busy to hold down a job"

"Are you sure you didn't just not turn up for work without giving a reason and then got fired?

"Uh……….."

"Sandra is my sister-in-law"

Oh no.

"So, what happened"

"I booked three weeks off to make my graduate film. I booked them, through Adrien, I really did. I came back three weeks later and was fired."

"So, why didn't you tell Sandra this?"

"Because Adrien cried and, to be honest, I hated working there, anyway"

"You know, I just bought the Fast Forward chain off Eddie and Sandra. We're going to rebrand those stores and this new one will be our flagship store."

"Well, I don't know if you're going to hire me now, but if you do, please don't make me work at the Marchmont one"

"No, I want you to work at this one"

"Really? That's great"

"Listen, I'll cut to the chase. I want you to be the manager"

"Uhhhhhh"

"Don't worry, you can go away and think about it. But this isn't Blockbuster and it isn't Fast Forward – this is a completely new video shop, which I think you can help me make into something incredible."

We shook hands – she had a good handshake! I left to wander the streets in deep contemplation. It seemed like I'd been handed my ultimate dream and my ultimate nightmare. I'd always wanted my own video shop and although this technically wouldn't be 'mine', it could be the shop that I built. I could take some pride in it. On the other hand, being manager of a shop is way different to being a part-time till-jockey. There's less goofing off. I wouldn't be able to be flaky or leave at the drop of a hat if I suddenly got a meeting in London. Also, my dad had been a shop manager since his late twenties and he never seemed to be having a whole lot of fun. At 23, I wasn't sure I was ready or willing to follow in his footsteps. But it was kind of exciting, and I was skint. So I went for it.

The shop itself was horrible. I wished I had got involved before the shop-fit because as new and clean as it all was, I hated it. Diane explained to me that the days of plastic walling (that moulded crap you see in video shops with spaces to fit videos with their covers facing out) were over and we were bringing in the new age – slatted walling. MDF wall covering with big gouges in it every 10 inches or so which you could hook plastic shelves into. The idea being here was an endlessly changeable set up, I don't think it changed once from the day it opened. Not only was the slat walling ugly, it was PINK. As was much of the shop in general. Hot pink. The logo, the signage, there was a pink neon light in the window. It looked, from the street, like a porn shop. I asked her why she had plumped for these colours and she explained that someone she had met had a very successful chain of video shops in London and she felt it was down to his branding. About a year later, on a visit to London, I realised that she had not just been influenced by this guy's branding, she had essentially nicked it. The logo was basically identical but instead of PRIME TIME VIDEO, ours read BOX OFFICE VIDEO. The hot pink actually made me yearn for the distinguished blue and yellow of Block-buster.

Despite the horrible colours, I was actually amazingly optimistic, here I was in a trusted, high-ranking position at the beginning of what was set to become a national chain of video shops that could end the horrible Blockbuster hegemony. Choices, practices and suggestions that I made could change the culture on a national, maybe eventually international basis. You know, it was exciting. Diane clearly had her sights set very high and that was amazingly cool to be around.

On my first day of work, Diane excitedly turned up with a bunch of big cardboard boxes which I helped her unload from her car. "The uniforms!!!" she cooed. I hadn't realised there would be uniforms. I actually thought everyone looked rather good in their own clothes, but I was willing to give her the benefit of the doubt. As she opened the first box, I breathed a huge sigh of relief that they, at least, weren't pink. They were blue. Blockbuster blue. Blockbuster blue waffle shirts, like they had at Blockbuster. In fact, in the exact place where on Blockbuster waffle shirts, there was a yellow embroidered 'BLOCKBUSTER VIDEO', these had a pink embroidered 'BOX OFFICE VIDEO'. In an almost identical size and font. I looked up hopefully for a laugh from Diane and confirmation that this was just a joke. But it wasn't. These were identical, but actually worse than, Blockbuster uniforms because they had pink on them.

"They're just like the Blockbuster ones!"

"Well, yeah! But the pink is a bit more eye catching!"

"I don't have to wear one, do I?"

"Not if you don't want to" relief set in for a second "you can wear a fleece!"

She ripped open another box and there, indeed were the Box Office fleeces. Shiny, silky, synthetically velvety blue zip-up jackets with that detestable pink logo on the breast. I opted for a fleece because I figured I could wear normal clothes and this on top, unzipped. People might not notice.

"Try it on!"

Mmmmm. Ill-fitting and itchy. It was like being home again.

I figured I'd let the uniforms slide for now – she was still excited about the whole thing. Maybe in a few weeks I could point out the excessive 'corparateyness' and we could scale it back a bit. Deliveries of new videos and DVDs poured in and the shop was open very quickly. DVDs were still way in the minority at this point and the films which made it to the format often seemed to be a somewhat arbitrary selection. The film which really bolstered the format was The Matrix. That was the first must-see DVD and inspired a lot of people to migrate to the format. Unfortunately, the initial DVD version of it was a tetchy wee bastard which resulted in an ever-expanding 'We regret to inform you that The Matrix does not work in the following DVD players' sign.

On my first day as manager of Box Office, Diane came in and spent the morning training her staff.

"When someone comes into the shop, you have to greet them IMMEDIATELY! – Hello sir! Hello madam!"

Oh no.

"I do NOT want staff taking home stock that could be renting out. Do NOT take new releases home under any circumstances"

Ugh.

"If you haven't sold a bag of popcorn or sweets or a bottle of Coke with each rental, you haven't done your job!"

Jesus.

Halfway through the training, one of the guys she'd hired – a friendly young student called Simon – pointed out to me that there was nowhere to sit down. I told him there were still a few oversights from opening so quickly and I'd make sure there were some chairs. When the hellish indoctrination was over, I approached a rather self-congratulatory Diane and asked if the chairs were on order.

"No chairs!"

"What do you mean 'no chairs'?"

"It looks terrible when you walk into a shop and the staff are just sitting around"

"But... they can't just stand up for an 8 hour shift"

"They do in McDonalds"

They *do* in McDonalds. I mean, she was right. Had I been over my shock at the idea of standing up for 8 hours a day, I could have formulated a response about how in McDonalds, they are always full of customers and the staff are moving about and have an amount of adrenaline and purpose to sustain them. And breaks. She was talking about standing up all day in an empty shop (video shops were only really busy evenings and weekends) with nothing to do. I mean, wouldn't Amnesty International have something to say about that?

"Just... standing up?"

"Well, I hope not, there's always cleaning to do, or stock-checking, shelf-tidying. I mean, there's no reason at all that anyone should ever just be standing about doing nothing. That would be terribly inefficient for the company."

Oh god. She didn't want to beat Blockbuster. She wanted to *be* Blockbuster.

She was going to out-corporate them! And because there was no middle management, shareholders or huge corporations going on, every time you didn't do the good-worker thing, you'd have to answer directly to the owner of the company.

After a few days of throbbing feet and blisters, I found ways around her nonsense. I purposely stacked boxes of empty DVD and video cases at such a height that we could all sit on them behind the counter. Luckily, with a bunch of other stores in Edinburgh to torture, Diane was only in the shop a couple of times a day. We kept dusters down there so if she came in unexpectedly and didn't see someone stood upright in a military fashion greeting her, you could pretend to have been dusting under the counter space.

I didn't get a say in the initial hiring as many of them had been hired before me. Generally, she'd chosen bubbly but infuriatingly normal young students. They seemed to be predominantly Irish for some reason, too. They were nice people but again far from film literate so the one most obvious topic of conversation went by painfully unaddressed and awkward silences were the order of the day. I actually abused my role as manager – imagine that – and ended any awkward silence with a request for whoever was making me feel awkward to go do some cleaning or some kind of menial work. Actually, thinking about it, that probably wasn't abuse of position – that's probably exactly what retail managers are supposed to do.

The one relief from the amiable drudgery of my staff was Ginger Ben. Ben was fantastic. He had been a couple of years below me at my film school. He was funny, articulate and loved film. In my eyes, the perfect video shop employee. In Diane's eyes – the opposite. He had no interest or aptitude in even the most basic parts of the job, he'd giggle when trying to provide the customer service Diane demanded and had a far lower tolerance than me for bad films – often commenting on or criticising customers for their choices. "OH GOD! WHAT? DON'T RENT THAT!"

After a few weeks, Diane called a meeting of all of the managers of all of her stores. We had to go to her big house in The Grange (the very poshest part of Edinburgh) one evening. I felt we should have been paid to attend an out-of-hours business meeting but everyone else seemed to think merely being in a big house in The Grange was payment enough. The way Diane chaired the meeting smacked of someone who had just read some horrible American book on how to host a successful business meeting. She put torturous effort into saying very buzzwordy things and asking us quite inclusive questions (in the style of 'this is YOUR company. How would YOU improve YOUR company?') but clearly was not even listening to our responses. You could actually see her ignoring all responses as she planned what her next speech or question would be. I didn't even attempt to hide my annoyance. After being subjected to her uninformed pontificating all day, I'd had to drag myself to her ostentatious pile to be subjected to even more. This woman seemed to live just to appear professional. I decided to tell her exactly what was going wrong in the shops. At first, she didn't notice I was speaking, so I peppered my speech with her name until she paid a bit of attention. She then went from not hearing to not listening. She was apparently just nodding in dumb appreciation of the fact that she'd inspired someone to talk. I gave up and just smiled politely like everybody else as she carried on.

As I was leaving, she called me back.

"You seem to have a lot of good ideas, Jon"

"Oh, you heard those?"

"I think you have so much potential. Why don't you put them all in a memo for me?"

"and you'll read it?"

"I'd be an idiot not to make the most of the manager of my flagship store!"

So I did it. Over the next few nights, I wrote one of the greatest documents of my life. With Jerry Maguire style passion and fervour, I found pouring out of me the template for the perfect video shop. It was exciting. I tackled everything – a better name for the store, better décor and branding ideas, a questionnaire for hiring potential staff, how to organise it, pricing structures and promotions. Philosophies about how to beat both Blockbuster and the successful indies. I covered every single base. It was a monolithic piece of work. I wish I still had a copy of it. I knew it would impress her. I also knew she wouldn't change a lot of the big stuff, but I was sure we could at least get the staff treated a bit better, the shop a bit better stocked and the customers slightly less patronised.

She had one thing to say about it the day after I presented it to her. It was this:

"I liked your idea for laminates on lanyards for the staff" – I'd suggested something saying the staff's name and their favourite movie or a catchphrase or something fun. It was part of my section on why staff shouldn't wear uniform. I reasoned that by wearing these things around their necks, customers would recognise them as staff but not as corporate peons – encouraging respect and better interaction between staff and customer.

"Ron said it'd be too expensive" she frowned. "But we will get name badges made up – so good work! We really appreciated your input!"

"So… we're scrapping uniform?"
"No! The name badges will go on the uniform!"

Great.

One day she marched in dragging a bin bag full of old videos.

"The shelves are looking empty, I thought you could use these to pad out the lower shelves around the shop"

I opened up the bag and found a treasure trove of rare and exciting films. I couldn't even disguise my joy.

"These are amazing! These are exactly the kind of films I was talking about in my proposal! If we stock this stuff, we'll get a lot more of the students coming in."

"Well, I've got another couple of bags in my car – I was taking them to the tip"

"THE TIP?!?!?! You were throwing them away?"

"They're old, not renters anymore"

"Bring them in, I guarantee these will rent!"

"I have more, maybe another 20 bags"

"WHERE DID YOU GET 20 BAGS OF VIDEOS? TO THROW AWAY?"

"Just in the backrooms and basements of all of the Fast Forward shops – if they didn't rent, they'd put them in the back to save on space"

Over the next few weeks, I added hundreds, if not thousands, of incredible films to the shop. Each bag came from Diane with some kind of disparaging comment about me sifting through rubbish bags like a tramp. She seemed amused by my enthusiasm and made no attempt to disguise the fact she was humouring me rather than understanding or respecting what I was trying to do for the shop. Even when the stuff started making money, she worried it might be at the detriment of the more expensive New Releases.

We were making OK money, but not great. This really frustrated her. She took it personally and seemed to blame it on our inefficiency. At this point, she came up with a two-pronged strategy. The first prong was to put New Releases on the shelves on

Fridays. New Releases came out on Mondays, stores receive their stock on Friday purely so it can all be added to the system and ready to hit the shelves first thing Monday morning. All retailers are specifically instructed by the studios and wholesalers that they must wait until the Monday to release the stock. If we were caught, there was an inherent yet probably arbitrary threat of legal retribution, they'd certainly supply us slower. I told her this, but she laughed at me. She said nobody would ever check up. I pointed out that Blockbuster was watching us like a hawk and that's all they needed to get us in trouble. She didn't care. The stock would go out on Fridays. I told her I took no responsibility for any outcome. The second prong of her attack – the magical move to make the shop suddenly run efficiently was to fire Ben. He only did three shifts a week and, although admittedly he was useless at banking, he was the only member of staff we had who the customers responded to at all. I said it wasn't fair to sack him without even giving him a warning, she disagreed and told me to fire him.

I flat out refused, I told Diane that if she wanted Ben fired, she would have to do it. She countered that it was my job to handle the staff and she was my employer and it was also my job to do whatever she said. We argued for about half an hour about the whole thing. I told her I would quit on the spot if she fired Ben. She told me it was my responsibility to sort him out and if I didn't she'd fire both of us, which was a dumb threat since I'd made it clear I would happily quit. Later that day, Ben breezed into the shop all smiles and giggles. I shouted at him until he cried. Didn't make much difference, though. I just got better at covering for him.

It should be said at this point, that hindsight and life experience have subsequently offered me a certain perspective on this which eluded me at the time. For all of Diane's failings, she was just a person trying to build a successful business by appropriating the current retail trends. This must have been made infinitely harder for her by the huge, furious long-haired beast she had contracted (and was sly enough to not do anything to actually break that contract) who didn't even have the decency to hide his contempt at her every utterance and who, at twenty three years old thought he knew far more than her about business. I... do.. still.. think I knew far more than her about business but I can at least recognise that I was also behaving like a bit of a tit.

A month or so later, Diane added a third prong to her attack. It might have been the stupidest prong I have ever been aware of before or since. She called another meeting. This meeting was a far bigger one. Ron was present, as were a lot of the other members of staff of all of the branches and some people I didn't recognise. She had told us she was going to make a huge announcement. I genuinely had no idea what it could be.

What she revealed to us that night was her fully formed business plan and the first steps of implementation of a sister project to her Box Office empire.

In60.

In60, we were told was a revolutionary idea that would change Edinburgh then, very soon, the country and the world. I was certainly intrigued. The idea was simple. It was a delivery service that delivered groceries, alcohol, videos and CDs (to rent or buy) within a guaranteed 60 minutes of receiving the phone call for free, 24 hours a day, 7 days a week. It was the 'for free' bit that I didn't understand.

"So, someone can phone up and order a pack of three condoms, and you'll deliver them for free?" I asked incredulously.

"YES!" Diane enthused.

"I don't understand!"

"What don't you understand, Jon?" Ron intervened.

"You're paying for a phone system, for people to answer the phone, for mopeds and drivers, I know it's not my concern, but where's the profit on delivering a pack of condoms?"

"People will order more than a pack of condoms!" Diane snapped back.

"There's a minimum order value?" I asked

"No, we might introduce one"

I just didn't understand it. I mean, pizza delivery makes sense because pizzas are cheap to produce and have a huge mark-up. The mark up on basic groceries is tiny. And paying staff around the clock to just be waiting on calls? I just couldn't process it. Even when Ron explained it was all to do with working in larger volumes, it just made no sense.

I got angry when I was told they'd be using stock from the Box Office stores for the rentals – rather than having their own separate stock. Indeed, within weeks, as I fully expected, Diane was angry at the drop in our takings and couldn't understand it might be because In60 was taking all of our most rentable stock away and adding the profits to their balance rather than ours. It just appeared to me this was another case of Diane having vision but no sense. I thought she was an idiot and I just found myself angry all of the time.

One night I had a dream in which Diane was a mouse. I picked her up and put her in a matchbox and then jumped up and down on it until dawn. This situation was clearly not good for me.

A few days later, she was showing a group of businessmen around the shop. I can't remember if they were journalists, investors, maybe she never told me. But she was bragging about a lot of stuff and taking credit for my work. At the point when she told them, in purposeful earshot of me that it had been her grand idea to introduce a large stock of older and more interesting films to appeal to students, I quit. Right there, on the spot. I was furious. I told her I quit. She wanted me out of the shop and not to have a spat in front of these visitors. She told me to take two days off – fully paid to make up my mind. My mind was made up and I filled those two days with joyous sleep, feelings of liberation and a little time set aside to write the most cutting letter of resignation possible. Angela, my assistant manager who took over as manager, saw Diane reading it and told me it had made her cry. I really let her have it with both barrels, stooping so low as to suggest if she treated her young children even remotely in the same way she treated her staff, they would undoubtedly hate her by the time they hit their teens. In my recollection, it was epic and glorious. It was probably just mean. I ceremoniously burned my Box Office fleece a couple of months later at our flat's Guy Fawkes party. Whatever it was made of, it burned quickly, gave off a foul chemical smell and vanished.

CHAPTER 9

THE LONELINESS OF THE LONG DISTANCE VIDEO SHOP EMPLOYEE

2000

My period of unemployment after Box Office dragged on for a few months. I half-heartedly hunted for a job that could utilise my Photoshop or film editing skills, but nothing presented itself really. I liked my (also unemployed) flatmates – Douglas and Dougie, The Douglae – and kind of treated that time as the big wind-down from 17 years of education, we lived like bums and enjoyed doing so. It would be half-true to say we lived in a squat but we actually paid rent to live in a run-down shithole that should have been condemned years earlier.

One day, I was cutting across from South Clerk Street to Marchmont, when I noticed a sign looking for staff at Planet Video.. I didn't even bother going in to enquire about the job, I went straight home, printed out my CV and marched straight into Planet under the assumption that the job was mine. At that point, the one thing I was completely qualified to do was to work in a video shop. I honestly doubt there was anyone else in the country that had such eminent qualifications for such a specific dead-end job.

Planet was it's own breed of video shop. Like, you couldn't get the measure of the shop by just looking around it. It was a pokey shop on a pokey side street. There was nothing corporate about the outside signage, the name of the shop was painted in funky colours above the door and inside, aside from the nasty plastic walling, there were handmade bookcases and everything had been painted funky shades of blue, purple and green by hand. It was clearly a proud independent but it wasn't stocked like an indie. Or like a corporate. It was a very strange mix. There were an awful lot of rubbish films on the shelves, stuff a normal indie would never touch and, because whereas Blockbuster may have one copy of such a film and 80 copies of something more significant, since Planet only had one copy of each title, the bad seemed to outnumber the good. But there were plenty of great films – the foreign section was comprehensive.

They had a copy of Leningrad Cowboys Go America. Leningrad Cowboys had, by now, become my test of a video shop's mettle. It was a cult film, but not a *cult* film, not everyone had heard of it, yet if you haven't heard of it and consider yourself a film geek, you should feel a rising sense of shame as I describe to you.

Directed by prolific Finnish director Aki Kaurismaki (probably the most satisfying filmmaker's name to say – give it a go. It's nice, right?). You'd be forgiven for not being up on your Finnish cult cinema, but the bulk of this film is located in the USA and it sports a nifty cameo from legendary US indie director Jim Jarmusch (Oooh, that's a nice one to say, too). The film is about a Siberian folk band of huge-quiffed and winklepickered chaps who tour America to find fame, embracing rock and roll along the way. It's a masterpiece of dry humour, understatement and eccentricity, yet I never fail to be surprised by how many film geeks have never heard of it at all. That said, it's inexcusable – *inexcusable* – for a video shop with cultural aspirations to be lacking a copy. Planet had a copy, most likely by luck rather than design, but if you looked hard enough, they had everything you could reasonably hope for.

I was interviewed by the manager – Juliette and a girl called Sarah who worked in the shop part-time, whilst also doing something in fashion. Which seemed contradictory since she was dressed in some kind of 80's power-suit and had her hair all froofed up into a pineapple looking arrangement. Indeed, I referred to her only as 'Pineapple Head' from that day on. I didn't really understand what Pineapple Head was doing there and she really didn't seem to like me. Juliette was alright, very chatty and friendly. We got onto the subject of films and they didn't really know much about them. Juliette had a good knowledge of the specific type of films she liked (modern French), Pineapple Head avoided the subject adeptly.

I asked about the story behind the shop and Juliette told me that until fairly recently, it had been a Fast Forward but when Diane bought the chain from her sister-in-law, she refused to buy this branch. The reason for this was pretty obvious, Planet was on a side street off a main road that had, equidistant and right around the corner from it, a successful indie – Vogue Video and the new huge Blockbuster. Sandra, not wanting to be left with one crappy shop, struck a very generous deal with her manager at the time – Gail, Gail had paid a very fair amount for the business, a recent business studies graduate, I believe, and had taken the corporate edge off it with a slight refit and a lick of garish paint. I suppose for the price she paid and with a head full of fresh ideas, the shop was a smart investment for a young woman but, I was told, Gail got bored quickly and grew homesick for the Highlands. So, back she went, invested in some really nasty looking holiday homes in Ullapool (she kept leaflets about them on the counter in Planet) and only thought about Planet when the banking was off or if she breezed into town to go clothes shopping. It turned out that the bizarre stocking policies of the shop came directly from Gail – she ordered one copy of every film that came out each week. Incredible. Literally the worst buying policy I have ever seen in any video shop. Anyway, Juliette and Pineapple Head both had other stuff going on in their lives and they needed someone who could cover a lot of shifts.

They offered me the job on the spot and I took it. It was basically full time, with my shifts scattered across days, evenings and weekends.

Other video shops I'd worked in were, in varying degrees, frustrating, fun, terrifying, depressing… but Planet was different. It was out and out boring. Not in a depressing way like Fast Forward, it was a nice shop and I never felt under scrutiny (apart from Pineapple Head's constant snipes about the way I did stuff, but I didn't care what she said, she was a stupid froofy pineapple head). There was just… nothing to do. Nobody really came in except for evenings and weekends so day shifts there were just kind of comfortable but pointless. Each day, the daily tasks started and ended with 'stock count', which required you to pointlessly print out a list of all of the films that were currently rented out and then check every shelf in the back-shop to make sure those films were indeed out and see if any films were out but not listed. I felt its inclusion was more as a token gesture to the god of work. It actually was kind of essential to one's sanity because it made you feel as if you had *something* to do. Some single purpose for being there.

There was a good-sized upstairs to Planet Video, with two large rooms and a bathroom. The door to the left was the office, although nobody used it as an office. Nobody used it at all. It was nice and bright and sunny (unlike the shop itself) and had a big comfy sofa in it, a desk and huge piles of timecodes.

Oh… timecodes. Timecodes were the holy grail of video shop life. Basically, the sales reps on their monthly visits to video shops, would drop off a pile of free videos. Free videos 3 months before they were to be released. That meant that the person who had access to timecodes had access to films which had recently been in the cinema, months before they hit video. The dream! There was, of course, a price to pay for such privilege, this being the dirty great timecode running throughout the film on the top or bottom of the screen. It completely wrecked the viewing experience. It rendered them pointless. Yet, somehow it wasn't about *watching* timecodes so much as *having* them.

It felt good.

Blockbuster timecodes never ever filtered down to the shops and even in indie stores, they generally remained the property of the management. The timecodes in Planet's office were almost exclusively films you've never heard of. TV movies, terrible abandoned studio comedies, nothing you'd ever care to see. Plus, the release dates were long past, there was nothing less desirable than a timecode past release date. It was a little sad, really.

The door on the right was a storage room and an Aladdin's cave for movie geeks – it was filled with decades worth of cardboard cut-outs, posters and boxes of Betamax tapes, the defeated carcases of the format war a decade and a half earlier.

Planet was the only video shop I worked in that actually had an actual porno section. Blockbuster had it's softcore 'Drama/Thriller' films but Planet actually had a modest shelf of real, actual, porn. British porn, it was sourced locally, I'll give them that. They had three volumes of 'Ben Dover's Sex Truck' and something called 'Pigs in Knickers' which I felt needed no further description to aid my avoidance. My stomach turns just thinking about it all. I'm not prudish or against porn or anything like that. I'm just kind of disgusted by the notion of rental porn. Timeshare wanking. I guess pre-internet, it was harder to be stealthy with your stash and, for some, rental was the viable option. My take on it is this... I didn't want to be near an object which had predominantly be handled by men who'd just had a wank. This was not a judgement call, it was a biohazard. These few videotapes were constantly being rented and returned like an anonymous community-wide game of Soggy Biscuit. For all of it's successes, one of VHS's bigger failings was the design choice of a ridged-textured fascia. These tapes became a veritable DNA archive of crusted spermy thumbprints. I didn't even want to touch the outer cases. I still get queasy thinking about it. Whenever one demanded to be handled, I'd have to lock the shop up afterwards and scrub my hands with a Brillo pad.

The challenge at Planet was to plan your day so as to avoid falling into the rut of boredom – staring wistfully out of the window. I broke my day down into easily manageable periods. I would leave my flat as close to (but never after) the shop's opening time as possible, meaning I could justifiably shave some time off the beginning of the day.

So:

9.54 – 10.30 – Travelling

10.30 – 11.30 – Opening shop, stock count, video returns from previous night, chores

11.30 – 12.00 – Morning poo with light reading.

12.00 – 13.00 – lunch hour: walk around shops, get fresh air, get baked potato from 'Potatoland'

13.00 – 15.00 – Movie time! Slowly eat lunch whilst watching a film.

15.00 – 17.00 – Fun time! I'd write or draw stuff, phone friends or friends would drop in to hang out.

17.00 – 18.00 – Customers would start to dribble in, I'd plan my evening. Then go home.

I think out of all of my video shop experiences, I never felt as much of an out and out slacker as I did at Planet. But those times were not to last long. I was still on the books of a web design agency and one day they found me a job – at a price I could not turn down. The web design bubble had yet to burst and even my questionable talents were worth the price of a day's wages at Planet per hour.

My flatmate Dougie had been recently made unemployed from his office job at Scottish Widows for writing ghost stories in the personal files of customers and he relished the chance to not have to wear a tie to work, so took my job. I still did a couple of evening shifts each week but, as it so often seemed to, it all ended nastily…

At this point, I had a huge personal collection of rare videos and a lot of the films that were being asked for by customers, we didn't have in the shop, but I had at home. I offered a deal to Juliette where we could keep a list in the shop of all the films I owned and if someone wanted to rent one, I'd bring it in the next day and would split the rental price 50/50 with the shop. It seemed like a good idea to me but Juliette was resistant. I didn't force the point. Anyway, through some bizarre twist of fate, she met Ben at a party (how does he always manage to get me into trouble?) and he mentioned the scheme, as I had to him, she got the wrong end of the stick and assumed I was already offering it as an under-the-counter service. The next morning, she fired off an amazingly angry email to me accusing me of all sorts of nefarious stuff. Catching me unaware and on a bad day, my reply was even more vitriolic and by the time Dougie stepped in to explain the situation to both of us, the damage was done and I couldn't be bothered with Planet anymore.

Video shop work was killing my soul. It was like always being behind a sheet of glass being made to stare at your dream on the other side. I was in these environments which I knew I could turn into something amazing and special but instead was always under the thumb of these visionless dullards who barely even saw film as being anything more than a commodity. It was frustrating beyond words. Little did I know then that this feeling is, essentially, the working experience of most adult human beings until they are granted the brief mercy of a late retirement and collapse thankfully into their graves. I was glad to be out, anyway.

Dougie fell right slap-bang into the depression rut of Planet and all the things he thought he'd love about it turned out to be his frustrations. He spent a lot of time making art with the photocopier there. He didn't watch films, really. He'd sit there watching endless tapes of Friends and get so emotionally involved he'd actually sit at work crying over key episodes. Dougie's knowledge of films didn't extend far beyond the chick flicks he relished and when faced with enquiries or requests for recommendations he'd say politely and honestly 'I don't really watch films'. He tried his best, though. He was full of creative ideas including 'advertising the shop' but Gail was deaf to them. Nobody cared, so eventually neither did he. He soon embraced my trick of arriving late to work, but managed to extend it to previously unscaled heights of tardiness. Not that anyone cared. In fact I think it was the lack of reaction or care about what he was or wasn't doing that really did his head in. Eventually he drifted back into temping in offices to preserve his sanity.

It was actually a relief to go full-time into web design. It was harder work, it was a less comfortable work arrangement (i.e. I was expected to *do* some) but the money was good and it was.. just a job. Not a heart-breaking tango around my thwarted dreams.

Throughout film school, I'd focussed mainly on directing and screenwriting. Screenwriting seemed a more viable career, I seemed to have a knack for it and it appeared less competitive than directing. Out of the blue, I got an email from Canada asking if me and my co-writer at the the time Andy might like to go out there and write on a bizarre softcore sci-fi comedy series called LEXX. We were on the plane within a week, leaving behind the UK and any notion of going back to web design.

After a few months of writing LEXX, we had great prospects and a bit of money in our pockets, but were fully aware that writing was not a secure career. Screenwriting jobs had to be chased after, pitched for, the career we wanted was one where we created our own series, this meant a lot of unpaid work being done on a project that might not sell or, even worse, get stuck in development hell. The only choice open to us for secure work would have been to try to get onto an established series, most likely a cheapo soap opera, but we agreed we'd rather not be writing than be writing for something we didn't care about.

This is when Dougie announces that Gail wants to sell Planet. Everything seemed to fall into place. Andy and I could buy the video shop, use the office upstairs as our base and writing room, convert the storage room into a plush viewing room for customers to rent out. We drew up a great business plan in which we would refit and revitalise the shop, market the hell out of it – make it the choice for Edinburgh's student population. I knew how to make it great. The only problem I could foresee was wanting to give all of my attention to the shop rather than the more lucrative writing side of it.

I powered full steam ahead. I had a meeting with the landlord, who was a lovely old guy, he agreed to not hike the rent and was very excited to talk about the building and how he had run a butchers there before he retired. I couldn't picture the place as a butchers at all, so he excitedly ran around, showing me where everything had been.

"You like smoked sausage?" He chirruped.

"I'm vegetarian!"

"Ah! Smoked fish?"

He bounded upstairs and pointed to a wrought iron hatch on the wall in the storage room that I had always assumed was an old safe. He wrenched it open and there was a smoking hatch. He proudly proclaimed that it still worked and spent half an hour demonstrating how I could basically smoke anything in there. His enthusiasm was so infectious I briefly considered the idea of a video and kipper emporium.

Gail had sent us the books and the figures were surprisingly healthy. Both mine and Andy's parents looked at them and agreed it was a worthwhile investment. Then Dougie looked at them and shattered my dreams with a simple 'Bullshit!' He just shook his head and said 'I see all the money that comes in each week and it's nowhere near this!' I forget the exact method of creatively presenting the figures which was used, but Andy's dad figured it out and the whole thing seemed way less viable. We offered Gail a lower price but her pride was wounded and negotiations were drawn to a close. Rather than sell us the business, Gail just closed it down. Another one bites the dust.

CHAPTER 10

CONFESSIONS OF A
VIDEO SHOP OWNER

2002

Again, at 25, I assumed that my video shop days were finally behind me. With nothing left to really keep me in Edinburgh, I decided that I'd follow Andy to London where, realistically, all the screenwriting work was anyway. I decided to spend a couple of months in Oxford first, acclimatising to the English way of life before jumping into the chaos of the capital.

Andy and I went into a highly productive period of conceiving and writing TV shows to pitch to the contacts we'd built up. But, in the uncertain haze following 9/11, TV companies just seemed to stop taking risks overnight. There's not much riskier than an unknown writing team being commissioned for their first series. The bottom just seemed to fall out and despite the frustration of that situation and the money quickly drying up, I was lonely. I had no friends in Oxford apart from angry Blockbuster Nick, who I shared a flat with but we were fast growing apart.

Any notion of moving to London evaporated, I needed money and a job I could drop at a moment's notice. So, once more back to the Summertown Blockbuster. Matilda and Carl were long gone, as were anyone else I'd ever worked with there. The new manager was called Jane, she was an OK person but an OK person after a few months under the Blockbuster thumb develops certain coping mechanisms that can be frustrating for everyone. She wasn't unfair, she just took the job too seriously, if head office gave her trouble, she gave us trouble in return. Actually, not even trouble, she just liked to run a tight ship. Which is, of course, no fun at all. The staff there were really nice, nothing crazy, just good people working part time to supplement their other minimum wage day jobs. Ed was an actor, a very bright and charming guy who rode a crappy little moped about 10 miles to work each day. Luis was a quiet but funny dude and Rowena was an amazingly loud and friendly lass who worked days in the travel agent two doors down and evenings in Blocky.

It was a kind of uneventful but comfortable period there for a couple of months, it was really nice working with the other part-timers (the full-timers were kind of like a weird ladies knitting circle that worked in all of the other branches in oxford in rotation) they were smart and interesting people and although there were no hijinks, there was always good conversation.

The closing of Planet Video really had coincided with most of those type of video shops closing down. Blockbuster had very much, very decisively won the battle for the UK video business. All of those initial shops set up by 80s entrepreneurs had been squeezed out of the marketplace. They couldn't afford to compete and didn't stand a chance against Blocky's aggressive marketing. The sheer volume of Blockbuster stores meant there was never one too far away. They had also successfully changed the culture of video rental. It was all, entirely about new releases now. Which meant the shop which won the customers was the one which could guarantee having that film in stock (for a while, if they didn't have it in stock, you got it free next time you visited) The early 00's really were the age of monolithic retail. Everyone was dressed in

GAP clothes, swigging Starbucks coffee and chatting on their Nokias. Blockbuster Video was all the vast majority of society needed. The middle ground was swiftly kicked away. Broadly speaking, the landscape was now huge monolithic corporate Blockbuster at one end and a handful of very hip, smart indie video stores at the other. Places like Twentieth Century Flicks in Bristol. Today is Boring in London and, of course, Alphabet in Edinburgh. Some of these places were longstanding, some brand new, but they were united in their comprehensive back catalogues, anti-corporate aesthetic and knowledgeable, approachable, relaxed staff. They were bespoke to their niche customer base.

Blockbuster at this point had essentially given up on the unprofitable and unsightly back-catalogue. Each store had an embarrassingly un-curated couple of units of older films, available to rent cheap, but they went widely ignored and were regularly emptied with little dignity into the ex-rental (sorry… PVT) bin.

I noticed more and more level-headed customers complaining about the lack of anything older than six months or generally worthwhile on offer. One man, after a brief chat about the state of the place pointed out that Summertown could do with a decent independent video shop, 'someone could clean up!' he emphatically stated.

And he was absolutely right.

By this time, my personal VHS collection was enormous and comprehensive. To walk into my living room was like entering the best video shop you'd ever seen. I'd put all of my effort and spare cash into it over the years – amassing a vast number of big-box ex-rentals from the dawn of video right up to modern day. In fact, it struck me that my living room was exactly what a video shop should be. And then I got really excited. A video shop like a living room. With furniture rather than fittings – bookcases. With sofas. With film posters on the walls, not advertising new releases, but the cool kind of crap I had framed on my own walls. And toys. Lots of toys. I was practically born with a Star Wars figure in my hand and could never resist movie memorabilia. We could fill every empty space with this crap and make it a quirky, fun, relaxed place with sofas and good music, things to see wherever you looked and the best selection of films ever assembled.

I mulled it over for a couple of weeks, then put a proposal to my dad, whose business had been faltering for a while. I put together a business plan showing that if he closed down his linen operations and we put a small amount of money and my considerable video collection into it, we could convert the shop into a brilliant indie video store and do pretty well.

Dad had a think and then agreed. It looked like he was close to retirement anyway and his business couldn't have survived much longer – he had nothing to really lose. The day he said yes, I was walking on air. My dream was going to come true – I was going to create, and more importantly own, my own independent video shop. From the day we decided to do it, my feet didn't touch the ground for months. The sheer volume of things to think about and organise were unbelievable. Dad took responsibility for the clerical side of stuff, everything else was my area and I threw myself into it gladly. I couldn't believe it was real. It was one of the happiest times of my life. Every job I'd ever had, I was fully aware that all of my effort was going to line the pockets of others, and usually people I didn't like. Working for myself was the most liberated I'd ever felt. The harder I worked, the more I'd profit and I was at the top of the chain.

I decided not to quit Blockbuster. I was in the utterly unique situation of having the complete inside track on my soon-to-be competition. I even started to spread rumours of an independent opening up in the area. At that point, my life became entirely list-based. There were so many things to consider and so many things I just didn't know or know to expect.

I had the location and the vision and that was really all. The first thing I thought about was shop-fitting. A huge amount of shelving would have to be built and a big, secure (but friendly looking) counter since late-night opening comes with a load of different issues of security. I phoned a bunch of shop-fitting companies and was rudely awakened to the world of big business. The figures they were quoting were so far out of my realm of reality, I spent a lot of time just re-reading them over and over again. Tens of thousands of pounds, to build a counter and some shelving and do a little electrical work in a little back-street shop. I figured I'd have to learn DIY. But then Dad found Peter. I'd never met anyone like him, I don't think there is anyone else like him. A hugely tall man in his late sixties, with a big mop of salt and pepper hair and one of those enormous moustaches that twiddles out at the sides. He was like something out of an issue of The Eagle, I could imagine him making gadgets for Dan Dare. He has this amazing truly English eccentricity to him, along with boundless energy and resourcefulness. He was retired and did jobs like this as much for the fun of the project as the very-reasonable rates. Peter had made his money by being the man who designed and installed the majority of the cigarette-manufacturing machines in the Far East. The way he told it, it would appear that Peter had single-handedly introduced cancer and pollution to the developing world. We contracted him to build a new counter (employing my brilliant idea to make all surfaces viewable to the public around the counter blackboard, so we could write our offers up and competition questions, etc), move some stud walling around to create a bigger back-shop, build all of the back-shop shelving and a dropbox. I personally wanted to hire an electrician to do the electrical work, but the mad professor barked at me that he could do it, so I let him (and made sure not to be there that day).

I'd say my one error of judgement, although I rather enjoyed it, was 'the pipe'. Once we had moved all of dad's old shop fittings out, I noticed a strange wooden column towards the back of the shop. I asked what it was and Dad told me it was to hide a pipe. He told me to leave it as it was. I got excited about it, though. The idea of an exposed pipe running across the shop seemed kind of funky. It was right where the counter was going to be built so I told Peter to get rid of the casing and build the pipe into the counter. I was expecting a nice shiny chrome pipe, I guess. What we revealed was a crappy combination of cobbled-together metal and plastic. I thought about spraying it with chrome paint but there were other more pressing concerns. Peter went ahead and built the counter around it and we just painted the pipe white like everything else. The day we opened, we suddenly heard a strange noise glugging through the pipe. I asked Peter what it was and he replied 'What do you expect? It's the sewage pipe from the upstairs flat!'. So every time anybody up there used the toilet you could hear it all whooshing across the shop and then disappearing down through the counter. It became known as the pipe of poop.

Nick and I spent what felt like weeks painting the entire shop clean, crisp white. Nick was actually brilliant during that whole period. He was working in HMV by then. As security. He got to throw a lot of people out.

One day, the videos started arriving. Oh, the videos. So, I had almost two thousand videos to put in to the shop – a fine collection, if I do say so myself. But the aim was always to end up with about six or seven thousand. I had to get in about three thousand films to open respectably and had

a very limited budget to do it on. I upped
my attendance of car boot sales, where you
could find almost any film, usually only
watched once – if that – before being safely
stored on a shelf somewhere for years. The
great thing about car boots were the prices, I
had become an adept haggler and could
usually score a film for between 10p and
50p. I rarely paid more than a pound for any
one film. And often managed to find
Ebayable bargains which could expand my
budget slightly (50p for a copy of the live
Billy Connolly film/documentary Big
Banana Feet – one of the UK's rarest films,
yet I managed to find three separate copies
at car boot sales and Ebay each one for
upwards of £60 a pop). I'd manage to pack 3
or 4 separate car boot sales into each Sunday
and would have to take a rucksack to fill
with my haul, regularly emptying it into the
car and going back out to refill it. I was
doing well, but not well enough. Car boots
were good but a bit of a crap shoot in that I
was mainly buying shelf-filler, all good stuff,
but not the important classic and cult notes
that I wanted to hit. Then I remembered the
video warehouse.

The video warehouse was a legend of my
youth. I don't even remember who told me
about it, probably Simon, the kid whose dad
owned Movies, but it was often discussed. A
huge warehouse somewhere not far from

Oxford where they had, as legend dictated, 'three copies of every film ever made'. Anything you could ever want, they had, and you could walk around and just buy all the films you ever dreamed of. I asked my dad to take me when I was 10 and he dismissed it as nonsense. And it did sound like nonsense – I mean, if it existed, why wouldn't it be advertised, surely such a place would be insanely popular. Eight times the size of HMV and stocked completely. So, I stopped thinking about it. A few weeks after I had moved back to Oxford, Nick and his mate Tristan were helping me alphabetise my video collection and get it up onto the new shelves in the living room. Conversation was fairly video-centric and Tristan suddenly mentioned the video warehouse. I called him on it and he said that it not only existed, but his mum – who had owned a shop that sold cheap videos – had been there regularly and taken him and that it was, indeed, the Aladdin's cave of legend. I wanted to go, but he explained it was trade only, like a cash and carry, you had to buy in bulk and it wasn't open to the public. I had just wanted to see it. But now, now, I could legitimately go there myself.

It took me a while, but I tracked it down. It was in a rural industrial estate, just outside Oxford, with spectacular views of miles of countryside. The units looked kind of like chalets and really not all that big. The video warehouse, or rather Home Entertainment Buying Group occupied just one of these. I was excited when I walked in and saw it full of crude shelves, stacked floor to ceiling with a huge variety of amazing films. The owner, Steve, was a lovely calm-voiced man who was amused by my excitement (I couldn't concentrate on anything he said to me as rare videos would suddenly catch my eyes wherever I looked). I told him about the legend and he laughed, I said how I was told that they had 'three copies of every film ever made', 'more like five or six' he responded. What? 'oh yeah, we used to have this whole estate, we were in every unit, we had everything'. Holy cow.

Steve was a smart cookie, at a time before blockbuster and supermarkets were selling videos at hugely discounted prices. He had created a secondary market. He would buy up private collections, businesses that were selling up or going bankrupt and all kinds of surplus stock, it all went to him – every unwanted video in the country. He'd clean up the tapes, put them in brand new plastic cases, shrinkwrap them and sell them on to companies who would sell them on as new. Remember how the big sales at the big high street stores would often have a seemingly random selection of films? That was because they were often buying them in bulk second hand from Steve and selling them on as discounted new – he had some huge clients and I was kind of appalled as I realised how sometimes I'd have bought films from those sales and just assumed they were brand new and I was getting a good deal, rather than repackaged second-hand. With the sheer volume of stock passing through his business, Steve also kept lists of rare films and had staff who specifically skimmed everything they received for these titles, so he made a great profit on selling these on to collectors. Every day, he'd get about 10,000 films coming through this unit, he employed staff around the clock to sort, clean and despatch them. One could no longer walk around picking and choosing, you would pay a set price for a set number of films, you could guide him in the selection (I begged for foreign films, classics, highbrow stuff) but it was essentially random and fantastic value at that. We agreed a deal and he, being a brilliant bloke, let me do 'swaps', which meant, I could actually achieve my dream of walking around and picking what I wanted and swapping it for ones that had been chosen for me. It was like a dream. As a film nerd, there were several points where I almost hyperventilated when noticing certain films.

This was smack-bang in the middle of the format transition. DVD had been established for a few years but it had yet to meaningfully replace VHS. For starters, DVDs were more expensive, seen as a luxury format, but also they weren't a practical replacement as for a long time, they weren't recordable. It would take the triple-whammy of cheap DVD players, Sky Plus and LCD TV's to force the bulk of consumers to move into the digital age. Back then, especially in Summertown where modern technology could be considered a little gauche, cathode ray screens and VHS sufficed. I was very conscious to build up our DVDs as we went along but upon opening, we needed a strong VHS back catalogue to appeal to our specific customer base.

Steve would phone me when an order was ready to be collected and grin at my enthusiasm as I saw what he'd managed to put aside for me. One day a huge order of rare kung fu films had come in and he gave us the lot. In fact, the day I picked that order up, a lad who owned a video stall in Camden Market noticed what I'd scored and had a little tantrum at Steve about it, who listened with a benign smile. He then tried to nick a couple of them as I was loading my car up, Steve dealt with it swiftly and in his even-mannered laconic, gentlemanly voice said to the guy.

"I helped you when you were starting out, let's help Jon now, shall we? I get thousands of films through here every day, you shan't be overlooked, so let's shake hands..."

Some of the happiest times in the setting up of the shop were visiting Steve, then driving home through the beautiful Oxfordshire countryside in a car that couldn't pick up any speed or really make it uphill at all as it was so tightly packed with so many videos.

There was nowhere for the videos to go. Dad hadn't yet closed down his linen store, I hadn't even quit Blockbuster. So they came home with me. The corridor of my flat was stacked to over six feet high down it's entire length, with boxes of videos. Nick was ok with it – he loved films, and had the pick of whatever he wanted to watch whenever he felt like it. But our third flatmate, Rachel, moved out. The mess and musty smell was too much for her. I bought a computer, got the same video shop software as I'd used in Box Office and set about the mighty task of getting every video on the system. For each individual video, I'd have to:

Remove the sleeve and remove any old stickers/damage to it. Replace the sleeve into a brand new plastic box. Add the film's information to the computer database. Clean up any old stickers on the tape/dust it off.

Put new chronological archival number stickers on the sleeve and tape.

So, you're looking at an average of a minute and a half per tape. Multiply that by four thousand and you'll know what I was doing with every spare minute I had from the decision to start the company to the very second the doors opened. But I kind of enjoyed it, it was actually quite relaxing, I'd always have films on whilst doing it and friends would come around for the evening and we'd get a little production line going. Those were happy times, people were excited to be a part of it, we were still young and this felt like an audacious attack on the grown-up world.

About a week before the shop was ready to open, Jane decided I should have a disciplinary hearing. The official letter arrived at my flat before she even mentioned it to me. The reasons listed were 'poor time-keeping' and 'taking a retail dvd home'. The retail DVD was Jerry Maguire, it wasn't sealed or anything and I wanted to watch the commentary. I'm down with Cameron Crowe. I'm down with that flick, actually, I'll take on all naysayers. Tom Cruise, in the hands of a great director, does great work. This was a film about the hollowness of corporate life, about how money had replaced heart in sports, it had something to

say and bags of charisma. Cruise is so good
as a man who's on the edge without really
understanding what edge he's on. Confusion and mania. I love it. So, the letter
arrives and I'm tickled by it because it was
only days away that I was going to quit
anyway. In fact, every day had been a
struggle not to quit for weeks. I read the
official rules and saw that the entire hearing
had to be recorded and that I was allowed to
have a witness with me. The date was set for
that week.

Rowena had enthusiastically agreed to be
my witness and I'd squared all of the rules
with Jane. My aim was simple. Mischief. The
idea of being able to drag out the bureaucra-
cy of a Blockbuster official ritual was just
heavenly to me. The hearing was conducted
in a place of suitable austerity – the stock
room. The stock room held about two
people comfortably. Crammed into it this
day were myself, Jane, the current manager
of Headington branch, a fearsome Nurse
Ratched looking character I'd never met
before, Rowena and a woman I didn't
recognise. I asked who she was and was told
that she was recording the meeting. I saw no
tape recorder. No, she was going to write
this all down. I asked her if she knew
shorthand. She asked if that was a horror
film or something. There only four
chairs in the room. Rowena was told she

would have to stand up. I made my first objection, I even shouted 'OBJECTION!' I pointed out that it appeared that this hearing was already geared against me if my witness was considered less seat-worthy than the company's witness. I demanded equal seating allocations. Jane pointed out there were no more seats in the building and the official court stenographer was sitting on one of those little wheely things you stand on to reach high shelves. She looked to confirm what she was sitting on and I asked if she had written any of this down. She said she hadn't and I claimed it to be utterly unacceptable as there had already been a clear incident within the hearing to show how it was angled against me. Rowena, realising that this wasn't going to be much fun and that she'd rather just get on with it announced that she didn't mind standing. I don't really remember what was discussed in the meeting as I concentrated purely on technicalities.

My goal was merely to drag the hearing out until they terminated it themselves. They had told me it shouldn't last more than 45 minutes but I knew I could stretch it to the 8 hour working day. Every point I made was salient and correct, asking for clarification on every single thing that was said and demanding evidence be presented to back up any claim or statement. And I do mean

ANY claim or statement. When the issue of my poor time-keeping arose, I protested vehemently.

"Could you please furnish me with the evidence of this alleged contravention?" I arrogantly enquired. I felt it important to use long words, to confuse and annoy.

"Evidence?"

"Yes, do you have time-sheets, do you have my clocking-in card?"

"We haven't got..." I was breaking her "look, I'm here every day and I KNOW what time you arrive!"

"So, it's just your word? Your... preju-diced... word?"

"I'm the manager!"

"That's anecdotal evidence from the prosecution" I turned to the poor wretch trying to write this all down "that's A-N-E-C-D-O-T-A-L. Oh, and prejudiced is P-R-E-J-U-D-I-C-E-D". It was hard to tell if she was appreciative or suicidal. I continued my assault on Jane.

"Is it not true that Blockbuster does offer a clocking-in facility on the shop's computer?"

"Yes..."

"Which you, as store manager, choose not to implement?"

She stopped talking and opted instead to smoulder with hatred.

And so it continued. If I couldn't find a point to argue, I'd ask for something that had been discussed earlier to be repeated from the official record of the hearing. That poor girl. They had told her that she would be recording key points, I insisted that everything be recorded. I wanted my words captured exactly. I managed to drag the hearing out to about 5 hours, by which time they'd agreed that I could be let off with a warning. I argued that having a warning was not being let off. They said the warning was final and if I wanted to contest it, I'd have to take it higher. They asked me to sign the notes that had been taken and that would be the end of it. But I couldn't read the furious scribblings that had been made. Most of the 9 or 10 pages were illegible to me. I asked her to read them all out then argued that she had misrepresented me or the discussion at most points. I managed to drag another two hours out of the redrafting of the notes. They asked if, once I was finally satisfied with the document that I would just sign it and that would be the end of it. I told them no, I wouldn't sign, I quit.

Jane's jaw dropped and I thought Ratched was going to rip my throat out. Rowena quit too, as I was hiring her for better money. It was amazingly satisfying.

Unfortunately Ed couldn't come over to Videosyncratic with us, he needed full-time hours at that point but he pledged his allegiance to the cause and came through with the information that not only was Jane going on holiday for a week when we opened but that the following week, the branch would be closed for at least 7 days for a refit. It was serendipity on a joyous scale. They wouldn't know what had hit them by the time they reopened.

We had papered up the front of the shop and remained tight-lipped as to what was going to open there. Summertown, being the rather posh part of town, didn't like the secrecy. I had to seal the letterbox as it was constantly flapping open to reveal the information-hungry eyes of middle aged women. Six or seven times a day, there'd be a knock at the door and some old bag demanding to know what was going on inside. My sister suggested putting a sign up saying 'COMING SOON – SUMMER-TOWN'S FIRST LAPDANCE BAR!' I did and, within an hour, had received calls from the city council and two local newspapers.

The night before we opened, all of my friends came to the shop and as a team, we got the whole place finished. We'd bought big bookcases from Ikea for the main shop displays, we had contests to see who could build them the quickest. Then there was stocking the shelves in the back-shop and dividing all of the display cases into genres and getting them up on the shelves in the front shop. There was a lot of work, but also a lot of pizza and beer and laughter and all those guys got free rentals for life.

10am, the following morning, the sign was up, the window graphics applied, the till and computer installed. My Millennium Falcon hung above the counter and the doors opened. The first member of the public to walk through them was a woman in her sixties. I thought to myself how it will have been a while since she'd seen such a fine collection of classic movies and forgotten gems from her youth. But she walked straight past that section. She marched up to the counter and, before I could even issue a message of welcome, told me "I do NOT approve of your signage, it is NOT very Summertown!". Then she left. She was the first of many old biddies complaining about us ruining the road over that initial couple of months. Most of them came back when they'd calmed down and realised that despite the big pictures of people with videotapes for heads on the outside of the shop, on the inside was a treasure trove of films they wanted to see. We won the place over eventually.

The design was a big issue for me, I wanted to proudly proclaim our independence and make it clear that we loved film and stocked every genre imaginable. I knew I wanted to work with our designer Heather because I'd seen some work she'd done for Scott Beiben's touring Lost Film Fest. Specifically, she'd designed a poster which was a skull and crossbones with the back of a videotape instead of the skull. It looked great and was so close to the style I wanted to convey. I came up with the idea of a bunch of characters with videos for heads and Heather ran with it. The main character, the guy with a video for a head, holding a Martini was just perfect. I still get a kick out of it. She backed him up with a keystone cop, glamourpuss, spaceman, mad scientist, soldier, cowboy, superhero and flapper. I think it summed us up nicely.

I spent most of that first morning waiting for one thing. Jane was on holiday and had been replaced for the week by Carl. I was waiting for Carl to come in. How long would it take for news to filter up the road and round the corner? At about lunchtime, he bombed down the street and stumbled in, mouth agape and utterly bewildered. Not just the shock of competition but I don't think he'd ever seen an indie shop before – it was a video shop that didn't even look like a video shop. I stood proudly behind the counter waiting for him to catch sight of me. Before he did, a flash of inspiration crossed his face and he removed his Blockbuster name badge. He was undercover. Then he saw me. He sneered slightly "You got a job pretty quick!" "I own the place!!!" His face dropped. I could see the frustration in his face, this was his week to prove to the Blockbuster brass that he was manager material once more and I come along to screw it all up for him. He's left in charge for one week and one of his ex-employees opens a rival business round the corner.

"What are ya… Why are you doing that for?"

"I don't know, I just felt like it"

Carl took a cursory glance around.

"You haven't got any new releases!" He scoffed.

"They're over there."

"Oh." He composed himself back into professional Carl "Well, best of luck to you"

"Yes, may the best man win!"

Panic flashed across his face and he left as quickly as he had arrived.

Two hours later, the Blocky area manager and some young whippersnapper with a notepad strolled in confidently with a rat-like Carl in tow. "That's Jon!" he whined, pointing in my general direction and they headed over. The area manager introduced himself (I hadn't met this one), but didn't tell me who his Boy Wonder was.

"Now Jon, this is your business?" The Area manager started.

"Yep", the AM nodded to his pal, who made a scribble on his notepad.

"You own it?"

"With my dad, yeah."

He smiled an arrogant, smug, detestable grin and nodded to himself.

"Are you aware that your contract with Blockbuster forbids you from…"

"I didn't sign a contract"

"What?"

"I didn't sign a contract, nobody gave me a contract to sign"

"I think you're bluffing"

"I've never been given a contract at any Blockbuster. Carl never made me sign a contract"

All eyes turn to Carl.

"I... did"

"You didn't"

The AM glared at Carl with such intensity, I swear the lights flickered. He turned back to me.

"What are your prices?"

"Everything's £2.50" – we were undercutting them by a third. He raised an eyebrow and smirked slightly.

"But the beauty of being independent is that I can change them when I see fit, I can make up promotions on the spot, you know? It takes you guys a couple of weeks to get things through head office, right?

He slowly nodded, gave me a smile and said "You've not seen the last of me".

That was the last I saw of him.

A few days later, Blockbuster closed for its refit. As the builders went home at 5pm each day, we'd plaster posters for Videosyncratic over the entire front of the shop and sit a member of staff outside with flyers, redirecting all of the thwarted Blocky customers to their new video mecca. To call our marketing aggressive would be a huge understatement. We had people on the main parade in Summertown constantly cheerfully harassing shoppers into visiting our shop. My friend Olly came over from London on one of the first weekends we were open and fashioned himself a hat out of Videosyncratic flyers. Then we covered him head to foot in flyers and he stumbled around Banbury Road goading people to visit us. When Blockbuster finally reopened from it's refit, it looked exactly the same as it had done, save for some wire rack shelving. It smelled the same too

I called my shop Videosyncratic and it was popular from the day it opened. Summer-town was a part of town where independent retail flourished and with a healthy mix of academics, well-to-do families and students, they appreciated that we stocked our shop to their tastes. Whereas I had watched these same people for months getting increasingly miserable, plodding around Blockbuster just trying to find the least bad film and having to settle for something merely acceptable, in

Videosyncratic, they were positively excited. DVD was still relatively new at this point, so they were finding films that had yet to be resurrected to a digital format – films they'd seen years ago and loved or had wanted to see and had forgotten about. That's what I loved about that early period – the excitement. One of our first customers howled with joy when he found the big box rental versions of The Goonies and Rocky. Being an utter nerd for those old black-bordered Warner Bros rental releases, I empathised with his primal outburst. He didn't care about stereo sound or widescreen letterbox editions, he just wanted to get them home and watch the old trailers then revel in the pan-and-scan delights. I joined him up and handed him his collectors-edition low-numbered Videosyncratic membership card (you could choose from one of nine designs for your card – each one featured a different tapehead character). "I won't be needing this anymore!" he said brandishing his Blockbuster card "Got any scissors?", I gave him a pair and he cut his card in half before giving it to me. I blu-tacked it up next to the counter under the box frame that contained my disciplinary hearing letter from Blocky and both Rowena's and my old Blocky name badges. So began a mighty collection. In each branch of the store we boasted a full wall of cut-up Blocky cards, all defaced and donated by their previous owners – our loyal customers.

Along with Rowena, I'd hired my friend Jamie – lead singer of local post-punk pop heroes Dive Dive and uber-slacker extraordinaire. I also hired Martin – one of my colleagues at the Oxford Film and Video Makers workshop, where I'd started teaching a few evening classes. He really knew his stuff about foreign and arthouse flicks. We hired Ben – also of Dive Dive within a few months of opening and, alongside my dad and I, he became the most recognizable member of staff there. He took surliness to new, previously unreached levels. I loved it. He seemed to have a pretty simple ethos – if a customer treats him with respect, he'd be open and funny and charming with them, if they didn't, he'd just not respect them right back. He was never rude, just brusque. Watching Ben work a Saturday night shift was a thing of beauty, whereas a huge queue would throw most employees into a panic, Ben worked at his own pace, treating some customers well and others with the derision they deserved. A masterful performance.

I also hired Gez. When I had left the Summertown Blockbuster and gone back up to Scotland at the end of the summer of '97, my job had been taken by Gez. Nick would phone me up and tell me excited stories about how cool Gez was and all the crazy stuff he would get up to. Like, one time Gez got angry and started punching the phone until it broke down into component parts. I was actually a little jealous of him and, when I first met him, suspicious of his shifty cockney ways but I soon warmed to him. On his first shift in Summertown, Gez had taken a bit of a shine to Becky and decided to show her exactly how cool he was. They'd closed the shop for the night, turned the lights out and were cashing up when a grumpy looking woman started banging on the window outside. "Piss off, you ratchet faced old bitch!" Gez shouted, turning to Becky for approval of his Noel Coward like repartee. "No!" Becky shouted "That's my mum! She's come to pick me up!" They were never more than friends after that.

Gez is one of the funniest guys I know, in a really horrible way. He is an encyclopaedia of bad jokes and will start to regale anyone with them the second conversation falters. When I say 'bad jokes', this is one of his:

"How many Sigmund Freuds does it take to change a light bulb?

Two. One to change the light bulb and the other to hold his cock.

I mean mother.

I mean ladder."

It gives you good incentive to make better conversation.

Actually, his Blockbuster story deserves to be told. First, I should give him some credit for creating a game that kept generations of Blockbusterers occupied during long miserable shifts. Video tennis – which was essentially tennis, but played with video boxes as rackets and a ball made of balled-up computer paper and Sellotape. You stretch blu tac, chewing gum or sellotape between the counter and wall, dividing the behind-counter area in two. Then play tennis. You get extra points for body hits and general destruction. Doesn't sound like much of an invention, sure, but Video Tennis is held very dear to the hearts of all who have played it.

Gez was – and is – an interesting guy. At that point he was in his late 20s, had been in a slew of fantastic bands and failed to find lasting success in any of them. He's an incredible songwriter and musician. He had no money, a very young daughter and was living in the loft in his mum's house (it hadn't been converted, it was just a loft, mattress on the rafters). He's a great actor too and always seems to scrape by on little roles in The Bill, adverts, gigs and the odd tour in a Buddy Holly tribute band.

The longer he worked there, the more disillusioned with it he got. He really genuinely hated it and as much as he liked Nick, felt horribly institutionalized by all of the Blocky crap. After Matilda and her replacement both left, the shop was managerless for a while. Nick – like Kevin before – refused to actually be made manager but had pretty much swindled a pay rise and perks without assuming any of the official responsibilities. Gez would swan in when he felt like it. Nick didn't care if the shop wasn't open on time – who was checking up on that kind of thing? So one day, Gez wakes up at around 11, makes himself some food, gets some stuff done, rolls up to open Blockbuster around 12.30. When he gets there, the door is open. Russ is behind the counter with a bunch of suits including Peter Lush. Gez, it should be noted, is probably in a Hawaiian shirt and almost definitely hungover – if not still drunk. Russ and the suits are livid with him and Gez is pretty impervious to their disappointment. Peter Lush asks where his uniform is and Gez replies that it's at home. Peter Lush composes himself and says "Go home, get into your uniform, come back and we'll talk about where we go from here". Gez nods and heads for the door. He reaches the door and thinks for a moment, turns around and says "To be honest, if I go home, I can't be bothered to come all the way back again. I think I'll just quit." He gives them a friendly nod and goes off on his merry way.

I don't know how many people there are who would give up their sole source of income because it felt like a hassle to walk half a mile, but I somehow doubt they pull it off with as much style as Gez. Gez was an obvious choice and worked the Sunday day shift for years until he quit, having finally found a real job. Actually, he quit constantly through all the years he worked for us but would usually come back a month or two later with a sheepish grin.

It should be emphasised, Videosyncratic wasn't just my shop – I was in 51/49 with my dad Michael. I'd insisted on the extra 1% because I knew I was always right and it was important that one of us be. The first few weeks were odd for both of us. I'd imagine to most 25 year old guys, their dad is an avuncular or frustrating figure to be engaged with a few times a year. My dad was an avuncular and frustrating figure who I was to engage with a few times a day. I don't know how best to describe my dad. The first and most striking thing when you meet the man is his unsettling physical similarity to Harold Shipman, our nation's finest granny-killer. With age, he's edging slightly more towards a scalped Colonel Sanders but a decade ago, we were very much still in the thick of people seeing him in the street and double-taking. As far as I know, that is where the similarities end. He's a quiet man and this means he must have secrets but I feel fairly confident in saying that I doubt they're of the dispatched pensioner variety. My dad's amazing. He's been enthusiastic and supportive of everything I've ever done, whilst retaining a cynical and exasperated edge at the way in which I've done them. My love of films undoubtedly comes from him. He was a film nut growing up, after graduation, he used to write film reviews for a newspaper in Leeds. By the time he had a family, he was already a keen amateur 8mm cameraman. Just home movie stuff, but he dug it and fed my obsession. He's a good guy. I enjoy his company a lot. Never play scrabble with him – the unholy combination of not being very good and not being very fast. Anyway, it's a strange moment when father and son face each other as equals. We both had a lot to teach each other and an equal amount of stubborn resolve about how things would be run.

The first battle was getting him to fit in. Part of me liked the idea of a hip young shop with an inexplicably old guy behind the counter but I cringed at thought of how smart-casual he'd be. In the last few years of owning his own linen shop, he'd downgraded from suit and tie to smart trousers and shirt with a maroon sweater. I'd ordered hoodies and t-shirts with the VS branding on them. So as to avoid ever being remotely like Diane, I had – firstly – had them designed to be ACE. We sold a lot of them to customers, they were gunmetal grey with the black and white tapehead logos on them. I gave all of the staff a hoodie and a t-shirt and told them that these were just a gift, if they wanted to wear them to work, that'd be cool, if they didn't want to – fine. Those that wanted to did, those that didn't wore them a lot when they weren't at work. It was a badge of pride. A T-shirt of pride. There was a certain amount of local notoriety that went with being a till jockey at the 'cratic. That probably sounds arrogant, but I'm fine with that. We were arrogant. Videosyncratic was basically – and I might be biased, but I'm pretty sure I'm right – the coolest place to work. I only hired cool people and I let them be themselves. It inspired a certain swagger even in those who weren't narcissists already. They were all narcissists already.

I told dad I wanted him to wear a hoodie and jeans. He dutifully went to Marks and Spencer and bought a pair of Clarksonesque denims and rocked the hoodie as only he could. With a button-up shirt underneath, collar fighting it's way through the neckhole and forcing both the hood and his neck into an awkward looking parody of 50 years of high street fashion. He was game.

We quickly realised that each of us was intractable on certain issues and therefore the division of responsibilities happened quite naturally. I did the show, he did the business. I knew what the shop should be – all of the branding, marketing, stocking and hiring was down to me. He knew business, all of the finances, legalities, paperwork and accounting was his domain. He was welcome to it. He liked it. I'd get a budget of how much I could spend each month and, I'd spend it. He'd track the figures on a daily basis, comparing them to anything he could find, we were both happy. Until the second one of us transgressed on the other's affairs and then it was hateful. I was incapable of doing even the most basic paperwork – end of day sheets, VAT receipts, petty cash slips. Well, not unable… lazy. And I harboured a perverse joy in doing things that I knew would frustrate him – as he did with me. Whenever I left the shop for more than a day, I'd return to find he'd set up a bargain bin of shitty, broken videos and filled the shop with signs, A4 bits of paper printed on MS Word version 1 in bizarre formatting offering confusing information. That fucking bargain bin, even if I threw it out and burned its contents, it'd magically reappear a week later with more dusty crap for £1. I was close to tears explaining to him that the whole bin, if it sold, would bring in about £8 and if someone bought a tape from it for £1, then they wouldn't also rent a film for £2.50. I offered to pay him the £8 out of my own pocket, but it fell on literally deaf ears. If not deaf, hearing-aid-conveniently-playing-up ears.

Dad's passion became confectionary. I respected this area of his life and left him to it. Each week, he'd go to the cash & carry to stock the drinks fridge, sweetie counter and not the ice cream freezer (he did this through wholesale deliverers) he meticulously tracked every bar of chocolate and box of tic-tacs. There were graphs. Reports. Obsession. The man loved film but I think, given the choice, he'd have run a sweet shop. I felt it my duty to use my five-fingered 100% staff discount as often as possible, if only to keep his accounting spicy. He would even spend his time coming up with elaborate stock control systems.

One day, I saw him leaning into the ice cream freezer with a felt-tip pen.

"Dad, what are you doing?"

"I've come up with a system of stopping shoplifting – I put a mark on the bottom of each tub and if somebody steals it, we'll know it's ours."

"If somebody steals it, it won't *be* here! Really – this makes NO sense, Dad."

He gave me a look of condescension and carried on with the task.

About a month later, I was working the till and noticed a guy grab a tub of ice cream and walk confidently to leave the shop. "OI!" I was over the counter and in his face within seconds. "I think you need to pay for that, mate!" "No," he protested "I brought it in with me, I got it in Sainsbury's!"

"Oh God", I sneered. My heart sinking as I realised what was about to happen. I grabbed the tub off him and turned it upside down. There was Dad's felt tip mark. I hated them both.

Of course, Dad's system only ever proved useful that once, so you could argue that the £3.95 saved in foiling that robbery pales in comparison to the man hours spent on a weekly basis felt-tipping every bloody tub but the application of logic to the actions of my father, dear reader, is the path to madness.

The shop quickly became my favourite place in the world. It had that living room vibe I was going for. It was such a relaxed space to be in. It was a comfortable place to just be. The sofas were upholstered in denim which felt like you were sitting on a great big lovely lap. You could spin the TV's around to any position so most afternoons you'd find me and any number of droppers-in just sprawled on the sofas watching movies, munching away the profit margin in confectionary.

Once the dust had settled, everything was done, loads of people had joined up and gave us their regular custom, the shop started to kind of run itself. I realised that, limited in ambition as I might have been, I had achieved my dream. This was my ideal lifestyle. I didn't have a boss but I had a steady job. I was the boss, not that I exactly wielded my authority, but I was answerable to nobody and if I thought something was a good idea, I did it. There were no real demands on me. I got to watch free films whenever I wanted. I got to stock the shop how I knew it should be. I got to employ my friends and work with my friends. And that work... was not work. We struck up a friendship with James and Martin, the guys at the Italian pizza place next door, they all got free rentals, we all got free pizzas. Yes. Free pizzas. If you're the kind of person who could be bothered to read this book, then you're the kind of person who will understand that, for a 25 year old film geek, to achieve a level of existence where he's his own boss, gets paid to hang out with his friends and gets unlimited free movies, pizza and sweets is as close to Shangri-La as humanly possible.

That's not to say there weren't flies in the ointment. There were of course... customers. Most were cool. Very cool, in fact. You didn't generally go into a shop that looked like Videosyncratic if you didn't 'get it'. There are a lot more cool indie shops of various types all over the place now – which is a great thing – but back in 2002, you didn't really get places with that kind of modern-indie vibe so much outside of the big cities. There hadn't been much of a counter-culture kickback and people were extremely comfortable with corporate uniformity. Had we embraced this – not unlike Diane had tried to with Box Office – we probably could have made an awful lot more money. But money wasn't a motivating force for me. I wanted it to just do it right. I wanted to turn the wrong people away. I'd worked video retail for years and I knew that I just didn't want certain people coming through those doors into my little idyll. I didn't want the horrible groups of teenagers who'd nick the video boxes, I didn't want the porno bastards who'd find blatant sexual thrills in being served dirty movies by female members of staff, I didn't want the people who'd rent films by The Wayans Brothers and then come in and say 'Mate, dat is da fuckin' funniest film I ever SAW!' before trying to explain to me the higher moments of the piece. It's a sad day when you learn that there is actually something less funny than a film by the Wayans's and that is an idiot trying to recreate the experience of a film by the Wayans's. One of my first executive policies was, in fact, no Wayans Brothers films. Ever. So, I didn't want any of these people through the door. Unexpectedly, the name itself became almost an elitist divider; people fell into one of two camps – either the name Videosyncratic was a delightful play on words which drew people straight in, or it was a baffling and unpronounceable assortment of random letters which provoked a confused but total dismissal.

But even those that 'got it' could turn out to be frustrating. Summertown, being the 'posh' part of Oxford and very much the place the more successful London commuter-routers installed their families, had a high quota of high-maintenance people. I remember we had a particular problem with DVDs of the TV show 'Friends' – one of the most popular rentals, people would work through the whole box set all the time. It was total comfort-food viewing, teenagers were crazy for it and teenagers minds are rarely on returning DVDs on time, so a lot of our dealings were with furious middle-aged mums...

A woman marches in and slams a Friends DVD down on the counter 'that's late' she declares. I check it back in on the computer.

'That's 31 days late' I tell her.

'Yes' she replies flatly 'Will there be a fine?'

'Well, officially the fine is £93'

'But it's not my fault!'

'Whose fault is it?'

'My children! They come in and take out films then go back to school for the term and just leave them in their bedroom. I don't see why I should have to pay for their mistakes.'

'Well, it's your account and you authorised them to rent, so you're liable. I can take their names off your account if you like?'

'Well, that means I'd have to come with them every time they wanted a film!'

'It's your choice, really. I'll knock the fine in half anyway.'

'You lot are quite clever, aren't you? It's all rather exploitative'

'Yes, we exploit your stupidity and the arrogant brattish lack of responsibility and the concept of the disposable value of money that you have instilled in your children and continue to by paying off a huge fine which they aren't even aware they have run up.'

I didn't actually say that last bit out loud. But I hope it was expressed in my mildly arched left eyebrow and hint of a sardonic grin. As she left the shop, I put a warning on her account 'INSUFFERABLE COW'.

I should explain the warning thing. I guess I'm going to tell you a bit of an industry secret right now, which is fine since the industry is now inarguably dead. We wrote stuff about you. On your account, you know? In every single piece of video shop software I have ever used or seen (which I'm pretty sure is all of them) there was a 'warning' feature. This is a little box that pops up when your account number is entered, created by another member of staff, to inform the person serving you of any pertinent information. Pertinent information is, of course messages like 'late fee scammer' 'speak clearly' 'must sign membership form'. Of course, it was seldom that such actually helpful messages would ever pop up.

My first ever encounter with the warning facility occurred on my first day of training in the Headington Blockbuster. I scanned the customer's membership card and a message flashed up on the screen 'SMILES LIKE A PAEDOPHILE!'. I instinctively looked up to be met by a leering grin of that exact description and had to swallow a laugh so severely, I thought I was going to choke. Other classics through the years have included:

'SMELLS LIKE FISH'

'WILL BE WANKING WITHIN FIVE MINUTES. MIGHT BE WANKING NOW'

The classic 'TWAT'

'LOOKS LIKE TRAMP, BUT IS MILLION-AIRE! SAW HIM ON TV!'

'THINKS SHE CAN FLIRT HER WAY OUT OF LATE FEES, LET HER TRY, BUT DON'T LET HER OFF!!!'

'PROBABLY A RAPIST'

'DON'T LOOK DIRECTLY INTO EYES. STRONG EVIL HYPNOTIST VIBE.'

The chilling 'UH OH, YOU'RE FUCKED'

HAMMERTIME!' for one particularly funky customer who always appeared in shades and baggy trousers.

'OH MY GOD, WHAT IS THIS BEAST SUPPOSED TO BE?'

'HER EYES MOVE INDEPENDENTLY OF EACH OTHER. PICK ONE AND STICK WITH IT'

'LIFE IS TOO SHORT TO ENGAGE THIS MAN IN CONVERSATION'

One of my favourites was the baffling but emotional 'SHIT DVD PLAYER??? SHIT CUNT!?!?!?!'

Then it descends into the more obvious.

'I WOULD!'

'I WOULDN'T'

'I MIGHT, I DON'T KNOW…'

(all three occasionally appearing in sequence on a single account)

'FUCK YOU!'

and once again 'TWAT'

You see, 'TWAT' is the most ubiquitous warning on any video shop computer because most customers manage to annoy us humble employees just to the point where we hate you but can't be bothered to remember you or type more than 4 letters.

Blockbuster's warning feature was extra special because if you entered a '*' into the text box, it made a 'diddle-ee-doo!' noise. I think I was the one who discovered that you got a diddle-ee-doo for each separate star, meaning if you entered a whole line of them, the computer would be making loud silly noises for the best part of a minute. This was both suspicious to the customer and embarrassing to the employee serving them. Fun fun fun.

The thing is, if you got a warning, you generally deserved it. It was a pretty egalitarian system, if you dressed nice and gave us a smile, you got a 'PHWOAR' (this might sound a little misogynistic but I can assure you there were far more 'PHWOAR's on male accounts than female), if you came in and kicked up a fuss, you got a 'TWAT'. I think part of the problem this is rooted in is that firstly a lot of people in this country have never worked retail (posh people are always FAR ruder than anyone else) and secondly, the corporations have done such a good job at presenting a corporate image that customers forget that they are shouting at and being rude to an actual person with feelings and pride. They seem to think they're shouting at the company, but all they're really doing is balling out a minimum wage till slave who is not responsible for whatever fuck-up you're blustering about. Damn right they're going to brand you a twat. You are one. Treat people well, Twat!

Besides that, once you get into the realm of independent video shops, you're dealing with a different breed of employee. This person you like to berate, patronise or ignore is probably as smart as you, if not smarter and definitely more interesting. The kind of people I've often been surrounded by at these jobs have been students, artists, actors, film-makers, musicians. People trying to do something interesting and positive with their lives. Surviving on minimum wage so they can devote their time and energy to their projects. Out of the Videosyncratic staff, I could list the following achievements:

Recorded numerous Peel sessions

Released a single with Jon Snow on vocals

Was briefly famous in Sweden

Starred in the west end production of Buddy

Starred in a Toyota advert in which he drove some aliens around Johannesburg in a Toyota whilst being chased by the mother-ship

Wrote some episodes of the Canadian sci-fi show Lexx (that one was me, remember?)

Was one of the original dudes at LYCOS and made out like a bandit with stock options.

A working artist with exhibitions/installations in Paris, New York and New Delhi.

A singer-songwriter who'd once had his song used in a big scene on the TV show The OC

Just this year, Ben – now a successful touring musician as part of Frank Turner's band, played lead guitar, headlining a sold-out Wembley Arena.

The talents amongst us included professional standard illustrators, musicians, filmmakers, electrical engineers, teachers, artists, photographers, actors, writers, the lot. Most of us had degrees too! We were very human and very awesome, if you talked to us, you'd find us quite delightful, if you were rude to us we'd misuse whatever power we had. And, as an employer who had languished on the shop floor for years, I wholeheartedly supported that. I encouraged that. I did that. A lot. And guess what, nasty customers, we didn't value or require your business. That standard bastard response was always 'I shall tell people about this and take my business elsewhere!' Well, we had thousands of customers who knew how to be polite and you hardly knew any of them! And, chances are, even if you did go and whinge about us to your mates, they'd only have said 'they've always been nice to me!' because they have manners.

Is it really so hard to understand the concept that if you're nice to people, they'll be nice back? Let's role play this:

CUSTOMER: (huffing and puffing) I'M A NASTY PERSON AND BLAH BLAH BLAH THIS IS COMPLETELY UNACCEPTABLE, YOU RUINED MY FAMILY'S EVENING WITH YOUR FAULTY PRODUCT! I WANT A REFUND!

ME: So, the disc wouldn't play?

CUSTOMER: (roar) IT FROZE ON CHAPTER TWO!

ME: Did you try cleaning it?

CUSTOMER: IT SHOULD BE CLEAN WHEN IT LEAVES THE STORE!

(I breathe on it, give it a wipe on my sleeve to remove big obvious greasy fingerprint, pop it in our dvd player and it plays perfectly)

CUSTOMER: I DEMAND A REFUND!

ME: I'm afraid, the product isn't faulty, you've had it for a whole week and it says clearly on the case how to clean it and to call us if you have a problem.

CUSTOMER: I WILL NEVER COME BACK HERE AGAIN THIS IS RIDICULOUS!

ME: (typing) t.....w....a....

Alternatively, same disc, right? Same problem…

CUSTOMER: Hello, we had a bit of a problem with this.

ME: Oh, I'm sorry about that, what went wrong?

CUSTOMER: It freezes on chapter two.

ME: Did you try giving it a little wipe?

CUSTOMER: We…didn't, to be honest, maybe we should have.

(I breathe on it, give it a wipe on my sleeve to remove big obvious greasy fingerprint, pop it in our dvd player and it plays perfectly)

CUSTOMER: Ooops! Looks like our fault!

ME: Look, take it back for another few nights for free.

CUSTOMER: Oh, we're going on holiday today.

ME: Well, I'll just put a credit on your account.

CUSTOMER: Oh, thank you so much.

ME: No, I'm sorry your evening was spoiled.

Wasn't that nice? I might even put 'NICE BLOKE' on his account. Or, if it's a lovely girl, she might have earned a 'NICE LADY!'. But best of all, they've not introduced negativity into the world, they've created a positive atmosphere, when we see each other in the street now, we'll raise a friendly eyebrow to one another. Next time they're in, I'll ask if everything worked OK and they'll thank me genuinely for teaching them the breathe and rub method of dvd repair.

I'll tell you the most legendary Videosyncratic event involving the on-screen warning, also one of my most embarrassing moments ever. One of our regulars came in, a good guy, bit of a fast-talking wide-boy phone-salesman type but totally not malicious or rude, I always liked him. So anyway, I wasn't even there to work that day, but was hanging out with Ben. The guy came in and I instinctively went to serve him cos we're on first-name terms. His account comes up and I notice a fine on it, I tell him and he queries it. I turn the screen around to point it out to him and he reads out (from the warning I missed) 'This guy deserves a slap?' The world stops. Three feelings coursed through the shop, the customer's hurt, my shame and Ben's sheer joy at being able to witness such an occurrence. I felt AWFUL and tried to do that thing where you make noises that aren't words and pretend nothing happened, gave him his film for free and let him go. Straight away, I sent him a letter of apology and put a bunch of credit on his account. On hearing about it,

Jamie – now my assistant manager – offered a more simple solution. 'When he said 'this guy deserves a slap', you should have just reached across the counter, slapped him, then deleted the message and carried on like nothing had happened'. See, we hired geniuses!

Jamie was generally hilarious. I think he'd have found the job perfect had he just been allowed to smoke indoors. Instead, he kind of set up base camp outside in all but the worst weather. He'd have his little station to the right of the front door, his chair, his guitar, a coffee and his cigarettes. He'd happily leave the shop unattended as customers browsed, telling them to give him a shout if they wanted serving. If people came to return videos, he'd just take them from them at the door. Occasionally, if he deemed a customer gullible enough he'd say 'Oh, I can take that for you' and then just run away down the street with it.

My favourite ever difficult customer was Rupert. I say customer, he didn't actually buy anything but he left his mark.

The shop was on the same road as a very posh boy's school. St Edwards. St Edwards was so posh, the pupils referred to it as 'St. Teddy's'. That's posh. One quiet weekday afternoon, one particularly loathsome young

Teddy's Boy stumbled into the shop and dropped onto the sofa by the front window, noisily conducting a conversation that sounded so slurred I couldn't figure out if he was uber-drunk or uber-posh. One of my multitude of pet hates was non-customers who came in off the street to conduct their phone conversations in a quieter environment, then leave once they were done. So I did my old trick to evict him – put a CD on and cranked it up loud. He was still there after one song, at least he hadn't left. I stood up to take a look and he was lying face down on the sofa with watery vomit EVERYWHERE. All over the sofa and floor. I get over there and ask him if I need to call an ambulance. He sits up and dismisses me with a wave of his hand uttering in a posh drawl.

'I'm fine, I'm fine, I just had too much vodka'.

He gets up to leave, I tell him if he's fine, he's going to stay until he has scrubbed that carpet clean 'Oh, mate' he protests. I lock the door and go to fill a bucket of soapy water for him. I come back to find him stumbling around knocking things off shelves. He whines some more about it being unfair, I tell him to be quiet, clean up the mess and that it'll cost him £20 for the cleaning of the sofa and the covers. 'I don't HAVE any money!' he shouts in that petulant way only the truly rich and spoiled can. 'Are you a St Edwards kid?' I ask 'Yes'. 'Start scrubbing!'

So I come back behind the counter and call his school to come and pick him up. He hears me doing this 'Noooooooo! Maaaaaaaaaate! No, don't do that!'. I ignore him and finish the conversation. He is furious and starts shouting at me, I calmly give him my look of fury and tell him to sit down, shut up and wait for his housemaster to arrive. He paces about for a bit in frustration, like a caged tiger, then runs at the glass door and with two kicks, kicks through it. He was wearing sandals. He clambers out through the bottom pane, cutting himself to shit as he goes. Broken glass and posh blood are everywhere, they cover the pavement and everyone in the street comes running out of the shop to see what the commotion is. It was very reminiscent of an episode of The Incredible Hulk where a stroppy Lou Ferrigno would run away in slow motion, leaving confused bystanders double taking between the carnage and the fleeing weirdo.

As he's halfway down the road, two teachers from his school turn up and watch him go 'Is that him? Did he....?' They work out what has happened, then sprint after him. They don't stand a chance, despite the obvious loss of blood and the fact he keeps stumbling off the pavement and falling into the road, the kid is fast. They give up and call the police. The men were very decent about it all and immediately arranged for an emergency glazier and a cleaning firm to come and clean the carpets and sofa. In the meantime, the school's head caretaker comes in and cleans up the glass and hoovers. He was a really nice man and it just struck me so foul that the arrogant behaviour of a 16 year old boy should have so many people cleaning up after him. Soon after, a parade of slack-jawed yuppy larvae paraded through to inspect the damage and go 'Oh wow, did Rupert do that? You'll be OK – he's MINTED!', 'is this the window Rupert broke? He's really rich, so I'm sure it'll all get sorted'. By locking him in and making him clean his mess, I'd rather hoped to teach Rupert a lesson but I get the feeling that by kicking his way through my window, he taught himself one – that he could puke anywhere he wanted and break anything he wanted as there were a squadron of people just waiting to clean up after him. That said, I heard he got expelled and his mother arrived that night in floods of tears, which was rather awkward for Ben who also had to field Rupert's plummy-voiced apology phone call two days later. If nothing else, I hope he learned the lesson about not kicking through windows if you're wearing sandals.

Generally, annoying customers went hand in hand with the issue of late fees. Late fees. I'll tell you about them but I'll keep it short because even now, years later, nothing annoys anyone who has ever worked in a video shop more than having to talk about late fees. So I'm going to explain why they were there, why you should've paid them and how you could have got out of them.

Do I really need to explain why they were there? Are there people out there who rent cars, return them ten days later and go 'that's ridiculous! I'm not paying for that! I FORGOT!'.

I always loved the use of 'I forgot!' as a valid excuse. 'But, I forgot!!!' Yeah, as opposed to all of those people who *maliciously* returned films late.

Late fees existed for two reasons – firstly because a video shop lost money every day on a film that could have been renting rather than sitting on your coffee table. Secondly, because if they didn't exist, it would be ANARCHY! People just wouldn't bother to return stuff ever unless they wanted something new to watch. So we had to enforce it! It was nothing personal. OK, it was often personal, but it had to happen or the business would have ground to a halt.

When Lovefilm started up, their genius masterstroke was the concept of 'no late fees ever' – obviously, they had to be a massive operation to make that feasible and they shrewdly mopped up what was left of the industry on that gimmick alone, but I'll tell you what – that made me a little sad. Modern culture is all about convenience and the absolution of customer responsibility. I personally think there's something rather nice and dignified about walking to a shop to choose something and then walking back there to return it punctually. It got you out of the house, got you some exercise and gave you a bit of social interaction. I've completely resisted signing up to any on-demand video services. It's too fucking easy and disposable for my tastes. I like to go to a shop and choose a DVD. At least to buy one online and enjoy the anticipation until it arrives and can sit on my desk awaiting viewing and then be filed alphabetically in my DVD collection. I never thought that concept would make me sound like a crotchety old-timer. Anyway, late fees…

When I didn't work in video shops, I always paid my late fees, and to be honest, many many people each week would bring in films and say 'this is late, how much will that be?' – which was utterly commendable.

Indie video shops didn't make a lot of money. Especially at the end. In fact, if you believe the information on wikipedia, even Blockbuster was losing over a billion dollars each year from 2002 to 2004, but, frankly, fuck 'em. The indies, generally were done out of passion, not profit, someone's neck was always on the line and every £3 late fee I dismissed set me back £3 worth of possibility of breaking even and staying open that year.

But we didn't always charge. There were ways of getting out of it. The first being, simply, don't return films late. The second was the fact that you would never be let off a late fee if you left the film in the drop box or ran in to return it and didn't mention it there and then. We knew every con, you'd leave it a month or so, then come back in and when told about the debt you'd say 'no, that's wrong! I brought it back on time'. We knew you hadn't. Even the most ramshackle video shop had a system for returns, we just knew when people were lying about this stuff and even if we let you away with it, we'd be writing 'LATE FEE SCAMMER' in your warning box, so not only would you not get away with it again, but every time you came in, the member of staff serving you would think you were scum. Talk to us! Pay us! Offer to pay! We often wouldn't charge late fees on old films that we wouldn't have lost money on if you were polite enough to offer! Here were my favourite ubiquitous defences that only ever strengthened my resolution to charge:

'But, I forgot!' – Yes, well, adults take responsibility for their mistakes.

'I could have BOUGHT it for that much' – Yes! Cheaper, probably.

'I'm weally weally sowwy!' – Have a little integrity.

'I wasn't told when it was due back!' – So, why didn't you ask?

'I got it back just after you closed!' – There aren't degrees of late.

'I was never told there was a charge for late return' – You should read contracts before signing them, then decide whether you want to be remembered as an idiot or a liar.

'It may be late, but it was faulty!' – Well, let's get the late thing out of the way first.

'It was my flatmate's fault' – you should have told him to get his own account.

'I'll take my business elsewhere!' – it's not really business if *you're* costing *us* money.

If you use ANY of those excuses, you'd have lost all goodwill with your video clerk. It's gone. Irreparable and instant. Understand that we heard that entire list all day, every day. We wanted to charge you just for having said that. It's like hearing the fingernails on blackboard for most normal people. Like the warning box, late fees are often the only power a minimum wage person had against an arrogant loudmouth who was patronising them. We relished this small amount of power and wielded it happily. Be polite and honest and have some basic human manners and you'd have done ok with us. Because either you'd get out of the debt, get it reduced or, worst case scenario, you'd have been supporting a struggling independent business.

Late fees at Blockbuster were a whole other corporate issue. It seemed to be fact while I was working for them that if any customer, no matter what they'd done or how much of an asshole they'd been about it, complained to UK head office, they would not only have their debt cleared but get 5 free rentals credited to it and, in some hilarious circumstances, an apology from Carl! That was always a giggle.

Despite the distractive niggle of a healthy customer base, I don't think I've ever been as happy as those early days of Videosyncratic. I'd done it. I'd achieved my dream. So, as it will, my mind swiftly focused on what to do next.

CHAPTER 11

VIDEOSYNCRATICS

2005

I just realised that I've been lying to you. I didn't mean to. I got carried away in literary devices, nostalgia and the romanticism of mundanity. Sorry about that. So, all that stuff I said back in that last chapter about having achieved my dream and having low ambition and all that? Yeah, that was pretty much bullshit. I had bags of ambition. And although, yes, one of my defining ambitions in life was to own my own video shop, I'd say that by close of business on the first day it was already, in some way, not enough for me. I think the day I started even planning the shop was probably the time I took a longer term view and hatched my plan for world domination.

Even in 2002, I could see the writing on the wall for video rental. As much as I adored the DVD format, from very early on I could see that it spelled trouble for the entire film industry. I could not conceive why the studios would back a format that was capable of being copied without losing a generation of quality. Let me explain, although piracy had been rife with VHS, a pirate video was a pretty shitty thing. Each time you copied a video signal from machine to machine, you lost a significant amount of quality – maybe 20%. So the average pirate video was usually 2nd or 3rd generation – 20 – 40% poorer quality than an original. Most people had no interest in seeing a film so degraded. The bulk of pirated videos were of films currently – or not yet – in the cinemas, so the value was in seeing something early, to some people a fair trade-off on quality.

DVD, being a digital format, had no significant visible quality lost when pirated to another digital format. Apparently, the studios had a deal with the technology developers that they would support the new format (which would have been worthless without their films) on the proviso that home DVD recorders would be held back from release for a few years. That alone was short-sighted and bizarre but I guess back then in the late nineties, they hadn't really considered what the internet would be capable of.

My mum had loved technology, we were the first family I knew by a number of years to have the internet at home (back then you paid by the minute for both the phone line and the internet service, one night I fell asleep at the keyboard and cost my parents the best part of £100). The first video I ever watched online was the trailer for the risible Stallone misfire Judge Dredd. It took hours to download, lasted 30 seconds and seemed to be comprised of about 12 pixels, each the size of my fist. But I knew that this was just the beginning. It seemed obvious to me that this would be the way delivery of film would go and as soon as I found out DVD was rippable, it was blindingly obvious that eventually video piracy, unless stringently safeguarded against would spiral out of control. The studios didn't see it that way. I guess they saw it as the first opportunity since the release of VHS to re-market their entire back catalogues. Which they did and, probably, to great profit. But they didn't future-proof it. Up until the beginning of this decade, if you wanted to see Casablanca, you'd have to pay around £10. Either on cinema re-release or buying it on VHS or DVD. Now, the very value of DVD has been decreased. Casablanca held its value for decades, at the time of writing, you can buy a brand new shrink-wrapped copy for £3 from Sainsbury's. As a film lover I find this both irresistibly fantastic and wretchedly sad.

Anyway, I saw this coming and from the get-go predicted that we had about a 7 year window with Videosyncratic. My plan was to build a local chain. Never national. I'm no businessman and although my dad understands the requirements and professional obligations, he'd crash and sink a national company in seconds, like a greased Titanic. I didn't want any more shops than I could personally visit every day and keep running smoothly. I figured 4, maximum. My long term goal was to build up a bit of a hip brand and move steadily into DVD distribution. I wanted Videosyncratic to be a DVD label, we could build that up over the 7 years and then, at the point the shops became unprofitable, we could cut them loose and glide effortlessly onwards as a global purveyor of amazing, idiosyncratic films. And that was my plan.

OK, I'm lying again.

The plan went a bit further than that. Once Videosyncratic the DVD label took off, I planned to launch Videosyncratic the production company. Where we could fund and produce low-budget, highly original films. I thought we could have a remit of first-time filmmakers only. I'd scour the film schools and film festivals to find undiscovered talent and set them up to have their first shot at making a feature film. I envisioned a Roger Corman style stable of unproven, raw but brilliant, actors, filmmakers, technicians, composers... That was my plan.

Some of it.

OK, I had a further plan. I thought once that took off, we could start a little studio – like Ealing and Hammer had been back in the heyday of British cinema. Our own studio, with full technical staff where we could continuously produce quality British films. Revive the flagging industry and give British film culture a solid kick up the bum. That was my plan.

I mean... yes, I envisioned our own cinema chain. I'll admit that. The most comfortable cinemas in the world, where people who talked, farted or even TOUCHED their mobile phones would be ejected by trained professionals with night-vision goggles (I planned to give Nick the head of security position for the entire chain) and banned for life. Where snacks would be neither crunchy, smelly or come with straws that could make slurping noises. Where ALL the lights in the auditorium would go off when the film started and toilets would be locked for the duration of the film cos it's only an hour-and-a-fucking-half, so go before you sit down or hold it the fuck in. I did think about the cinema chain. Which would have been very successful.

So, inevitably we would have diversified – invested in emerging technologies. I'm not saying that Videosyncrat-O-Vision would have outclassed the current 3D technology sweeping our land but I like to think it would have caused fewer headaches and been projected at a more appropriate level of brightness.

So that WAS my plan. I swear I didn't once think of becoming so powerful that I could crush companies like News Corp or Starbucks or that company that supplies all the frozen food that the pubs microwave and serve under the guise of 'home-cooked food'. I in no way envisioned VIDEOSYN-CRATIC CORP as a mighty yet benevolent overseer that guided culture and, indeed, society towards my own personal and political ideals.

I didn't even consider the notion. Not for an idle minute.

Where was I?

Oh yeah, what was next for Videosyncratic? Well, it was obvious that we needed to open a second branch – people were crying out for it. Some people made weekly treks the whole way across Oxford (even Oxfordshire and some dedicated folks made weekly pilgrimages from other counties entirely) but most just visited us once and found their initial joy being replaced by stroppy jealousy that they didn't have anywhere like this where they lived.

I didn't want to set up in the centre of town because, despite terrible parking facilities, Simon's dad Leo Edwards' last video shop Movies was still doing great business. I respected him and I had no desire to tread on his toes. I was happy to blast a Block-buster out of the water though, and the obvious target was Cowley Road.

Cowley Road was the Greenwich Village of Oxford. When I was growing up, it was a pretty scary place for a pudgy middle class innocent. It was a run down but incredibly vibrant and bohemian place. All cultures lived and mixed there, mainly because they had no choice. Back then, if you had money, you didn't live on the Cowley Road. All of the streets coming off it were full of rundown terraced housing. A vast quantity of the buildings were squats (even the shops and cinema), the rest was welfare or cheap housing or homed dangerously large numbers of people in dangerously small numbers of rooms. To some, it was the home of culture and vibrancy. To me, it seemed like a place you went to get stabbed. I went to see gigs there and to see films at the Penultimate Picture Palace but you couldn't get me off the street and into the venues quick enough.

Since I'd returned from film school. I'd seen a huge change in the area. The gang culture had been sorted out, maybe I was just a little more sure of myself, but the place seemed safer and culture seemed more predominant than stabbing. I spent all of my social time there and had moved there during Videosyncratic's second year. The last proper squat on my street was busted a couple of months after my arrival (to the street, not the squat) and the area was getting quickly gentrified. Since the Oxford Polytechnic had been allowed to change it's name to 'Oxford Brookes University' it had seen a huge upturn in its fortunes. Now every brainless child of a rich family was dispatched there upon finishing school so their parents could say 'Oh, Rupert and Finella are both studying at Oxford' without technically lying. Just like Greenwich Village, and many places since, the people with money wanted to live in the 'cool' part of town, descended upon the Cowley Road and sparked off a cash bonanza for the landlords.

There were an awful lot of huge vacant shops on the road and I wanted one. I knew that a big, bold Videosyncratic would just do incredible business there. It took a year to find a location. Despite all of these shops being empty and on the rental market, the owners had been infected by greed. The rates they were charging were more akin to trendy areas of London and the condition of the buildings themselves dictated that you'd have to spend many tens of thousands of pounds just to make the building safe before you could even think about starting a business and making money. It was a truly frustrating period as I was sure that someone was going to see how well we were doing in Summertown and try to replicate our success in Cowley. I was very vocal that we would be opening on Cowley Road soon, just to try to cut any potential usurpers off at the pass.

Our saviour came in the form of Ash, a landlord who, with his father, owned a considerable amount of the property in the area. He owned the best and least practical shop on the road. A sprawling and highly visible corner property made up of various internal nooks and crannies, having previously formed a shop and storefront offices but having, over the years, been kind of, oddly, opened up into one sort-of space. It had loads of window space and bags of character. Its last incarnation had been a vintage clothing shop. Ash could see that we weren't just an upstart, that we were local and wanted to create a business that would sit well in and serve this community. We got on with him, so he took a punt on us and said he'd completely renovate the space for us if we took a 12 year lease. This was longer than I thought practical but Dad pointed out to me that a 12 year lease on one of the best shops in this fast-gentrifying area was actually a rather shrewd investment. If we wanted to get out, in a few years people would pay a premium to take that place off us. It just made sense. So we went for it.

My vision of the new shop was big. It was different to Summertown. It had to be. Summertown was a cool experiment, this had to be a bold statement. That was scary though. Summertown didn't cost much to set up, I had a decent stock base before we started, it was easily fitted on the cheap. This new shop was twice the size and far more prominent – being on a busy main road and not a side street. Speculate to accumulate, right? We had to get a bank loan. This absolutely terrified me. Although I'd never really had money, I'd also never really had money problems as my parents had warned me consistently growing up about the dangers of indulging in credit and loans. I didn't own a personal credit card. I still don't. My student loan was my only debt and.. well, that still doesn't seem real, really. A business loan and a 12 year lease were a huge stress to me but Dad seemed confident about it all. And neither of us would have taken the step if we hadn't done our research and been optimistic about it. So we signed with the bank and we signed with Ash.

As brilliant, if eccentric, a job as Peter had done fitting the Summertown store, I didn't want this one to be shabby chic. I certainly didn't want it to be corporate but it struck me that this was the frame of reference people had at this moment in history. Cowley Road, although steeped in a fug of hippy haze history, just wasn't really that place anymore. I didn't want that living room feel. There was no way I was going to put sofas in this one – I knew Cowley Road, you put sofas in and you'd instantly be a drop-in centre for misfits and nightmares.

One thing I could never resolve having worked at so many different video shops was the glaring fact that customers spent more money at Blockbuster. It was an unassailable fact. In every indie shop I had worked, the average customer transaction was one video rental – so maybe £3 or £3.50, whereas at Blockbuster the average spend was at least a tenner. They'd rent a couple of films and grab a bag of popcorn and a bottle of coke. I had tried to emulate this in Summertown – we had a permanent offer of rent 2 films, get a third free so that we could try to ensure a basic transaction of at least £6 from each customer. Whenever we tried to bring food or drinks into the deal, it just didn't work. When I looked at my own shopping habits, I was aghast to realise that when I went into my beloved independent book shops or comic shops, my spend was generally FAR less than when I just popped into Borders. Likewise, I found that when I was at my weekly farmer's market, for some reason I was very aware of prices and acted with frugality, whereas in a supermarket I didn't even look at price, I just slung whatever caught my eye into the basket. It's a curious phenomenon but what I came up with is the notion that this is some kind of consumer psychology. Some environments just make us want to spend money. Make us feel expected to spend money. Anaesthetise us to it. This kind of thought was a bit alien to me and made me feel a little ashamed of myself but, for the first time, I felt a huge adult burden of responsibility. Our rent was high. We had a big loan to pay off. Summertown, in comparison, was a hobby for me and a lazy retirement for Dad. This was business. It was livelihood. It was scary.

So, I realised the shop had to be airy, professional, clean (like it was ever going to stay that way) and a spending environment but swirled in with our brand of anti-corporate punky mischief. It had to have the counter-culture heart with a corporate sheen. My god, I'm just a massive fucking sell-out, aren't I? Well, who fucking isn't. At least I was never a profiteer. I wasn't shucking people or lying or playing with independent imagery to bolster my margins. In fact, quite the opposite – I was a true indie with true indie ideals playing with corporate imagery to ensure survival. Yeah. That's the ticket. I wasn't so bad. Don't judge me.

In Summertown, we had seriously wounded the Blockbuster and I wanted to target their Cowley Road branch. It was right across the road from us diagonally, a 30 second walk away and I knew it was a part of town where we could take them on and probably win. I was spoiling for a rumble.

The renovation Ash did was excellent, it created one big, but oddly spaced shape. I heard about a local fitter called Barney who supposedly could do anything. I liked him. He was painfully young and worked with an incredibly old furniture designer – Neil.

They were the strangest double act I'd ever seen but they got it instantly and did amazing work. We had beautiful wood flooring put down and over that, Barney and Neil filled the shop with custom built shelving units. All in red and grey with adjustable shelving. They looked fantastic. Modern but quirky and designed to display DVDs in the most attractive and intelligent way. No plastic walls. They built a stunning and monolithic counter which cut across most of the length of the shop and behind that they designed an incredible series of bookcases on castors, like something out of some secret government archive buried miles below the ground. We knew they were the most efficient way of storing all of the stock in its rental cases but we weren't sure they were going to actually work. The units were massive and heavy. They did work but I lived in fear of a health and safety assessment which might judge them a technical physical abuse of my staff. They were a bastard to pull out. You could spot a Videosyncratic worker in the street as one arm would always be a Schwarzenegger-esque mass of muscle and sinew whilst their other would hang pale and limp at their side. Everyone had a different method of getting the things to pull out. I favoured to plant my left hand on the next unit along and use that as a grounding on which I could use my body as a fulcrum, spinning, letting my chest muscles take the brunt of the tug. Elliot would stand facing the unit, planted to the ground and let his bicep take the strain in one mighty yank. Little Humphrey would grab the handle with both hands and fall backwards, using the dead weight of his entire body to get the wheels moving.

We had inordinately high ceilings so I hired Rowena's little brother Robin to do some art. Robin was about to head to art school and was the only person I knew at the time who had Banksy as a point of reference. He did a series of beautiful film-related stencil graffiti all over every spare surface in the shop. It looked amazing. A huge Easy Rider piece featuring Fonda and Hopper on their bikes, a massive King Kong, a tiny Alfred Hitchcock at the bottom of a column, The Three Stooges, Hepburn, Jay and Silent Bob, Ferris Bueller, The Karate Kid, a massive Robbie The Robot by the front door, Frankenstein and his Bride, Dirty Harry, a Stormtooper and my personal favourite, a life sized Woody Allen sat in the window. It was really beautiful work.

The place looked great, anyway. Above the units on the shop floor, we put plenty of toys and ephemera and I spent a bunch of time at film conventions getting signed photos. I'd visited The Carnegie Deli in New York a few times in the previous couple of years and a big part of the fun of that experience is that every spare bit of wall space is filled with photos of its famous customers, all signed to the deli. I'd never seen a video shop do that, so that became a bit of a mission. Of course, we didn't exactly have celebrity customers. In Summertown, our celebs began and ended with Susie Dent from Countdown, the drummer from Radiohead, Jeremy Paxman and Raymond Blanc (mistaken for a tramp at least once by every member of staff at some point). Rory McGrath jogged past with his big red face occasionally but never stopped in. Oh, and Richard Branson came in once looking for an opera video that we didn't have. Rowena pointed out that they might have it at the Virgin Megastore in town.

We didn't have any celebs at all at Cowley Road. In our first week, John turned away Mickey from Supergrass because he didn't have the right ID to sign up. But I forged ahead anyway. I'd discovered what my girlfriend at the time coined as 'nerdfests' – these crazy events where a company would ship a load of B-list celebrities (B is generous. There are some B's but generally it spans C to Z) over from America, sit them behind trestle tables and charge the great unwashed anything from £5 (blokes who appear in single frames of a Star Wars film) to £60 (Shatner, blokes who appeared in most of the frames of a Star Wars film) for a signed photo. They're quite the most curious of happenings but irresistible to a true film nerd. Over the years, we amassed a vast collection of items dedicated to Videosyncratic and the shop became all the more popular for it. My high points were a License To Drive poster signed by BOTH Coreys (R.I.P. Haimster), An Army of Darkness poster signed by Bruce Campbell (Yo, Videosyncratic, Get Busy!), a Dawn of the Dead poster signed to us by Romero. We had a great signed pic from Burt Reynolds who was a joy to meet – resplendent in a mustard coloured suit, he was chuffed to bits to hear that his films had their own shelf (I didn't tell him it was actually labelled 'BURT REYNOLDS/MOUSTACHES' and also had a heavy Tom Selleck quotient). We had Sam Jones – Flash Gordon himself, who wrote 'To the customers and staff of Videosyncratic, I'll save everyone of you – with the help of God!' which was a bit creepy, but fair play. Everyone from Danny Trejo to Tony Curtis, it became a mission. We had a signed poster from Terry Gilliam who, after asking what Videosyncratic was held up the line to chat to me and tell me that independent video shops were the last frontier and that he and filmmakers like him depended on guys like us to get their work to their audience. The place was full of signed pics, it was really cool and customers would bring visiting friends in just to show them.

To stock the shelves, I headed back to the Video Warehouse. I found a very changed environment. The operation had been pared down considerably. Steve was a bright entrepreneur but his business had been hit hard by DVD – firstly, many rare films were no longer rare as studios reissued their entire back catalogue on the new, cheaper format. But then DVDs did something strange to the whole industry, they cheapened it. Cheap to produce, selling at a high volume, the public just aren't prepared to spend the same amount on them and they are very quickly discounted. There just wasn't such a place in the market for Steve anymore. We did stock some VHS, but nowhere near the quantity we had in Summertown and in many ways it was more for the aesthetic. By now, it was DVD people wanted and we honoured that well.

I eschewed the notion of stocking confectionary. We were surrounded by newsagents and cheap grocery stores, with a massive Tesco up the road and I knew people were more frugal here. I also knew there'd be more shoplifting and couldn't be bothered to pay it the attention dad did in Summertown. But I did want to be more than a video shop, so I dedicated a section of the shop to film memorabilia. We sold action figures, posters, t-shirts, gifts, just cool shit. It wasn't a huge money spinner but it was steady. We were the only place on the road other than the record shops where you could buy a decent birthday present. I also had Barney fit a big glass section in the counter where I could stock my bizarre obsession – vintage trading cards. I found that on Ebay, you could buy full unopened boxes of Topps trading cards from the 70's and 80's – you know, the ones that came in Wax paper with a stick of nasty bubblegum – for between £5 and £30 each. Since each one had 36 packs, it was actually a profitable little sideline. We sold them at £2.50 a pack – which is a nice price for such a bizarre but joyously retro film artefact. We had a huge selection – Alien, Rocky 2, Howard The Duck, Moonraker, Elvis, Superman, Star Wars, A-Team, Knight Rider, we even had some Garbage Pail Kids. Every christmas, we'd get cleaned out as they were perfect stocking fillers. We also sold local music, all of Oxford's record shops were closing down and soon we were the only place were local unsigned bands could sell their wares. Since they were all customers and many of them were staff, it seemed the least we could do.

Staffing proved relatively easy. I took Jamie with me from Summertown as assistant manager. This was a role that required no extra responsibility on his part whatsoever but carried an extra quid an hour as some kind of recognition of seniority over the new boys and girls. Then I hired Dan. Dan was a film geek I'd known for some years, I'd taught him at OFVM when he was a teenager and was impressed by his knowledge and wit. He'd been languishing in the Rose Hill branch of Blockbuster for years and since I could only offer him a couple of hours a week at Summertown, he couldn't afford to quit. In Cowley Road, I could match his Blocky hours so successfully either stole him away or liberated him, depending on how pompous I feel. Dan, immediately became my actual assistant manager in terms of being the only person in the shop who did any work or gave a shit about the place. I mean, everyone was proud to be a member of staff at Videosyncratic – it had a certain cool cachet locally – but most of them could barely operate the till, let alone the broom. I once watched our crazy Wednesday night guy Scottish John snap a broom in half trying to brush a concrete lintel away. Dan cleaned, he was fastidious about the paperwork, he kept the place in shape. He was amazing, really.

I also liked Dan because he was a bit of an enigma. Not to me, really, I always felt we had a good understanding and friendship but there was something enigmatic about him to others. He had a reputation for silence which people found, at best, off-putting and, at worst, terrifying. That kind of silence carries a certain gravitas with it which was in no way intentional on his part but hilarious to observe. He was just a quiet guy. In fact, he wasn't even that quiet if you bothered to speak to him, but whatever. Along with the silence, he rocked an arched eyebrow and a wry grin. Again, people read an awful lot into that, but it was just his face! He couldn't help it. So people thought he was mocking them or being snooty but he was never doing either. Dan's face had this magical quality where essentially it was like a mystical mirror where whomsoever looked into it would see all of their worst insecurities reflected. I was immune to it. Dan rocks.

When people found out we were opening on Cowley Road, we really had the pick of everybody, we opted for a combination of film geeks and hipsters. We figured that's what the customers would want. The film geeks were dependable, fun and awesome, the hipsters got fired one by one for never turning up or giving free films to beautiful girls. It all worked fine and we became quite the merry band. Being on Cowley Road, the shop quickly became a hang-out and there were always brilliant people there. Interesting people, funny people, argumentative people. It had such a great vibe, an ever changing gaggle of counterflys (like barflys, I'm coining a phrase here!) shooting the shit. I loved it.

The new staff quickly found their own little customer service personas and in no time flat, the complaints were rolling in. From accusations of Dan's brusqueness to the little German man who wrote me a 2-page letter, having run out of the shop screaming 'YOU ARE HURTING MY EARS!' at Liam's choice of music and refusal to turn it down. My favourite customer complaint, however was one against Hanna, one of our few 'bubbly' members of staff who was, quite wonderfully, accused of being 'polite to the point of hostility'. Bravo, Wiggins!

Liam had actually replaced Hanna. When she quit to go to art school in London, she insisted I give her job to him. I was terrified of Liam. I'd never met him but I'd seen his metal-goth-gospel-punk-ska band Suitable Case For Treatment and, despite being one of the best live bands I'd ever seen, I couldn't see quite what use I might find for a howling, screaming, bellowing, grunting untamed beast of a freak with a maniacal, tooth-missing grin. Of course, when he turned up he was smart and funny and not in any way like his stage persona, so he got the job. It turned out there was slightly more of his stage persona to him than I had realised but I really enjoyed watching the customers have to deal with that. Liam's default expression was one of wary suspicion. I'm not sure he was even conscious of this but as anyone, apart from friends would talk to him, he'd cock his head to the side and back, furrow his brow and look down his nose with curious intensity at whoever was speaking to him. Late fees were often paid to him mid-explanation. They'd just give up, whatever they were saying would tail off and they'd leave sheepishly. Liam also stood out from the other employees in his almost total uselessness. Not only did he know impressively little about films but he couldn't fulfil even the most basic function required of him – his presence. I made no real demands on my staff at all other than they actually be in the shop when they were supposed to be working. I liked Liam a huge amount and genuinely gave him about 30 final warnings 'you do it once more, you're fired! On the spot!' the day I finally did it, we were both a little in shock. It's tough, though. You're over a barrel with this kind of thing. I genuinely liked all but 3 of the people we ever employed in Videosyncratic (nope, I'll never tell you!) Liked, even loved, if we weren't friends before they were hired, we became friends pretty damn fast. You don't want to fire people you care about. Especially because I couldn't imagine anyone else ever hiring most of them. Firing them felt like a death sentence.

The only person I ever sacked on the spot was Jim. Poor Jim. Young Jim. At the end of the initial round of Cowley Road hirings, Jamie and I were left with a dilemma – two final suitable applicants and one job to fill. Should we go with Tim, who knew loads about films but seemed a little awkward, or Jim, who knew demonstrably less about basically everything but had what Jamie defined as 'Cowley Road hair'. We decided we had enough introverted film geeks in the company, we were going to give the girls of Cowley Road some eye candy. Actually, it turned out we were going to give the girls of Cowley Road so much more. We were going to give them free rentals. I say 'we', I mean, of course 'Jim'. One day, a sweet and friendly young lady walked into the shop and asked where the 'blonde guy' was. I told her Jim had swapped shifts today. She was cool and we talked about films. After she left, I took a look at her account to see the kind of things she'd been renting. It was all pretty respectable, but then I noticed something. Well, technically I noticed nothing. In the cash column. All of her transactions were recorded as 0.00 – she'd had free rentals for months. At first I thought it was a computer error, but then I realised that all of her visits coincided with Jim's shifts. I made a note of Jim's hours and then trawled through all of the computer records and pretty quickly managed to construct a clear link between his schedule, free rentals and the hotness of certain female customers. He was giving free films to pretty girls. I called him in that night and confronted him with it. He chuckled in a cheeky manner and said it wouldn't happen again. I agreed that it wouldn't as he was sacked. He was stunned. I tried to explain but he sincerely couldn't see why that was a sackable offence. He protested that it wasn't stealing and I tried to illustrate that it wasn't so much raiding the till as barricading it but it was still costing me potential sales. These girls were all customers who were paying actual money when he wasn't about. So he WAS costing me money. He didn't get it, but he shuffled off anyway. We never heard from him again until the week that the shitty horror film 'The Deaths of Ian Stone' was released. Dan took it home and phoned me to tell me I had to watch it. It turns out Jim is in it! And he gets brutally murdered! We were so proud. Awww, Young Jim.

We settled into a rhythm with Cowley pretty easily and it became a great place. We still had the grumbles you'll always have – mainly customer based. It's probably a good time now to address the most tired piece of comedy material that always gets thrown against video shops. That being the ID required to sign up. The bane of the video shop clerk, especially on a weekend evening, is the new member. I understand completely that it'd be a weekend night where you'd go 'let's hire a video!' so troop down to the shop, it was just the worst time to join up. There'd be a huge queue of people and we'd have to stop to do data entry and explain stuff to the new customer without showing our frustration and alienating them from giving us lots of lovely money.

Here's the problem, though, people never had the right ID to join up. All we'd ask for is proof of their Oxford address (so bills or bank statements – these work as they have obviously been posted to the person and we can see how recently by the date on it) and a credit or debit card (which they authorize us to debit if they nick our films and don't respond to phone calls and letters). If you had just one of these forms of ID, you can put down a £20 deposit that either sits on the account or you can claim back if you bring in that ID at a later date. So, it was a pretty simple arrangement. It was all worked out. It just never seemed to go smoothly. I would have thought that if you asked any normal person whether they were carrying proof of their oxford address and a credit card, they'd be able to say 'yes, I do!' or 'oh, no, I don't', that just wasn't what happened ever. For proof of address, we were offered library cards, prescriptions and, the ever annoying passport. There was no would-be-member more exasperated than the one clutching his passport. Passports don't contain addresses and can't be debited so they're worthless to us. Is that really so insane a concept? Shitty comedians would build entire routines around that. The concept that a passport wasn't enough for a video shop. Every day there seems to be a new red face blustering 'But it's a PASS-PORT! This is the ULTIMATE form of ID! I'm offering you a PASSPORT and you want a GAS BILL????' Instead of credit/debit cards, people generally tried to offer us their cash card details which are, obviously, of no use to anyone and, frankly, what kind of grown adult doesn't even have a debit card? If the bank doesn't trust you to deal with your own money, I'd really rather not let you borrow any of my property. So, when their ID had been declined, rather than removing themselves or going home, they'd stand their and make an arse of themselves in front of a whole queue of customers.

Handbags are emptied on counters in the desperate hope that maybe a tampon or breath mint might somehow fit our membership requirements. Men would assume that the more they shout, rage, tut or raise their arms in the air to the almighty, the more likely we would be to change our minds and let them join up with just a stick of chewing gum and some belly button fluff.

I've been accused (by such idiots) of taking a perverse pleasure in seeing this happen and, I must admit, they were astute in such observations. I always enjoyed seeing idiots behaving like idiots. It amused me when someone pays the price for behaving like a fool and, if they were nasty and aggressive, all the better! Also, it always gave me licence to use my favourite of all the catchphrases which sprung up in Videosyncratic, Jamie's classic – 'Who are you *really* angry with?'

In all of the hearts of those of who worked at the Cowley Road branch, there was only really space for one particular angry customer. Tony Easterbrook. We didn't find out his name for about a year, we just called him 'Pissy' because he was always furious. And he smelled of piss. We actually grew very fond of him, he'd come in to bother us most days and, after seemingly snubbing us for a week or two, his neighbour came in one day to tell us that he'd passed away. I wrote this obituary for the VS blog:

Yesterday, all the staff here at the Cowley Road branch of Videosyncratic were deeply saddened by the news that, this weekend, our favourite customer had passed away. I wanted to write a few words about him, as he had very much become a part of this place and we're going to miss him horribly.

In fact, horrible is probably the right word to start with because, in so many ways, Tony Easterbrook was absolutely horrible. He had a horrible taste in films, a horrible taste in music and a horrible temper. Although there was also a glory attached to each of these attributes, of which I will go into detail later.

My first experience of Tony was just a few months after the shop opened, he wandered in – as so many of Cowley Road's nutters do – in a filthy, stained coat, with a confused grimace. He looked around for a couple of minutes with a look of utter disgust and disappointment. "IS THAT IT?" He shouted at me with his old Oxford farmer drawl. "Is what it?" "THAT'S ALL THE FILMS YOU GOT?" I nodded. He sighed deeply and looked crestfallen, shook his head and pointed around "I've got more films than this in my fucking house!" Then he left.

He next came in a few days later, I thought he was drunk but it later dawned on me that this is just the way surly people behave once they hit their seventies. He walked up to the counter with a warm smile "Now, 'ave you got the film 'Orrors of the Black Mausoleum'?". I check the system, "No". His smile drops all the way down his face into a disbelieving sneer. "Well, what fucking use are you?" He asks and dismisses me with a wave of his hand.

"I might be able to get it!"

"Oh yeah?"

"Yeah, What's it about?"

"Well, it's that man Michael Gough. He's in it. And in the opening scene, this woman, right, she gets a parcel from a secret admirer. She opens it up and it's a pair of binokkelers (I have to write some of this phonetically because he had a beautiful way with words) and she goes to look out the window with 'em, adjusts the focus dial, and these fucking nails shoot out of them right into her fucking eyes"

He laughs like a drain for a moment.

"What happens then?"

"I don't know, I fucking turned it off, didn't I? I'd just fucking ordered a pair of binokkelers, had to give 'em to me mate to try out before I'd fucking use them!"

"OK, well, the film's available, I can get you a copy!"

"I DON'T FUCKING WANT A COPY! I TOLD YOU, I 'AD TO TURN IT OFF!"

And once again, he stormed out leaving me frozen in a half-shrug of confusion.

Later that week, Jamie asked if I was aware of a 'piss-smelling man' coming in regularly, asking about obscure films, shouting and then leaving. I confirmed that I was, as did other staff members, until we realised that he had started coming in daily.

Tony, (or 'Pissy' as we now called him, more because of his attitude than aroma) turned out to be a well-known character on the Cowley Road, every day he'd walk a circuit of it twice – first walking his dog Teddy, then by himself, popping into several shops for a quick chat or, in our case, to berate, confuse and annoy us, then leave.

One day I was bored and decided as he stormed into the shop shouting the odds about one thing or another to actually engage with him. To steer him into conversation. It turned out he was an old-school film geek of the highest order. He only really cared for horror films, but his knowledge was encyclopaedic. He knew horror films like nobody I had ever met. Right from the Tod Slaughter films of the 20s up to the most obscure straight-to-video twaddle of the last few months. He loved it all equally, horror was his obsession and, combined with his previous career as a grave-digger, we tried to overlook how potentially terrifying he must have been as a younger man and embraced him as our favourite visitor.

Tony had fallen in love with films as a child and, pre-empting the video era by some 30 years, the first thing he bought himself when he started earning a salary was a 16mm projector. Every week, he'd go into London to a shop on Tottenham Court Road and buy the latest horror films on celluloid (or 'sellaloy' as he'd call it). Sometimes he'd hold screenings for friends but generally he was happier on his own in his own private little cinema. He told me that by the late 60s he'd racked up a huge collection of film prints, most of which he sold, as rarities and collectables, for a great price when home video surfaced.

Video seems to be where Tony flourished. He often told me that he had thousands of videos at his house. I took that as exaggeration until the day his roof fell in.

"My FUCKING roof's falling in! I've got to clean my FUCKING house out! Do you want some of my videos? I shan't have time to watch them again at my age and if you don't want them I'll sling the fucking lot!"

"Yeah, we'll take some"

"There's a lot!"

"OK"

He told me to take my car round to his house at the end of Alma Place and to wait outside. He came round from the back with bag after bag of dusty old ex-rental videos. That first visit, he gave me about 200 tapes. When I got them back to the shop, I couldn't believe it. Although DVD had rendered video of little financial value, these were some of the rarest tapes ever. I don't even know where he got these from. These weren't even collectable-rare, they were just weird! He had a copy of a film called 'Rambu' – an Indonesian Rambo knock-off. He had bizarre little sci-fi films that starred Klaus Kinski, original pre-certs and video nasties. Exploitation films that Tarantino would freak out for and some of the craziest, sickest box art I've ever seen.

The films didn't stop coming, Tony gave us over a thousand and was still calling me up to pick bags of them up from his place on Friday. Which was the last time I saw him.

In return, I'd scour the internet to find him DVDs of the films he'd loved as a young man, bizarre rubbish horror films that nobody else would get through ten minutes of and any films in which Hercules or some other mythical Adonis would fight big monsters. He'd come to me with a list of titles and ask me for a synopsis (or 'snipopis'), I'd usually get a sentence in before he'd stop me ("Ilsa is a beautiful young girl with a secret, she loves the taste of blood and will kill…." "THAT'S ENOUGH, I'll have it.").

He'd order his DVDs in batches of five and, from the moment the order was completed, he'd be demanding to know where it was and why it hadn't arrived yet. This perceived slowness of delivery could drive him into an absolute rage. My enduring memory of Tony will always be the image of his face pressed against the glass of the front door with raised eyebrows, asking without words whether his order had arrived, when I would shake my head, he'd launch into a tirade of pointing, shouting (which I couldn't hear as the door was closed, but judging by the reactions of passers-by, was peppered with his trademark salty favourites) and fist shaking. Then he'd wave both hands down to the side, mouth 'well you can FUCK OFF' and storm away. The angriest I ever saw him was when I was half an hour late opening the shop, he'd not only been waiting but had seen the postman put the 'sorry, we missed you' delivery slip through the door. Tony was so angry, he couldn't even find words, just facial expressions and bizarre experimental poses of rage, punctuated by grunts and whines.

But he wasn't just an angry old man, as often as he was comically furious, he was also quiet and sweet and decent. Offering bits of advice, asking strange and random questions ("Have you ever eaten one of them pizzas?", "You got toothache? Why don't you have 'em all pulled out? I did! Makes things much easier!"). He took great pleasure from mocking us and trying to get us in trouble with each other. He'd often come to me with stories about how Jamie or Liam (or Jeremy and Lee-mo as he insisted on calling them) had been shirking their responsibilities. Equally, he'd go to them and tell them I wasn't fit to run a business. I once played him a song from one of Jamie's albums and he made sure to tell him "I thought a fucking cat was being strangled" the next time he saw him. He particularly loved to torture Dan, often holding him responsible for the failings of myself and the Royal Mail. There was always a twinkle in his eye, though.

Aside from film, Tony's other love was Alma Cogan. The 'voice of the valleys', a Welsh singer from the 50s and 60s. He adored her. He used to go to London whenever she was performing and would fight like a maniac, throwing people out of his way to get her autograph at the stage door. It's my one regret that I never managed to track down a cd for him with the track 'Ricochet Blues' – he had been looking for that for years.

His most memorable moment, and the phrase we most fondly attribute to him was on a day much like any other, a couple of us stood behind the counter. He marched in, stopped looked suspiciously between each of us and demanded "What do you two fuckers know?" The last time I saw him, he'd received an incomplete DVD order, one of the films (the wonderfully titled 'Children Shouldn't Play With Dead Things') had been out of stock. Three times he reminded me to chase it up and not let them forget we ordered it. His last words to me were "Don't let the fuckers pull the wool over your eyes!" Words to live by.

Tony never married or had children and didn't have any living immediate family, but he leaves behind his dog Teddy (who will hopefully be cared for by his nearest relations) and some good friends. He is already sorely missed by all of us at Videosyncratic and we'll very soon be creating a special memorial section for him containing the cream of the video donations he made to the store.

If there is a heaven, I actually like to think that Tony isn't there. I prefer to think of him stood just outside the gates, pointing, shaking his fists and shouting at everybody inside that they're a bunch of useless fuckers. I kind of think he'd be happier that way.

Tony, it was a pleasure to have known you, mate.

Tony's family somehow got hold of the blog and really liked it. They invited us to his funeral, so Dan and I got into our suits and went along to see Tony on his way. It was a strange but lovely service, full of middle-aged men who looked suspiciously like Tony for a man who'd supposedly never had any children. To my shock and confusion – at the family's request – the Vicar used my obituary as the eulogy. Swearing and all. A vicar, in front of a coffin, effing and blinding the place up. Tony would have loved it.

Our other most significant customer would have to have been the man-child Richard Morley. It's hard to explain Rich without using words like 'puppy-dog', 'loyal', 'excitable' and 'possibly simple' – he was a Somerset lad of boundless enthusiasm but restricted intelligence. He became the shop's mascot and, we worked out, apparently spent more time in the shop per week than even most of the full-time employees. He became a real friend and we even would take him on our staff nights out. The most memorable being one Christmas event which ended back at his house. He'd been supposed to go out with his girlfriend but had opted to join us. It turns out he'd told he had to stay in to revise, so when she turned up in the early hours of the following morning and found us all sat in a circle watching Rich dance in a sombrero and then vomit into a wicker waste paper basket, he was in trouble. She clipped him hard round the side of the head, then dragged him away by the ear. We all sat, far less drunk and unsure what to do. 'Do you think we should leave?' asked Dan. 'Fuck that' replied American Steve 'I want to see how this plays out!' Rich stumbled back into the room, just as drunk but with the stunned expression and dripping clothes of having been thrown into the bath and cold-showered. He reached straight for a vodka bottle but his missus was back in the room with paranormal speed. 'You can all FUCK OFF' was apparently her hint that we should leave. He was a good guy, Rich.

Those first few years of Cowley Road Videosyncratic were the halcyon days for me. That was the video shop dream. Both shops were operating well and, to me, it just felt so good to have these two places, one each side of town where I could go any time of the day or night and find the sustenance of free food and free films on tap and, more importantly, the sustenance of the best company Oxford could provide. On both sides of the counter, there would always be a revolving squad of smart, acerbic, questioning minds to sit down and shoot the shit with. I can't even express how proud I was of my staff. Proud to have assembled them, proud to know them. When I sat down to write this book, I fired a group message off to the lot of them on Facebook, asking for their recollections and favourite moments. They shared some fond memories on the group message and then, one by one, individually private messaged me to brag that they'd each got laid at some point behind the counter. One of them 'awkwardly' 'in the VHS'. I remain proud.

CHAPTER 12

JERKBEAST

2006

With both shops now ticking over fine, 2006 became the year I was ready to move Videosyncratic up a gear. I adored the culture of independent DVD labels in the US. Criterion in particular were buying up an incredible catalogue of films, producing the best transfers, filling the discs with intelligent and informative bonus features and packaging them in beautifully designed artwork. I knew I wouldn't be able to compete with their titles for a while. I set my goals a little more modestly and aimed to be a British version of the Anchor Bay label. Anchor Bay seemed to be putting out a mixture of great forgotten genre stuff, cool new releases and cult TV. Most indie labels seemed to stick to one genre – there were scores of horror labels and some sci-fi or exploitation ones but I couldn't think of one which did what I wanted to do, which I'd sum up as 'light-cult'. Videosyncratic was a quirky and, yes, idiosyncratic brand which wasn't based around traditional notions of what was cool but more the notion that if you're passionate about something, it becomes cool.

Our staff were always famed for, and indeed employed on the basis of, their film recommendations – that was a big part of the interview process for me. As a film geek myself, I've often been annoyed at other film geeks for falling into what I perceive as obvious cultishness. As much as I love Star Wars, Aliens, The Evil Dead, Blade Runner and Goodfellas, I think there are WAY better films out there which maybe didn't hit their mark commercially or have simply been forgotten. I wanted to create a label that guided Woody Allen fans towards the directorial efforts of Albert Brooks (to this day only one of the seven incredible comedies he's directed are available on DVD in this country. Many didn't even make it to VHS), I wanted to release the Martin Rosen animations, I wanted to bring the Leningrad Cowboys to DVD. Old music documentaries, stand-up. Special editions of existing DVDs which hadn't been done justice to. I loved what Rhino Handmade were doing through their website with records and wanted to do the same thing for DVD.

My first move was towards Japan. None of the Godzilla films had been released on DVD in the UK. I couldn't understand that, considering how iconic they were, I figured the rights must be tied up somewhere, but in the research I did, I couldn't find out any suggestion of that being the case. So I contacted Toho Studios in Tokyo, the producers of the films. They were friendly and immediately keen to cut a deal. They sent over a file of information about each of the films along with some beautiful prints of the original poster art for each release. We agreed that a good starting point would be to release the daddy of all monster films 'Destroy All Monsters' – We discussed a basic potential release strategy and I started getting incredibly excited. Then we started talking money and it became a lot less exciting. It just wasn't so attractive a deal. They wanted a fairly hefty sum upfront as an advance and a big percentage of the gross before any deductions whatsoever. I was pretty sure I couldn't agree to that without putting the whole company at serious risk so I wimped out of the deal. Got to keep those poster prints, though. To every film geek cloud, there's a film geek silver lining.

I was putting the word out everywhere I could that I was looking for an unknown film, something with cult potential. Not too mainstream but with some real attitude. I got offered a bunch of zero-budget horror films, which admittedly are the commercial way to go if you're just starting out but I didn't like them. I wasn't going to release anything that I personally wasn't excited about and happy to endorse genuinely.

One day, I was speaking to my friend Jess in Seattle and mentioned what I was on the look out for. She didn't even pause "JERKBEAST!" "Are you... calling me a Jerkbeast?" I didn't even know what that meant. "No, it's a film – JERKBEAST – that's what you should release" and I knew immediately that she was right. I'd never heard the word 'Jerkbeast' before but I just knew it was a great word. I would pick up a DVD that had the word JERKBEAST on the cover and getting someone to look at, let alone pick up, a DVD cover is half the battle won.

"Tell me about Jerkbeast!"

Turns out Jess had lived with this guy Brady Hall who was the creator and performer behind Jerkbeast. He and his friends had started a live public access cable TV show in the mid-nineties where he dressed as a big red monster called Jerkbeast and people would phone in to insult him and he would out-insult them right back. It apparently became quite a cult in the Seattle area and people would stay in on Saturday nights just to watch this angry red monster with a southern drawl cuss idiots on the phone. A few years after the show finished, Brady and his pals had been messing around making films. Their first feature was called Polterchrist which told the story of Jesus coming back as an angry ghost and killing a load of kids at a bowling alley. They'd almost sold it to Troma. I loved the idea of a film that Troma had passed on. That has to be a level of bad previously untapped in cinematic history. For their Sophomore effort, they decided to go back to the well and make a movie about Jerkbeast – telling the story of his band Steaming Wolf Penis. I hasten to add that Steaming Wolf Penis was a real band that played for years and released two albums. With Jerkbeast on drums.

Jess put me in touch with Brady and he sent me a copy of the US DVD. The DVD had been put out in the US by Film Threat under a deal I didn't fully understand. It seemed that Brady and his co-creators Calvin Lee Reeder and Brian Wendorf had been obliged to produce and manufacture the DVDs themselves, Film Threat paid them nothing and took them off to sell. Something like that. They'd made no money and the DVD looked like crap. The thing about Jerkbeast is he works in concept (admit that you're not already into the idea!) and he works in practice but if I were to just show you a photo of him, you'd have no interest at all. He's a crappy papier mache monster head painted gloss red with wooden teeth and an old rug for hair. Imagine Frank Sidebottom after being beaten to a bloody unrecognisable pulp. Of course, once you see the character come to life, his technical shortcomings are his strengths – it's all part of the joke. But Film Threat had a put a crappy photo of his head in the middle of the cover. It looked cheap and shitty. I mean, the film IS cheap and shitty – that's its charm – but that's no way to market it.

I watched the film and loved it. It was rough around the edges. And the centre. But Jerkbeast himself is such a hilarious character along with the wild James Dean with a head-injury stylings of Calvin as the necrophiliac Sweet Benny and the confused participation of Brian as bunny-hammering Marty. I thought it was great. I booked the Ultimate Picture Palace on the Cowley Road and put on a free midnight screening of it, asking the attendees to fill out a multiple choice form after it. Everyone thought it was shit but hilarious. Dan really loved the film, so I went for it.

We cut a deal where I'd put up all the money and handle the whole thing and we'd do a 50/50 split on any profits.

I immediately hired my favourite designer to work on the project. Nolen Strals from Baltimore, who has since gone on to great success in the design world. He recently wrote and had published the definitive book on fonts and lettering. He's amazing and so much fun to work with. I told him that I wanted something iconic. I wanted it to be logo based and I wanted that logo to be so fucking cool that even if you hated the film, you'd want it on a t-shirt. I knew that one of the biggest pulls this film had going for it was it's title alone. JERKBEAST. It's funny and striking and odd and cool. Nolen worked his ass off coming up with concepts and I wouldn't let it go until it was perfect. We came up with this crazy Jerkbeast shaped cartoon silhouette, holding a club with a nail in it with JERKBEAST hand lettered on his body in red. It's still one of my favourite pieces of design work I've ever seen. We kept the DVD cover completely white with the logo bang in the middle. It just looked so striking and fantastic and defied you not to pick it up to read the back cover where we just went for the hard sell about all the cool stuff in the film. Brady produced a vast amount of extras for the DVD – to the point where I decided to make it a 2-disc set. We had a full SWP gig on there, a couple of commentaries, the highlights of the TV show, just a ton of stuff. It was definitely value for money. I had a few thousand DVDs produced without thinking about where I would store a few thousand DVDs. The day they got delivered to the shop, Dan walked in, looked at the wall of DVD crates, looked at me and arched an eyebrow. The bastard.

We set the film's release to coincide with the UK's biggest nerdfest at the Birmingham NEC. We booked a huge stand there and went in as if we were a big distributor. We had T-shirts and hoodies produced, promotional badges, amazing shaped vinyl stickers of the logo and Jerkbeast red plectrums. I had a massive cardboard version of the logo made to put on the top of the stall, you could see it from anywhere in the hall. We flew Brady and Calvin over and spent the weekend at the nerdfest.

It became obvious quite quickly that nobody was in any way interested in us whatsoever. The first few hours were not just dispiriting, they were embarrassing. I didn't know Brady or Calvin at this point, I'd flown them over to sit in a huge room as if they were celebrities. They were, and are, both unassuming guys with no trace of ego about them and it was just mortifyingly embarrassing. I felt like I'd brought them over to publicly demonstrate how un-famous they were. On top of this, I was surrounded by stock I'd spent a fortune on in, in a stall I'd spent a fortune hiring in bloody Birmingham of all places. I'm not a natural showman, but something kicked in and I realised that this film was simply never going to sell itself. If I wanted it to be a success, I would have to sell every single copy individually. I'd have to put it in people's hands and sell them on it and not let them go until they were a tenner poorer. I turned into a circus barker. It was my neck on the line and I wasn't going down without a fight.

I'd cut a trailer for the film, which we were showing on a loop on a TV screen. The trailer ended with the greatest shot in the film – a shot of Calvin on a stage calmly throwing a guitar right into someone's face. It's like something out of Jackass, you can't quite believe what you're seeing and that shot alone always elicited an 'OOF!' or a cheer of joy from anyone watching it. I started targeting people in the throng. Anyone who looked vaguely punk or metal, I'd call them over to the stall 'OI MATE! YOU! YOU! MATE!' they'd wander over.

'This is your favourite film and you don't even know it yet' 'yeah?' 'I promise you, watch the trailer – it's only a minute long!' – they'd stand and watch the trailer and on that last shot they'd go 'WOAH!' I'd be straight in there 'today only, we're doing it for a tenner, you get a free poster, sticker, badge and plectrum and these are the stars of the film, they'll autograph it for you' 'go on then!'

It worked a treat. I barely took a break all weekend, I lost my voice, my entire body ached but I sold a load of them – enough to cover the expenses of the weekend and bringing them over. On the Sunday night, SWP played a gig in Oxford. Ben filled in on guitar for Marty. He's still proud to be an honorary member of that band, even now with the success he's found as Frank Turner's lead guitarist. Recently I saw Frank headline at Wembley Arena and when Ben played his big solo, I knew that he still had his Jerkbeast sticker on the back of his guitar.

Once Calvin and Brady had gone home, it was time to really spread the word about Jerkbeast. Unfortunately, like everything I do in life, I'd gone into this whole venture naively and idealistically. I'd done my homework, but I'd studied the wrong subjects. It doesn't matter how good a film is, Hollywood is built on shitty films, what matters is how it's marketed and distributed and I didn't really have a clue about either. I had a fun cool film with a great cover. That wasn't going to open any doors. I had assumed that film magazines would cover any film that got released – since only a handful came out each week, I figured it'd be news. It was their job to tell their readers what was being released, right? Right? Nothing. I sent out hundreds of copies with free t-shirts to every reviewer or celeb I thought might dig it in the country. Nothing. Not a word. One of my guys gave Simon Pegg a copy and a shirt at another nerdfest, he apparently was 'polite' – I doubt he took it home. Why would he? I'd been an idiot. Most of the sales we were getting through the website were for T-shirts and hoodies and were coming from Seattle where Jerkbeast already had a following.

I wasn't done fighting, though. At the end of that year, there were a clutch of nerdfests happening around the country within a few days of each other, so I booked them all, brought Calvin, Brady and Brian this time, over we booked some gigs for SWP too and did a UK tour. I did as much publicity as I could, a couple of promoters helped out too. We got a good gig booked for a popular London metal club on Oxford Street and some indie radio stations and magazines were showing a bit of interest. The nerdfests were hard work again but they were working. People dug what we were doing. In Birmingham, people who'd bought the film last time round were coming back to tell us how much they liked it and buying extra copies of the DVD as Christmas presents.

In London, I was focused on getting Britain's biggest-selling film magazine Empire to cover us. I'd had an email conversation with someone there who had essentially said 'piss off', they weren't interested in actual film journalism, they were set up to kiss the studios arses, get the biggest interviews and sell advertising. Jerkbeast wasn't going to do much for them, so why should they be interested? Since we had Brady in full costume in central London, I planned a raid. We went straight into the EMAP building, got in the lift and got to the Empire floor. Brady was amazing. As Jerkbeast he berated all of the journalists for not covering his film and having an agenda. They loved it, took photos, and then put it in their email newsletter stating how pathetic we were and how we had no chance of making it to the magazine. The gig that night was pretty disappointing. It was badly set up and Brady got too hot in the costume. I think they did three songs before he stormed off. In a quiet moment, Calvin and I were stood outside on the street and Mick Jones walked past us. That somehow made everything seem OK.

Manchester was the most fun and bizarre part of the tour. At the show, we found the celebs were generally pretty bored and gravitating towards us because we were kind of the only cool stand there. Everything else was toy dealers and junk, they liked our attitude and I think found a certain comfort in the kinship of their fellow Americans. This huge American biker guy kept lumbering over to us and rabbiting on about stuff. Brady hated him, Calvin and Brian found him hilarious. It took us most of the day to realise that he was one of the 'celebs' – a guy called Andrew Bryniarski who'd played Leatherface in the Texas Chainsaw Massacre remake. Brady watched him walk away 'Can you imagine giving that idiot a chainsaw?' The other guy we befriended was a lovely chap called Ari Lehman, who'd played Jason Vorhees in the first Friday The 13th – when Jason was just a kid, not a hockey-masked psycho yet. He was a lot of fun to shoot the shit with. He asked what we were doing that night and I told him about a gig we had booked there. 'I'll try to get along!' he said in that way that you do when you have no such intention. "Can I play with you guys?" asked Andrew. "Sure" said Calvin adding "I hope he meant musically" once he was out of earshot.

It was a small venue putting the gig on and we expected a handful of people, we'd been booked by a kid promoting his first gig who loved the film and begged SWP to play. When we got to the place, it was heaving. Loads of kids there, they immediately swarmed Brady, Calvin and Brian, who were lugging their gear in. "What's going on?" I asked the promoter "Everyone's so excited for this!" he laughed "Jerkbeast is huge here!"

It turns out, he'd bought a copy in Birmingham and then become completely evangelical about it in his hometown. When I checked our online sales when I got home, I realised I'd been oblivious to the fact that I'd sold so many copies by mail order to Manchester. These kids couldn't believe they were going to get to see Steaming Wolf Penis play. As the support band were playing, Andrew Bryniarski exploded into the room, stormed on stage, took the guitar off the guitarist and started jamming horribly. These poor kids on stage were terrified. We hadn't actually expected him, so hadn't mentioned it. To them, they were being terrorised by some crazy enormous biker. I got to the stage and explained to the singer who he was. They couldn't believe that Leatherface was there! It turned into one of the best nights of their lives – especially when Ari showed up too and started stagediving. During the break, Andrew and Ari were lovely with the kids, they signed loads of autographs and posed for photos but that couldn't compare to the tension building up for the headline act. The crowd were chanting 'STEAMING! WOLF! PENIS! STEAMING! WOLF! PENIS!' I asked Andrew to introduce them and he did a sterling job. When he brought the band out, the crowd went apeshit. It's all on youtube in a video entitled 'LEATHERFACE VS FACE' (it starts with Andrew's anecdote about meeting and threatening Dirk Benedict from the A-Team) It was an amazing gig, the crowd sang along throughout to all the hits and even demanded a repeat performance of 'Looks Like Chocolate, Tastes Like Shit' and it just kicked ass. Brady, years later, emailed me to show me a clip he'd found on Youtube from 2011 of a band from the UK performing a Steaming Wolf Penis tribute act. They'd built their own Jerkbeast and everything!

When people talk about cult films these days, they're creating a contradiction in terms. People think worldwide hits like Rocky Horror, The Big Lebowski or The Blues Brothers are cult films. Sometimes they'll apply it to low-budget worldwide hits like Clerks or Plan 9 From Outer Space. It always seems wrong to me. I'm so proud to have been associated with a genuine cult film. A film which is intensely loved by the very few people who have seen it. I still get the occasional email about it and that always makes me happy.

Of course, we lost all of our investment on it. It didn't have legs. The second tour cost a lot of money which we couldn't make back and since none of the media had even a passing interest in covering it, it just failed. I still have over a thousand copies sat in a lockup out in Witney. Let me know if you want one.

Videosyncratic 'the label' was mothballed, its only release being 'VIDSYN001' – I doubt we could ever have really topped that, though. How could you top Jerkbeast?

CHAPTER 13

THE FALL OF
THE HOUSE OF SPIRA

2007 – 2010

Although I carried with me a notion that the video rental industry had just 7 years left in it when I started Videosyncratic, it hadn't taken long until evidence had started popping up to support that and make my suspicions credible. Just two months after we first opened doors, the first nail was hammered into the coffin.

Training Day. Not even a good film. Denzel Washington and Ethan Hawke in a dull machismo-parading-as-drama exercise which, like so many cop dramas of that era, was apparently shot through a shit-smeared lens. Warner Home Video was becoming the wildcard studio in rental terms. They could see the future and they were impatient for it. Video rental was an outmoded concept which had long overstayed it's welcome to the studios. It wasn't exactly a cash cow for them. Back in the dawn of video, it was expensive to produce video cassettes and not many people owned VCRs. It made sense to sell tapes to video libraries, it seemed far-fetched that many people would need, or even want, to own a film. But that had changed. Sell-thru video was a thriving market now, and with the explosion of 'home cinema', people were opting to amass a collection of their own. The average price for us to buy a rental tape or DVD was between £20 and £40. When the DVD was being released to buy in shops 3 or 4 months later, the cost to the public was between £15 and £20. Really, it was preposterous that the studios let this go on as long as they did. If they were charging essentially the same to rental shops and the public, why would they bother giving the rental shops a 3 month advance window when they could close that and capitalise on the ongoing buzz from a more recent theatrical release?

I suppose ironically, the answer to that would be Blockbuster. Blockbuster was a huge operation at this point, a huge company, and they bulk bought the vast percentage of the rental tapes. I would imagine it was this buying power that kept the rental industry alive at all. But there were rumours. Trade magazines were publishing stories of Blockbuster's struggle. It was a company that couldn't modernise. There was no place for them in the future. They had been slow to embrace the shift in the industry of rental-by-mail and Netflix in the US and LoveFilm in the UK were to fly past them wearing jetpacks. I remember one hilarious announcement from the company stating that they were considering fitting their stores with 'download pods', meaning people would have to go into their shops to download films. Kind of missing the point of download. I'm sure I even read an article which said they'd planned to offer a service where if you took your DVDs in, they'd rip them for you and give you an iPod file. Whatever. They were a shot elephant, still moving forward but it was just a case of how and where they were going to fall and who was going to get squished.

The release of Training Day changed the industry in the UK. It was the first film released to rent and buy on the same day. Not only this, but they were releasing two versions of the DVD. One which was RENTAL, the other RETAIL. The only thing that separated them physically was a big warning at the start of the retail DVD saying that if the viewer had rented it to report the person they rented it from. The other thing that separated them was the price. We were still paying around £40 for a film you could buy in HMV on the same day for £15. A lot of indie stores refused to stock it. I knew it wouldn't make a difference. They didn't need indie stores. I don't know what deal Blockbuster negotiated but I knew that we were only a few years from the point where they'd be releasing films that were illegal to rent at all.

I'd watched the industry shift even before this. The wholesalers seemed to be floundering. There were two main DVD wholesalers in the UK – THE and Golds. Every shop I'd worked in before, including Blockbuster, had used THE. I instinctively signed up with them when we opened but within a year it was apparent that our business really meant nothing to them at all. We'd end up getting films two weeks after their release date, if at all. Two weeks was huge in the video industry.

Customers knew what was coming out and when, they came in specifically to see the new stuff immediately. On an average film, you had to at least break even on your investment in those first two weeks or it was a failure. THE just didn't seem to give a shit. Quantities would be wrong, deliveries just wouldn't be despatched. I'd phone up and complain but the general sentiment seemed to always be that the few hundred quid a week they'd receive from me really wasn't in any way important to them and, in fact, maybe it'd be less hassle for them if we'd just take our business elsewhere. So I did.

S Golds and Sons was a family-run company and one thing they did that I really dug was to send reps out to you. I just liked that, there was something so old-school and classic about a slightly down-at-heel guy in a suit turning up with a briefcase, bitching about the traffic on the A34 before opening his briefcase and displaying his new selection of products for you. Technically, of course I could just put an order together online each week but I just really looked forward to the monthly sales visits.

Our first rep, from THE, was a guy called Barrie Berns. I could never place Barrie's accent but if you do a 'comedy nerd' voice, then drop it down a few octaves, you're kind of there. Barrie must have been in his early fifties, he had a moddish haircut and dishevelled brown suit. He seemed to love his job and had a kind of a pre-crash Willy Loman feel about him, he resided comfortably in the mindset of an era when a suit and a briefcase were a sign of great character rather than a sign of huge mistrust. He carried himself with his head held high and seemed to regard sales as the worthiest of jobs. He just seemed so happy. Going through the orders with him was always hysterical. He pimped every film. Hard! He didn't have a bad word to say about any of them and usually had an anecdote for each title too.

"The Fast and the Furious, now let me tell you, I don't like racing films at all but my boy, he says 'Dad, you HAVE to watch this! Just five minutes and if you don't like it, I'll turn it off' So I say 'OK, just 5 minutes' and I'll tell you what, I watched the whole thing and THOROUGHLY ENJOYED IT! This is, if not THE best film ever made, it's up there, I'll tell you that much!'".

"Now this one, this doesn't look good, does it? No famous people, No famous director, the cover looks awful, you've not even heard of the title. But I'll tell you what, it IS good. My wife – who usually hates watching films – she watched the whole thing and she says to me 'that's one of the best films I've seen this year!' – and she doesn't even like films. WOMEN. LOVE. THIS. FILM"

"Now I know what you're thinking! Charlotte Church? In a film? I thought exactly the same – she's a singer! But I'll tell you what, the girl can act! THE GIRL CAN ACT! She is....DELIGHTFUL."

I actually bought a copy of that Charlotte Church flick. That's a testament to either his patter or my utter stupidity. And I'll tell you what… it's the only new release we ever bought in that never even rented even once.

I was never sure if Barrie was just practicing an antiquated and awful form of sales patter or whether he was being absolutely honest. Like maybe he had a family with such insanely low standards that they were all genuinely shocked by the quality of absolutely any old piece of wank. I pictured them all sat in the Berns front room holding up DVD boxes with suspicion and mistrust, then popping the films on and being blown away by the faintest trace of quality. Proclaiming 'I'll tell you what….' To each other.

Whenever I'd pass on one of Barrie's recommendations (which was basically 95% of the crap he tried to peddle), he'd cock his head, look down at his paperwork and say 'Well, I think you're making a mistake on that one, but let's move on'.

One day, Barrie came in with a younger guy and told me he was training up his replacement. When I asked him what he was going on to do, he was fairly non-committal in his answer. His replacement was younger, sharper and a bit more 'Essex' where Barrie felt kind of 'Wolverhampton'. We never actually saw him or his replacement again. THE just stopped sending reps out to us. That's one of the reasons I ditched them.

Our Golds rep – Frank, was a happy-go-lucky London geezer and was always fun. Unlike Barrie, with his zip up portfolio, meandering fondly through his photocopied sales sheets, Frank would slap his laptop on the counter with a 'plug that in, won't ya?' and flip through titles onscreen at the speed of light with an appropriate commentary.

"That's crap, that's crap, that's crap. You'll want one of those, crap, crap, crap, might go in Summertown, crap, crap, crap, crap…."

"Wait – go back, what was that one?"

"It's crap, Jon"

"No, I want it!"

"Alright… crap, crap… crap…"

Frank would also do the main thing I hated THE for not doing. He fulfilled my inner-twelve-year-old's need for crap. He'd bring piles of posters, massive cardboard cut-outs and loads and loads of timecodes. I mean, we had a no-cut-out and no-poster rule at Videosyncratic, I didn't want to look like a shitty little video shop. Even though I had no need for them, I still WANTED them. He got that. Eventually Frank's visits became pretty sorry affairs. Mainly it was him apologising for late shipments or missing shipments. Golds were struggling and had been for a while. They were the UK's largest and longest serving independent entertainment wholesaler. They went into administration and then they were gone forever.

We'd stopped buying our new releases from them months earlier. I like to think of myself as pretty loyal but they simply couldn't get them to us in time for release. I kept on buying all of the back catalogue releases from them, mainly out of loyalty to Frank and to support another indie business. The truth is, it would have cost effectively the same to have just ordered that stuff from Amazon. The new releases, we bought from somewhere I never expected to and somewhere I hated doing so.

Sainsbury's.

For me, the killer blow to the UK video rental industry came from the most unexpected place imaginable. I assumed that the studios would just ban the renting of their product or that piracy or download would supersede us. Everybody else I knew assumed we'd be hammered out of existence by LoveFilm, the new postal rental service which promised no late fees and had a sweet opening offer of free films for a month. I never once sweated LoveFilm. I knew that it was only attractive to a very small percentage of our customers. Most people didn't consume films in that way. It was great for those who watched any film any night, but for most people, rental was an impulse thing and you wanted to see a film you felt like watching at that precise moment. Lovefilm wasn't immediate like that, you had to plan ahead and also, they just sent you films off a big list you kept with them. You weren't guaranteed to see the film you wanted to see at the exact moment you wanted to see it. Obviously that's all changed now with Netflix and video on demand, but we were safe from it generally, even if it was eroding the coastlines of our business.

No, the one thing I truly didn't see coming was the supermarkets getting involved. By 2007, most of the studios were following the precedent set by Warners with Training Day. Not only were all of the major films being released for retail and rental on the same day but the actual products now differed wildly. We were still paying at least double the price for rental versions, but the retail versions were better! The rental releases were film-only. The retail were two-disc special editions. That meant that real film fans wouldn't touch the rental versions,

they'd already seen the film in the cinema,
what they wanted from the DVD was the
bonus features. The commentaries and
deleted scenes. That's what I fucking
wanted! *I* didn't even want the rental
versions! To add insult to injury, Warners
(of course!) started packaging the rental
versions in flimsy slimline cases – a third as
wide as a normal DVD box. This meant you
couldn't display them spine-out, they'd just
disappear on the shelves. At one point, they
stopped even printing the titles of the films
on the spines. I was livid. I phoned them up
to complain as if I had any chance of talking
to anybody who could make the slightest
difference. I just sounded like an idiot.

What was worse was the day the supermarkets got clever. They realised they could sell
new DVDs as a loss-leader. They could sell
at wholesale or even below-wholesale price,
this would entice people into their store
where they would inevitably do enough of a
grocery shop to offset the loss. It worked
very well for them.

I don't blame the public one bit. It was
irresistible. The big one for us was the
release of Casino Royale – the reboot of the
Bond series, Daniel Craig's first outing. That
should have been a huge renter. Sainsbury's
sold it on day of release for £7. When you
think that video shops were charging £3.50 a

night for a new film, well it's obvious. Why risk late fees and the hassle of venturing to a video shop when for an extra measly £3.50 you can just keep the thing forever?

And that's when people stopped renting films.

We were in decline. Cowley Road had been a massive investment for us and although for the first couple of years, it was doing well, that soon changed. I'd depended on the business there coming from students and frugal families, video rental was the choice of people who couldn't afford a big night out and Cowley Road was rife with such people. One other thing I hadn't predicted was the boom of high-speed broadband and the massive ubiquity of BitTorrent. People who couldn't afford to rent or buy films were downloading them and watching them on their computers or burning them to DVD. Summertown was beating the hell out of Cowley Road on profit. Its overheads were way lower and it just brought in more money. It was a more moneyed area, we did well there on rentals, on late fees (in Summertown, if a film was late, the member would return it and hand over a credit card nonchalantly, in Cowley Road if a film were late, the member wouldn't bother to return it and would disappear into the night, keeping the fucking DVD. The credit cards were no longer security, the credit card companies would no longer let you conduct an unapproved transaction), Summertown even did a roaring trade just in ice cream and bottles of water.

I told Dad we should bail, we should cut our losses and get out but at that exact time, Blockbuster started closing branches all over the country. The Summertown one disappeared overnight to our great elation and we got a much-needed surge in business. We kept hearing that the Cowley Road branch – the flagship Oxford store – was in desperate trouble. Dan's girlfriend's mum was the manager, an awesome woman, who would come and tell us how much she hated the place all the time. I knew she wasn't spreading misinformation and she kept telling us how tenuous that branch's future was. We kept hanging on. I started to feel that Cowley Road was a luxury we simply couldn't afford. The shop was massive and we still held a lot of VHS stock. I thought we could sell that off cheap, squeeze the shop into two thirds of the space, put up some stud walling and let out the side of the shop, which had it's own separate entrance, to another business. We had a bit of interest but nothing worked, nobody was biting. So the choice was to change or stop. Dad felt there was life in it and I'd had a tentative plan which started to look like a go-er.

Oxford's only comic shop Comic Showcase had closed down the previous year. It blew my mind that a town like Oxford now had no comic shop and no record shops (apart from the HMV in town but that's not a record shop as record shops should be). I figured that a comic shop and video shop have a certain crossover appeal, a certain kinship. I thought I could integrate the two. So I did. Cowley Road became half-comic shop, half-video shop. We brought Barney back in to adapt half of the shop for comics and collectables and it worked pretty well. We brought in a whole new customer base and the two concepts actually worked symbiotically – the comic geeks started renting cool old films on impulse and the video customers were impulse buying graphic novels. It was also refreshing for people to have a comic book shop open until 11 at night. I was always amazed how many graphic novel sales I seemed to do to people walking home from the pub.

It was good, we weren't close to paying off the extra investment it had cost yet, although business seemed steady. But I wasn't enjoying it. I loved video shops because you got to sit around and watch films or talk about films. There wasn't a whole lot of work to do. Once a month, you'd put an order together, once a week you'd get the new release delivery onto the computer (I didn't even do this myself, it bored me so I got Dan to do it. I was getting so sick of everything that generally I'd just announce to Dan that I was promoting him – he did make assistant manager once Jamie left – but I'd give him weekly promotions which extended his responsibilities and job title but not his pay. By the time we closed, Dan was the Senior Executive Executive Executive Senior Executive Assistant Management Co-ordination Management Co-ordinations Assistant Manager. I hope that's on his CV), you'd do the returns, you'd do the banking and that was your work done. Even as manager there was little actual work to do. With a comic shop, it wasn't just work, it was stressful work. I took to putting the stock on the computer myself as there was so much that could fuck up with it, I was obsessed with knowing the system microscopically. With DVDs, I just ordered whatever I wanted. After a decade or more in the industry and as a lifelong film fan, I had an innate understanding of what would rent and how much and on the rare occasions I was wrong (Charlotte bloody Church), I knew it would all balance up anyway. There was no risk.

Comics were pure risk. To begin with, I knew nothing about comics. I read the occasional graphic novel but I was nothing even approaching a comic geek. I hired two wonderful guys who'd worked at Comic Showcase – Elliot and Cody and they helped as much as they could but there was no rhyme and reason to it. You could predict maybe what you'd shift in Batman and Spider-man titles, but that was about it. If you were lucky. Every customer had different needs and wants, it was so hard to predict. And although graphic novels would sell steadily (especially Watchmen), comics themselves were a total crapshoot. If a comic didn't sell by the Saturday of it's week of release, it would never sell. So you had three days to shift the stock or it was a loss. There was a 100% mark-up, which was nice but you still only made about a quid profit on each item. If I ordered 10 copies of a comic, I had to sell 5 to break even. If that didn't happen, I was out. With at least 30 titles coming in each week, each of them on a knife edge of even breaking even, and with my lack of financial nous to hamper me, it was just incredibly stressful. I felt the stress just every single day.

It wasn't all abject misery, we had some great times – especially on Free Comic Book Day, when I insisted all the staff (and Rich Morley!) dressed up as superheroes. And, you know, the comic geeks were nice – some of them I really looked forward to seeing, but a lot of them were just the worst type of geeks. Socially uncomfortable, demanding, intrusive and I felt bad because I couldn't be the guy they wanted and needed from a comic store owner. I should have been that enthusiastic guy with the encyclopaedic knowledge. I should have relished the question 'who would win in a fight, Red Hulk or Grey Hulk?' instead, I found my face generally sank into a hollow-eyed contemptuous countenance.

Summertown was supporting Cowley Road. That was not a good situation to be in. Things were difficult, although always fond, between me and Dad too. Dad's a wonderful father to the degree that he'd try to protect me. I've never had a great understanding of business and numbers are my complete failing. At school, one teacher observed that I excel at any subject that doesn't have a right answer. I was happily oblivious to the actual figures and depended on Dad completely to handle that side of things – which he did. But he wouldn't ever give me a realistic view of exactly where we were. Some days he seemed worried, others he seemed cocky, but no matter what, he'd tell me not to worry. I started worrying all the time. I knew we were going down. My first plan was to get into smaller premises.

Cowley was cripplingly expensive and in Summertown we were given a rent review which came with a whopping 100% increase. Business was still brisk and I figured a smaller unit in Summertown and a smaller unit in Cowley Road could get us back to break-even. Maybe we could even make some money selling the Cowley lease on – it was a hugely desirable location now. I also had been noticing these DVD rental vending machines cropping up all over London. I thought we could even scale business down to a few of those around Oxford which could operate easily on almost pure profit. Again the upfront investment was too high and Dan eventually pointed out that the only reason I was still even considering the idea was that I'd fallen in love with the name 'Videosyncratic-o-matic'

We looked tirelessly but we couldn't find alternative locations. We came close on both sides of town, but it wasn't happening. In October 2009, Dad and I both took a morning off and sat down at my house to properly discuss our options. I'd always said that I didn't want to be the kind of bitter asshole who goes down with their ship. I'd seen it before. A failing business pulls your soul down with it. I was already stressed but I'd been swimming as hard as I could against the tide. I was always looking for solutions. Dad's never really worn his heart on his sleeve, he's not easy to read. I know that he loved the lifestyle of independent retail, that he was probably unemployable at his skill level for his age in the wider world (that's why he'd started the linen shop 15 years earlier) due to his age and had no hankering for retirement. He argued that it was still possible to carry on. I called him on it but he had nothing. I could see he was prepared to throw good money after bad but I knew there was no point. Our 7 years were up. We talked and worked out that if we could offload both leases and sell our stock off, we could probably get out of the whole thing relatively scot-free. So, that's what we decided to do.

I didn't want to tell anybody yet. It felt like subterfuge, not even telling Dan. I realised that although the video business was dead in the water, the comic shop had a life. Not with me. I couldn't face that. If it wasn't a video shop, the idea of working retail was ridiculous to me. I still did freelance film work and script editing on the side, I could probably cobble together a living from that for a while. I tried to sell the business. That Cowley Road branch should stay as a comic shop. I tried to sell the business to both the Forbidden Planet chain and Gosh comics. Neither even got as far as negotiation. They just weren't interested. I thought that was a real shame but I was dealing with it all.

You know how sometimes emotion just hits you out of the blue and flattens you? I was watching a DVD one night on my sofa. I thought I was relaxed and out of nowhere I suddenly realised that I was going to have to fire my staff. It hadn't even occurred to me before but all of a sudden I couldn't think about anything else. I'd fired a couple of people before but they were mostly assholes who were ripping me off. The only person I'd ever fired that I'd cared about was Liam but I had literally given him 30 official last chances to stop missing shifts and he was on his total total no-bullshit-I'm-not-even-joking last chance when I finally let him go. These guys were my friends and they loved the shop as much as I did. This was a part of their identities. They were my guys. It wasn't just that I wouldn't get to see them all the time. These were their jobs. This is how they paid their rent. I was going to fuck up their lives. Who the fuck was going to ever hire Humphrey? What about James? He was an uber-film geek, this was literally his dream job. It just fucking engulfed me like a fog. How do you even do that kind of thing? I started imagining it in my mind. The notion of firing Dan made me well up and before I knew it, I was crying. I cried most of that weekend.

We knew it would be stupid to close down before Christmas – that would be a final boost in sales, especially with the comic book stock, but also we did a bundle deal at that time of year on rentals where people could take any 5 films for a tenner for the whole of Christmas and New Year, meaning people stocked up just in case. It always did well. So, realistically we'd close some time in January.

We decided to close the shops early one night in December, hire a minibus and take the whole staff of both branches on a treat. We drove them to London and took them to see Avatar at the IMAX in 3-D. This was a big deal. It was a hot ticket, crazy expensive and I had to book like lightening the very minute they went on sale. For film geeks, this was nirvana – James Cameron's return to sci-fi and the first of the new 3-D technology. It was a lovely drive out there, everyone had a blast and it was so rare that everyone was in one place at the same time. We had such a good time. We all drank in the bar before the film started and Dad blew that week's slender profits from Summertown on popcorn and drinks for all. As soon as we took our seats, I felt physically sick. Not because of the all-encompassing 3-D and not because Avatar quickly proved itself to be a massive turd of a film. But because I knew that after it was over, I had to tell the staff that we were closing the shops. Part of me was glad that the film was as punishingly long as it was and part of me wished the film would tear in the gate of the projector and I could just blurt it out to them. I'd hoped to get them all back in the bar but as we left, I couldn't find the words to make it happen. They were all in high-spirited bad moods – they'd hated the film, their arses ached from sitting down so long so we all drifted back to the minibus that we'd parked on Waterloo bridge. I had the keys. Once we were all there, I went to open the door but knew that this was the moment. It was freezing cold and the exposed bridge attracted a suitably icy wind. I told them all to shut up and that I had something to tell them. I clocked Dan and at first his face dropped but then turned into a supportive smile. He knew what I was going to say. I glanced at Gez and he knew too. He winked at me. I could feel the emotion working up through my guts and chest like vomit. I don't even remember what I said. It wasn't planned and wasn't eloquent but it was heartfelt. There was silence. Dad said something too. He so rarely showed emotion that hearing him talk about how much they all meant to him made my face burn and my hands shake. They were so incredibly lovely about it. They hugged us and each other and someone demanded we take a group photo. It was real. It was a relief. I kept myself together until I got home.

I posted this on the internet on 27th January 2010.

My top ten film endings ever – in no particular order

The Breakfast Club – They leave detention a little cheesier and a little happier, freeze frame on Judd Nelson punching the air triumphantly. What has he succeeded at? I have no idea, I'd have thought getting all soppy was a failure on his part but a freeze frame of Judd Nelson punching the air triumphantly is a brilliant thing. More films should finish with them.

Life of Brian – A brilliant final image. So dark but so funny. Rows of crucified people dancing. Best musical number in a film ever, even if the song is utterly cringeworthy when removed from that context.

The Muppet Movie – Crazy Harry blows a hole in the soundstage roof, a rainbow comes in, Kermit sings 'life's like a movie, write your own ending – keep believing, keep pretending', which might be the sagest advice ever. Then the camera pulls out to reveal THOUSANDS of muppets singing 'We've done just what we set out to do, thanks to the lovers, the dreamers, and you!' I hope I never become too cynical to appreciate the Muppets.

Poltergeist – The traumatised and filthy Freeling family check into a cheap motel. As the camera pulls away, we see the door open and the TV is unceremoniously pushed out on to the balcony. Am I reading too much into it or is this the most perfectly succinct comment about on the forces that are really destroying family life?

The Last Waltz – Ends at the beginning. The first song we see them play is actually the last song they ever played together. Don't Do It. My favourite film of all time.

Rocky – everyone forgets that he actually loses the fight. But he's won. And everyone knows it cos he went the distance. Makes me cry.

Don't Look Now – I'd love to see how it's written in the original screenplay. 'and then she turns around, it's not his daughter – it's a fucking terrifying witchy-faced dwarf with an enormous fucking knife. She looks at him ruefully then stabs him in the throat'. It should be the biggest 'you what???' moment in cinematic history, yet it seems to make perfect sense as the last piece of the rule-defying filmy jigsaw.

Watership Down – The rabbits finally in their new safe home, the first new generation of baby rabbits frolicking about, Hazel watching them old and tired from the distance, is quietly visited by the rabbit spirit. 'I've come to ask if you would like to join my Owsla. We shall be glad to have you, and I know you'd like it. You've been feeling tired, haven't you? If you're ready, we might go along now.' and then Hazel lies down, breathes a couple of dying breaths and follows in spirit into the sun. Like the film itself, relentlessly sad yet uplifting.

The Graduate – He steals the girl away from the wedding, she's already married, though. They run out of the church with everyone cursing them, get on a bus, sit down grinning and slowly the smiles fade. A happy ending silently made bittersweet by letting the camera roll just that bit longer than the usual freeze-frame moment. Beautiful. BEAUTIFUL.

Sullivan's Travels – Preston Sturges's film about a popular film director who decides to take to the road 'slumming it' in research for his next film – a serious film about the suffering of humanity. When eventually, assumed dead, he finds himself as low as he can go – as an anonymous convict in a deeply rural place he finally sees the real people he craved, uneducated, damned prisoners watching a Pluto cartoon and loving it. It's there that he comes to the conclusion 'There's a lot to be said for making people laugh! Did you know that's all some people have? It isn't much but it's better than nothing in this cockeyed caravan!'

Yeah. So, this is my roundabout way of telling you that the one place in Oxford where you could actually find all of these flicks is facing its own finale. Death scene. Unexpected twist. Denouement. End titles. Closing number.

Videosyncratic is closing.

Just before Christmas it was apparent that we'd completed our tumble from profitable to OK to break-even to loss, and there's no point chucking money into an independent video rental business. It's an outdated concept, right? Going out and renting a video. Who would do that now you can download them or rent online or illegally torrent them for free, or buy them below wholesale price at the supermarket. Or just watch something from the ten billion hours of crap stored on your Sky Plus? It's funny how quickly something can go redundant. But things move on and change and that's absolutely how it should be. Like powdered egg to our grandparents and Saturday cinema matinees to our parents, we'll one day tell our confused and uninterested kids about how we went to choose and borrow films from the local 'video shop'.

Video shops have been my favourite places all my life. I practically grew up in the video shops of Headington – Bogarts, Ritz and the brilliant Oxford Video. When I went to film school, I discovered Alphabet Video in Edinburgh – the best video shop I'd ever seen, two rickety floors of forgotten classics. And a fish tank. Then there was the recently departed Mister Stacey's Video Emporium in Cambridge. Possibly the world's only leather-panelled video shop. I love video shops. I worked in them from the age of 18, loads of them, and it was my lifelong dream to own my own indie.

I'm really fucking proud of what we did with Videosyncratic. From the incredible selection of films we stocked to the surliest yet sharpest staff ever assembled. From the beautiful logo to the signed photo from Burt Reynolds. The stencilled artwork on the Cowley Road branch's walls. The 'ill judged forays into acting by rock stars' section. The celebrity customers (Paxman! Branson! Dent!). The legendary battles between customers and staff. The in-store gigs. The private school kid who puked everywhere then threw himself through a plate glass window. The cultural elitism. Rich Morley dressed as Wolverine. We did alright and we had a lot of fun.

It's pointless to pretend I'm not sad at having to pull the plug. VS is the best thing I've ever done and I think I'll miss it a lot. I'll miss the people. The regular dropper-ins – the Morleys, Ramages, Nixons, Marlers, Searjents and legion of others who prop up the counter for a chat. I'll miss them. And most of all, I'll miss the staff. I don't know who else would handpick such a ragtag bunch of misanthropes but they made the company what it was. They defined it. I got endless complaints about the lot of them and every moaning letter or phone call made me proud of my guys.

But hey, there are new challenges, the idea of a life free from the general public, complaints about late fees (I suppose I can reveal now that the way to get out of late fees is… to be nice. Who'd have thought of the wonderful results basic human decency can have?) tramps wandering in to get warm, brainless Brookes students and the eternal fretting about finances sounds pretty OK to me. One of the things that does bug me is being one of the alarmingly frequent closures of cool indie shops in Oxford. I hate how this town is changing. The rents are too high, there's a recession, global corporations are putting the squeeze on the little guys.

Independent businesses, set up and operated because of the passion of the people who establish them, are beautiful, precious, and increasingly rare things and should be cherished. Every single purchase makes a difference. So, if you're one of the people who'll be sad to be reading this, remember that if you want cool indie places to exist, you have to support them. If any of our customers defect back to Blockbuster, I'd be very sad. There's one last indie video shop in Oxford – Movies on Walton Street. They've been the longest running indie vid shop in Oxford and it's absolutely right that they be the last ones standing. You should give any business you would have given us to them, they're awesome. And make the effort with the other independent business- es. Fratellis and Atomic Burger, Uhuru, Ryouki, Gameskeeper, Meli, Music Box, the book shop in Summertown, the Cowley Road and Wolvercote farmers markets. There are good people doing the right things for the right reasons. Supporting them is a joyous thing and if you don't fucking do it, you're looking at a future where every town is just a massive Tesco with a Nando's and a Carphone Warehouse either side.

Enough ranting. To those of you who were members – Thank You, even if we were rude to you, we genuinely appreciated your support and hope you had as much fun with your time in our shops as we did. Keep your membership card in a safe place because it forever marks you out as one of the cultural elite. If you weren't a member, tough titties, missed your chance, loser.

Now, onto the fun stuff. As any of you who have closed down a business before will well know, it is a scary, scary thing. The cost of closing the shops, settling accounts, getting sorted is thousands of pounds. Which, as you may guess, we really haven't got. SO. We're having a bonanza. Summertown branch will cease trading at close of business on Sunday night. Starting on Monday, at Cowley Road branch, we're selling EVERYTHING off. VERY CHEAP! ALL the DVDs, ALL the comics, ALL the graphic novels, ALL the T-shirts, even ALL the VHS (which will be very, very, very cheap). If you want shelves, we'll sell you the shelves! If you've been looking for a Humphrey, WE'LL SELL YOU HUMPHREY! Always had your eye on our life-size Gremlin? HE'S YOURS FOR A PRICE. So, a HUGE DVD and comic shop sale. I figure if we sell even two thirds of our stuff, we can pay off all of our debts. So, please forward the word onto every one you know in

Oxford or the surrounding areas (London is an easy bus ride away). Email them, Tweet this, Myspace it, Text it, whatever you have to do – anyone you know who likes films or comics, it'll all be very cheap and very awesome!!!

Thank you so much for your support over the last nine years. It's been brilliant.

Happy endings are bullshit. Here's to an ending that makes us think.

Jon VS

CHAPTER 14

REQUIEM FOR
THE VIDEO SHOP

People did forward that message, it went a
bit crazy. I had lots of requests for interviews in print media and radio which I used
to state the sentiment that I hoped could be
derived from this turn of events. It was too
late for us but if you enjoy even just the idea
of indie shops of any kind, you have to
support them. Not that I didn't feel
supported. For us, it was an inevitable
industry change that consigned us to history
but for other small businesses, every pound
in the till keeps them open. That's how it
was for us at the end. We were fighting just
to break even. The phrase I found myself
repeating ad infinitum was 'Use it or lose it'

It was weird knowing that I had only days left. I couldn't imagine a life without video shops. They'd filled my thoughts since I was a kid. I wasn't going to join Blockbuster and I was always against illegally downloading. How the hell was I going to see films? Some of our customers were very sweet and emotional about losing us but I found an endless stream of people I simply didn't recognise coming in to commiserate. I mean, I worked there all the time, I knew who our customers were and these people, although I'm sure well-meaning were kind of freeloading on our sadness. It drove me mental. Dan came up with a brilliant scheme. Our friend Matt Halliday designed a beautiful little button badge with a broken heart that said 'I MISS VIDEOSYNCRATIC' on it. I gave them out to all of the staff, our friends and customers but every time someone I didn't recognise came in to tell me how much they'd miss the place, I made them put their money where their mouths were and sold them a badge for a quid. By the time we finally closed the doors, we'd made £300 on badges alone. Years later, I still see the odd person at a gig or walking down the street with one of those badges on their lapel or bag strap. It always gives me a warm feeling.

Two days before the sale, I took my pick of the stock. If I wasn't getting free rentals anymore, I was going to stock up. Once I had my pile secured, I let Dan take his pick, then the rest of the staff got to take what they wanted. We all got our favourites and there were thousands left for Joe Public. The VHS collection I'd started the business with was kind of redundant now. I'd moved to DVD and had nowhere to store all of that VHS which, frankly, was beginning to degrade now anyway. We ended up selling all of the company's VHS as a bulk sale on Ebay. For £65. Somewhere in the region of 6000 tapes. One of the best collections of films in the UK. A collection I'd started as a child and built my future on. A doughy-faced woman from Hull came and took it away in a transit van.

The plan was to transfer all of Summer-town's DVD stock over to Cowley for the sale but on the last day of business there, some people got wise to it. We decided to let them buy what they wanted, it saved us lugging it all across town. In an unofficial sale, we took more money than we ever had before. Gez, Ben and I worked that last night together. That meant a lot to me. Barney helped me work through to morning putting all of the discs back into their original cases and driving them in his van across town. I got about an hour's sleep before having to get to Cowley to prepare. We were opening at 10am but from 6am, there was a queue outside the shop. By the time we opened the door, the queue stretched down Cowley Road and round the corner into Princes Street.

The queue didn't end until after midnight. The average wait to get served was 45 minutes. The shop was so dangerously rammed that James and Martin, our friends who had worked at the Summertown pizza place, who by now owned two restaurants of their own on the Cowley Road came and worked as door staff – operating a one-in, one-out policy. Almost all of our staff past and present came back that night and all jumped behind the counter to work the last shift. It was chaos. It was beautiful. It meant so much to me to be with them behind that counter one last time. Even some of our loyal customers crossed the threshold to help us out. Our friend David K. Lord mucked in with a huge grin for hours, he said it had always been one of his dreams to work there. Jamie and his wife Minnie had just had their first baby Molly a week or so earlier and Jamie rolled the pram straight in and took pictures because he wanted for her to have been in the shop.

Richard Walters, from the Summertown branch, asked if he could arrange live music for that night and he did a stellar job. Favourite local bands The Family Machine,

Ute and Stornoway played, as did Richard himself, Humphrey's band did an amazing set and Nick and Mark Cope from The Candyskins – my favourite Oxford band as a teenager – headlined playing their hits acoustically. Ben Walker opened the night and performed a song he wrote about Videosyncratic. That gesture alone made me well up with pride and tears.

We said a lot of fond farewells that night. And sold most of our stock, not quite enough to get us out of debt. Most importantly, we gave it the ending it deserved.

And then it was all over.

EPILOGUE

It's been seven years since Videosyncratic closed its doors.

To begin with, it wasn't easy. It takes a while to find your place in the world and those shops were my place. For the first year, I really didn't know where to go or what to do. I'd lost my sense of purpose.

Worse than that, actually, I felt like I had exhausted my purpose in this world. If I wasn't Video Jon, who was I? If I didn't have the shops, didn't have that life, what did I have? The week after we closed, I cut my long hair short and shaved off my beard. I just didn't want to still be that guy, didn't want to be recognised.

It wasn't much later that I realised, for the first time since I was 19, I was going to have to pay if I wanted to see a new film. That felt like a cold, cold indignity. That truly robbed me of my status.

Worse than that, I needed a job. Having spent so many years in the video jungle, I was unsuitable for the workplace – too restless, too lazy, too entitled and the only form of communication I was able to utilise with work colleagues was brutal sarcasm and scathing deconstruction. For a while, some friends gave me some work in their office and were generous in their under-standing of my anti-social ways and slowly took the edge off my awfulness and gave me the basic skills I needed to get along in normal, polite, professional society.

I was employed but still very lost. I yearned for a place where I fit in, where I could be myself and where my actual skills had some value. Luckily, filmmaking came back into my life. A documentary I had been making about the Oxford music scene got some traction and a cinema release, I started getting freelance filming work and that would lead to a full time job at the British Film Institute making documentaries about film and interviewing the stars and directors I'd spent so long obsessing over. All those years nominally wasted in video shops had armed me with an extraordinary breadth of knowledge and understanding of cinema and the BFI was the place where that had value and meaning and usefulness. Finally, I was having those energised, enthused conversations about film again but I was having them with the people who actually made those films. My knowledge of obscure films was not just of value, it occasionally even seemed to be completing the circle for the people who had made them.

When I had the chance to interview Mike Hodges, who generally is called on to discuss how he directed either Get Carter or Flash Gordon, I went in depth on Morons From Outer Space – he was resistant at first, questioning whether it was a film worthy of the BFI discussing and telling me it had been a bad experience for him and he hadn't actually seen it since it was completed. But we kept on talking and he started to remember why he had got involved and what he had been trying to do with that film. An hour later he said "You know what? Maybe I should watch it". He should. It's a wonderful film. And I'll fight you if you disagree. And I'll win.

I interviewed Peter Fonda and put in a request with his people that the interview be entirely about a bizarre low-budget sci-fi film he directed in the early 70s called Idaho Transfer. He arrived in the room with his hand outstretched and a smile "Jon, I've never talked about this movie before and it's the one that I've always wanted to talk about! Let's do this!" and for the next 45 minutes, he unloaded about how important this film had been to him to make and how he felt vindicated that all of the social and ecological issues he predicted in it have become the key issues for the world right now.

I felt like I was paying back. As useful as I'd been to my community in those little video shops highlighting the films that people should make a point of seeing and appreciating, now I was getting to do that on a national and international basis.

I was getting to see films for free again, too. And this time in the best cinema in the UK. My video shop heart healed and left a beautiful scar and life rolled on.

Last summer, I found myself in Austin, Texas where I was told there was somewhere I had to visit. I Luv Video is recognised as the world's oldest and biggest video rental store. I'd heard of it but had no idea it was still open. I couldn't have been more excited to not only finally see the apex of the industry I had dedicated so much of my life to but also to step back in time and feel the warm nostalgic hug of actually being in a video shop once more.

The building was undeniably impressive – a huge, cavernous space on many mezzanine levels. But my girlfriend and I were the only two people there. It felt desolate, abandoned, worthless. It was filled – rammed full – of probably every video and DVD to ever have been made commercially available. But there had been no upkeep. The cases had become tatty, and broken and dirty, many of the covers had faded. Nobody had cleaned or dusted this massive space in seemingly years, the floors were spongey, sticky, bits of the building were falling apart and it smelled like mildew. I just thought the place should be bulldozed. I wanted to set the owners and staff free. It wasn't a step back in time, it wasn't retro or nostalgic or a perfectly preserved slice of social history. It was a sad, rotting corpse of something that I had loved, that had had great meaning to me. I don't think we spent more than ten minutes in there. The world has moved on. And so have I.

I'll admit that I've struggled to embrace Netflix and Video On Demand. There seems to me something too easy about it all. There's no emotional investment on the part of the viewer if they can literally just watch anything, any time. It amuses me that as wild as I had been as a young man in video shops, I palpably missed the discipline of traveling across town to a shop, choosing a specific film, having a finite amount of time to watch it in and having to travel back across town to return it. It sounds like an unbelievable hassle now, in this age of convenience, but it was special. It made your film choice special. You had literally invested in it. So you sat down, turned your phone off and you watched it beginning to end. We rarely watch films like that now. We dip in and out, we get distracted by social media, we don't make it to the end and gradually just add to the 'continue watching' playlist on our accounts.

Film is becoming less magical.

For the average consumer, it's no longer a treat, it's an entitlement. For a low monthly direct-debit charge, all the films they could possibly want to see are right there on their phones, tablets and TVs, taken for granted. Films have their Netflix debut days after their cinema premiere, many don't even get a physical release on DVD or Blu Ray now. The notion of actually paying to see a film at all has now become a bit archaic.

Sadly, I think all of this is something of a step backwards, with the loss of physical media, to some degree, films are pushed back into the ether that existed pre-video. Netflix does not house or stockpile films, each month it seems to remove as many as it adds. As DVD players become obsolete, we are being forced to a digital platform. All we need then is the entirely conceivable shift in which Youtube finally cracks down on copyright issues, the illegality of file sharing becomes enforced and streaming replaces download/ownership entirely. At the BFI, I learned that digital archiving is actually one of the least reliable forms of preservation. Films which have been shot and edited digitally and have existed only on hard drives are at almost as much risk as films from 100 years earlier which exist only on nitrate prints. I do worry about swathes of films disappearing once more, but my days of collecting, curating and putting them in peoples hands are over.

The space in which the video shop once existed is gone and we already have a generation of children whose brows would furrow and eyes would widen in incredulity if you were to tell them that to see a film in your day, you had to actually go to a special shop, walk around for an hour, choose a film, pay for it and then take it back there the next day.

But what special shops they were.

APPENDIX

TALKING SHOP

A conversation with Chris Stacey, owner of Mister Stacey's Most Excellent Video Emporium in Cambridge.

My friend Simon says the link between video shops and their owners is as visible as that between dogs and theirs. So, whereas the happy-scrappy bright colours, shelves of toys and graffitied walls of Videosyncratic are a perfect projection of my inner chaos, the refined, classy leather-panelled walls and beautiful wood counter of the Emporium seem to reflect the calm, sophisticated coolness of Chris Stacey. Chris started the Emporium around the time we opened our second branch and spent a bunch of time in Oxford with me, asking questions and learning the ropes. He went on to create a shop with more enthusiasm and intelligence than I have seen anywhere else in the industry. I'd go out on a limb and say his was the last indie to open in the UK and will probably retain that title. Before we met up to have this conversation, I felt a little guilty, having encouraged him so strongly to follow his video shop dream and knowing that it wasn't pulling in the money it should be. His viewpoint was quite different, though. This conversation took place on the 28th of March 2007 in the backroom of the Video Emporium and is a nice little snapshot of where our minds were at the time. Also present was his right-hand man Mark – the Emporium's most senior member of staff and resident DJ.

Js: Ok. So first of all, I want to know your background, before you came to video shops, before you came to any of that kind of thing.

Cs: Art school.

Js: Right.

Cs: Went to art school – Chelsea School of Art – sort of muddled around that, fell into working for art galleries, which basically, ultimately, meant becoming a posh builder for other artists, some of whom I went to college with. By that time, I'd become completely disillusioned with art as a medium and I always thought films were much better. And I was looking for something to do, I wanted to get out of the art world and I was just sitting at a friend's house and someone said 'there's no decent video shop in Cambridge!' and everyone looked at me. I was like 'what?' And that's when I introduced myself to you.

Js: So, had you had any history with films at all? Like, you thought that you wanted to go and be involved with that?

Cs: No, never! No, I mean I'd always just watched them in a very pure way and I'd always thought it was more of a thing, that it was a much more successful art form than visual arts. Cos I think visual artists are basically amateurs and, you know, if you watch 'A Matter of Life and Death' or 'Goodfellas', then that's a professional job.

Js: And there's an artistry to it and it's also found its audience, it finds its place in the world.

Cs: Yeah, and it's not elitist. It's not the cult of personality, it's none of those things, you know? Which art is. Certainly Brit-art in the last few years. And those are the people that I was working with, I was working for Charles Saatchi and the like, so it was all Damien Hirst, The Chapman Brothers, Tracy Emin – it was all those people.

JS: Right. And was that good money? Was it a good living?

Cs: Yeah, it was better than this!

(both laugh)

Js: So, when the idea first came in about doing a video shop, you saw that as like a bedrock, as kind of like security?

Cs: I wanted to do something that was mine. I wanted my own business, because, you know, it became increasingly obvious over a ten year period that I really hated working for other people.

Js: I've been there, I know.

Cs: You feel the same.

Js: So, before you started The Emporium, what was your relationship with and experience of video shops?

Cs: I do remember when I was growing up that there was a little one in the town next to us. A little tiny smoky room and I always thought back on it when I started reading about Quentin Tarantino. It was run by an absolute film geek, he was in there every day just watching films and it was this little smoky horrible little shop that my mum hated going in to.

Js: So, what year would that have been?

Cs: I… don't know.

Js: Pre Blockbuster?

Cs: Yeah, yeah! It was a little independent one in Essex. Um, so it would have been twenty odd years ago?

Js: So, when Blockbuster came in, were you aware of that?

Cs: I remember in London, later on that there was, and what was it? Apollo? The one that Blockbuster bought out big style, what was that?

Js: Ritz?

Cs: Ritz! I remember that. I don't recall going to them that much. I mainly remember watching films – the films that I really remember – is when they used to do Saturday matinees on BBC2. I mean, I think that's where my whole cinema information comes from. Watching The Apartment, watching Irma La Douce, A Matter of Life and Death, watching anything Billy Wilder, I remember I really grew up with that. Saturday afternoons.

Js: I wanted to ask you about the run up to starting this place.

Cs: Mmm.

Js: About the research you did…

Cs: Talked to you! Went to Today Is Boring, um, mostly talked to you, I think! Had a look around a few. But, you know, you were so informative and supportive that it was basically you.

Js: You're making me blush.

Cs: It *was* you!

Js: Cool. But then you started working at Blocky?

Cs: Yeah, the banks loved that! They absolutely loved it! 'so, what are you doing now?' 'working at Blockbuster!' *'really*? Oh no, you poor thing!'

(both laugh)

Cs: They thought I was the dog's for doing that!

Js: And how long did you work there?

Cs: Just a couple of months. That's all I could take.

Js: Right.

Cs: I mean, I wanted to know how not to do it, obviously. But they also get a lot of things very right. Like their locations, one thing they have got is that they're in the right place. So that's why I knew I had to be where they were cos if they're not there, there's no point in being there!

Js: That's it. Also, for us setting up indie shops, it's where people already come for films! So where's Blockbuster in relation to us now?

Cs: There's a shitty little one over the bridge, we can go and have a laugh at them. He hates me cos he thinks I sprayed my name on his shop! but, um, there's another big one in East Road – it's by the university.

Js: And that's the one you worked in?

Cs: No, I worked in one in a village in a market town in Essex. Really nice little shop, actually.

Js: and what did you get from that? What did you learn?

Cs: That the people who worked there weren't as stupid as I thought.

Js: Yeah.

Cs: I actually offered the manager of the – the guy I worked with there, the guy managing that shop – the job of managing this shop, actually. I was just trying to do everything properly from the outset and, actually, the way it's grown, we've got people like Mark here and Mark's really got into it as well. The personality of the shop is as much to do with Mark – and how it's developed – than how it has to do with my initial thoughts about it.

Js: It finds its own kind of natural balance, doesn't it? With the people who are involved.

Cs: Well, yeah, I would never have considered people drunkenly roller-skating or having decks on the counter. It's not something you think about.

Js: Is that all Mark's doing?

Mark: There's lots of like 'Imagine if we did this….'

Cs: And I go 'alright, then, I'll pick you up, we'll go to Sainsbury's and we'll do it – Saturday!' It's been organic. (To Mark) I'm saying that there's as much of your personality in this shop as there is of mine. Especially as I fucking hate videos and people.

(All laugh)

Js: So, how would you describe your customer base?

Cs: I thought it was going to be students but, on Saturdays you see all the piano-in-the-front-room people coming in – the families who can afford the house prices up Kingston Street. That's... there's a lot of that, isn't there? I don't know. I mean, it's predominantly local. But, no, I don't know, if you look through the postcodes... *I don't know!* Who the fuck *is* our customer base? We don't get chavs, do we?

Mark: Not particularly, no. There's a couple, but not... no.

Cs: We do get all sorts of people in here.

Js: So, if it's not students who are coming in...

Cs: There are students coming in but I imagined there'd be a lot more.

Js: But it's not predominant? Cos, I'm in the same boat. I imagined that when I opened on Cowley Road, I was opening there because it was a student area, but students don't make up the biggest part of our customer base at all. So, what do you think is happening? What do you think has changed with students? Because students used to be the traditional renters.

Cs: (noticing a customer in the shop) See! It's people like that! The lady in the raincoat – old lady. Don't frighten her, Jon! She just went round the corner. There – look. We get people like that in here! All sorts!

Js: Yeah, that's totally what we get. Well-meaning, supportive… yeah.

Cs: and lock up their bikes with the big wicker basket outside, you know.

Js: You wouldn't expect it at all, would you? Like I really think that both of our stores are set up to attract a younger, funkier crowd.

Cs: I really thought…. Maybe it's just that the students don't give a fuck if they go to Blockbuster or not.

Js: That's it! I think what's changed is the students have changed. This is my theory that students changed and traditionally, when I was growing up – I mean, I don't know how much younger I am than you, I'm 30 now – but, when I was growing up, students were pretty right-on, pretty educated people who had a certain amount of politics going on behind them. They were smart people as well. When I look at the students now, I see a bunch of kids who don't really give a shit, who are just kind of holidaying.

Cs: they're not interested in anything but doing coke on a Saturday.

Js: I don't think they're even particularly smart; in fact, the ones that I find are most student-like to my definition of student are the foreign students – who we do get a lot of. Even the American students. I think if they're prepared to travel to study, they tend to be more interesting people.

Cs: Mmm.

Js: And we have a lot of American students and French students and Spanish students and they're very smart people and very supportive of us and very interested in film. They're exactly what I expected, when setting up in a student area, I expected that – but British. But I found that the British students are actually pretty... thoughtless.

Cs: I thought combating that by being cheaper would do something, but it doesn't.

Js: I don't think they care. I think the corporations have made their brand on them.

Cs: Only one person mentioned anything when we raised our prices last year – only one!

Js: Well, I think it's very strange being – I think being an independent video shop in this age is a strange thing. That's what I've come up with. I've come up with the idea that the students now – they've changed, they're not the same people that they were, they're not what students traditionally were – and this is a generation who have grown up under the corporate watch, so they don't even necessarily think about it. They'll go to Blockbuster.

Cs: People cherry pick. I mean, people cherry pick belief systems. They'll take a bit of Buddhism, they'll take a bit of this, bit of that, bit of new age nonsense, you know? They'll go to Blockbuster if they've got a copy of The Prestige, they'll come here if we've got The Dam Busters. You know? Whatever. There's no allegiance.

Js: Retail's weird, isn't it? It's like; it's a strange thing to get in to if you've had any kind of creative background because you find yourself in touch with the public, which is in itself quite strange.

Cs: I enjoyed it initially but I shy away from it completely now because I'm just too fucking grumpy.

Js: Yeah.

Cs: I let Mark take over because he's much better at it than I am.

Js: I've hit that point as well. It's a really strange thing, isn't it? Where once it's kind of first set up, you're totally just kind of like 'This is my shop! Welcome to my shop!'

Cs: 'Come in! I love you!'

Js: 'Let me serve you!' – Yeah, totally! And you're also kind of like, I remember when we first opened Summertown, there was this bizarre kind of feeling where it was like they were doing us the hugest favour by coming through the door.

Cs: Yeah, it was brilliant!

Js: I was so grateful for it.

Cs: The first person who came in before I'd advertised and spent money, you just think 'Yes!' and then people walk in now and you're just like 'oh, what do you want?'

Js: Exactly!

(Both laugh)

Js: That's exactly it, it's just like 'you can fuck off.'

(Both laugh)

Cs: We should do this more often.

Js: I know! Well, now I know how to get here... I love this shop!

Cs: its cool isn't it?

Js: It's fucking brilliant!

Cs: You see, sometimes when I get bored, I bring people back here. We all sit in the back, drink vodka.

Js: That's what I... I hang out at the shops all the time. My friends work there – I love everyone who works there – some of the customers just become your friends. Who's your favourite customer?

Mark: we just keep having new favourite customers, don't we?

Cs: Not just pretty customers! An actual favourite customer! Bad Mum – she's pretty good.

Mark: Yeah, she's good.

Js: Bad Mum?

Cs: first thing she ever rented, she'd just moved in around the corner, little kids like that (indicates they were small) – South Park The Movie. We were like 'Fucking hell! What are you doing to your children, woman?' and so we called her Bad Mum.

Mark: You did tell her, though, didn't you?

Cs: Well, I don't know if I did. I don't know if I did. Then she came back the next day going 'Oh, have you seen this?????'

Js: She thought it was a normal cartoon?

Cs: Can you imagine showing your kids that and it's all 'unclefucker' and stuff?

Js: So does she know she's called Bad Mum?

Cs: No. She's called Yvonne really. But she comes in here a lot. Gets lots of Asian films. But who's our favourite? I don't know. That taxi driver who says 'Never go in there! They always charge you late fees!' 'ONLY COS YOU BRING IT BACK LATE!'

Mark: I still think we should ring his taxi up, leave him sitting outside the house for three days and see how much it costs. 'Oh, I was in someone's boot! They only just found me!'

(All laugh)

JS: OK, I want the list. The list of the marketing things that you've done.

Cs: Right. Things that didn't work as well?

Js: Everything!

Cs: OK. Things that didn't work are all forms of print advertising.

Js: Absolutely.

Cs: Things that did work is: Identify your local market and places who you think might share a customer base with you and dump loads of flyers on them. Put flyers through doors. But you can only do that so many times, I think.

Js: Yeah, people get pissed off.

Cs: I hate to get flyers through my door.

Js: Exactly, it can put you off a business.

Cs: Well, how I countered that particular thing, cos most of the stuff that comes through your door is flimsy and you can screw it up like that. My flyers you couldn't screw up. Also make them out of something – this is very important – which is roachable. Cos it'll stay on someone's table for months!

Js: Wow! Yeah!

Cs: You can even put the little indentations, so it's easy for them. So yeah, roachable! So, don't make it shiny and it'll stay on someone's coffee table for months! And they'll be staring at it; it'll be ingrained in their tiny little minds. We did stickers – loved that – all the viral stuff, I'm particularly into. So you just put stickers on all street furniture – lampposts, a lot of them get taken down but you just put them back up.

Js: And you never get any trouble from that?

Cs: Apart from from Blockbuster but we did rather a lot on their shop.

(Both laugh)

Js: We did that when they closed down to have a refit, we papered the whole front of their shop everyday once the workmen had left.

Cs: Shop window, use that as the biggest piece of advertising, myspace, obviously you're much better at that than me, uh, website presence, uh, animate it! People loved it when we animated it. Badges, always badges, people just love them and they're cheap as chips. Uh, talking to people – we've got this resource here because Carly comes from the Bodyworks dance studio, so we have these people come and work here, sometimes we get these people in just to do promotional stuff. So, if I know that the shop's going to be quiet – for instance, there's this thing called Strawberry Fair, the shop dies – it's like Christmas day. Everyone troops down Mill Road. If you've got a couple of girls standing outside when they come back, in roller-skates and one of your hoodies giving out flyers, giving out champagne, you're gonna pull some people in here who would have walked straight past. Everyone likes seeing fit twins on roller-skates.

Js: Were they twins?

Cs: Yeah, the twins are the ones we use the most. They're lovely as well; they're just really good at it. If you had someone (half-heartedly going) 'video shop', it just wouldn't work. You want someone who engages you and does what Blockbuster doesn't. I mean, this is what you said to me – 'do what Blockbuster don't!'

Js: Yeah.

Cs: Talk to people, create a nice environment, and stay open late if there's someone in the shop.

Js: So you do the free champagne?

Cs: Yep. Every Saturday – Champagne Saturdays. That's how it works. We were thinking about sort of Mogadon Mondays or something. There's no V so we can't do valium.

Js: You've got the optics in the back, but that's just for staff.

Cs: Yeah, but it looks fun! People say 'this is a nice place! There are people here!' you know, we do the thing with decks. I went to the Selfridges in Manchester, never been in there before, got up the escalators to the men's department and, if you think what Selfridges have got – high end – whatever you buy, you're going to spend a lot, first thing you see is a DJ. Like that, when you're coming off the escalators, you think, 'oh, this is cool!' – Even if he's a northern monkey playing shit – you think 'this is cool!'

Js: So, where do you set the decks up?

Cs: We just move all the stuff required to run the business out the way and put the decks on the counter, we just sort of shift things around a bit.

Js: And what's the response to that?

Cs: I dunno, I think people just like that you can do that.

Js: It's something a bit different.

Cs: Yeah! And people know him anyway (points at Mark), he's a well known sort-of face around Cambridge, so... But I DJ occasionally here as well. The other one – filling the shop with balloons, we must do that again!

Js: You filled the shop with balloons?

Cs: Filled the shop with balloons! People were going 'what is this?', they were all just spilling out on to the street and people were going 'what's going on over there?' The other thing we did think of recently – just on the viral thing – Mark and I were looking through books of these personalised marketing things. You were quite keen on the what?

Mark: I was quite keen on loads of stuff.

Cs: The lighter, we thought – little Bic lighters?

Js: That's a great idea.

Cs: Nobody ever keeps them, people always steal them. If you've got your logo and it's nice enough, it's going to change hands an awful lot. Another thing we did start doing, which we never really got on to was stickers on the back of people's phones. Get my stickers on the back of people's phones, people put their phone down in the pub, others go 'what's that?' They've got to agree to it obviously.

Mark: Have you got The Gingerdead Man?

Js: Yeah! Gary Busey as the gingerbread man who kills people!!!

Mark: Has it rented?

Js: Well, yeah, maybe 8 or 9 times.

Cs: Mark and I had a deal, he wanted to get it in, I said 'you buy it, you can keep any money you make from it, it's yours to do what you want with.' So, we put it in New Releases even and he put a review on it and people would look at it and he'd go 'oh you know if you get two, get the third one for free, why don't you....it's only an hour long!'

Js: How much did you make out of it?

Mark: I think it's up to thirty odd quid, isn't it?

(All laugh)

Cs: You know, it's been really quiet the last couple of days?

Js: Yeah?

Cs: Has yours been quiet?

Js: We had an awful day – yesterday was ok – but the day before was shocking.

Cs: Mm.

Js: we took fifty six quid.

Cs: I had a day like that recently. No, we just had a couple of hundred and twenties.

Js: Well, I can deal with that, in the week I don't really care, but if we have a bad weekend after having that in the week, then I'll get angry. I'm finding that, well, when we started Cowley Road, I was very much like 'I want to be there! I don't care how much it costs, that's where to be!' but I'm paying the price for it now.

Cs: Mmm.

Js: Because we've not got the trade there to sustain it at all. In fact, Summertown's been supporting Cowley Road sometimes.

Cs: Yeah, but you're only in your first year.

Js: Two years, but it's like we were talking about before, it doesn't feel like it's growing, it feels like it's just, you know, existing.

Cs: Well, we're up on last year but last year was the first year. We're trying to get a bigger slice of a declining market.

Js: Yeah.

Cs: Which is fine, I mean that's when boutique things open. I mean, what we were talking about the other day – when THEY [Blockbuster] go.

Js: I mean, do you think there's going to be like, because this interests me is what's happening with Blockbuster, the idea that they could vanish any day, they could suddenly just pull out.

Cs: Mmhmm.

Js: Do you think there would actually be a sudden new wave of people like us? Because I think that me, you and Today is Boring...

Cs: I'm sure there's a couple of other ones – little boutique places. Because, you know, people did say to me – and this is why I opened – 'if only there was a decent place to rent movies'

Js: Yeah, but do you find that, I mean, what's your view on the way the market's going? I mean, what do you think is happening to the video rental industry in the UK? What's going on?

Cs: I don't know, I mean I think every-thing's… all markets are fragmenting, I would have thought. Everything's a specialist market now because we're not a supermarket, you know? And we're not a big online delivery thing, so I think, I mean, my hope is that there'll always be a small scale market for niche products. Which is what we are. It's just a question of how big a niche product we are.

Js: I'm scared of the industry closing in. This is my biggest fear, I feel at the moment of being at the whim…

Cs:…that people will stop renting?

Js: Not just that, but that they're condition-ing people not to rent anymore. When Asda, last week, were selling Casino Royale for £7 I was terrified. I was terrified. I mean, they've devalued it! They've devalued film! In a way, it's almost like…

Cs: Which is what we talked about initially, isn't it? That back catalogue is equally, if not more important, than something new.

Js: Definitely. Yeah, and that's the ethos that both of our shops are basically built on! Which I think people do respect but the problem is that the industry itself isn't respecting it. I mean, you've got HMV at the moment selling Gladiator and a bunch of other ones for three quid each and you've got the newspapers giving the DVDs away free as well.

Cs: Yeah.

Js: I mean, that's an issue that worries me. The idea that when video rentals started…

Cs: You've got to be able to get this content. I mean, yeah, the day that I'm able to go 'I want to watch Lemming' and I click a button and I watch it – we're all dead then.

Js: So basically, when what happens with iTunes happens with film.

Cs: There are still cd shops, you know, HMV aren't doing very well but Fopp are expanding.

Js: HMV are doing the same thing as Blockbuster. They came in so big they were able to kill the independents and now they can't sustain the size they are.

Cs: Fopp's growing! They're opening new branches!

Js: That's true.

Cs: People like Fopp because everyone understands them to be independent. Even though they're not. But people go there, people like it, people don't like going to HMV, and that's part of the reason why we're here – people don't like going to Blockbuster! That's the way I advertise – I don't say 'we've got Casino Royale', I say 'WE'RE NOT BLOCKBUSTER!' You know? That's the only advertising we can seriously do – 'We're not Blockbuster!' and that's why people come here.

Js: You know, their new slogan is the most offensive thing I've ever seen. 'Don't let anyone else entertain you'! I mean, that's not even a slogan, that's an order! I've never seen anything like that before. It's not even like an invitation, it's not warm. There's nothing to it, it's just 'DON'T. LET. ANYONE. ELSE. ENTERTAIN. YOU' You know what I mean? Where is that coming from? Who are the people who are coming up with this stuff? Because they're not clever people, they're not smart people. It's a real kind of thing that gets me, the idea that when – I mean, we've both worked for Blockbuster – and you get this feeling that from the bottom to the top, Blockbuster UK, specifically, is rotten. There's no one that gives a shit in that entire company.

Cs: Apart from those mad yelping reps you get in the morning on the answering machine going 'COME ON GUYS! IT'S GOING TO RAIN TODAY! COME ON, LET'S GET AT 'EM!'

Js: Oh, I never had that! Is that like the emails? Because we used to get the email, the inspirational email.

Cs: Voicemails! And they were going 'COME ON! WE'VE REALLY GOT TO MAKE A DIFFERENCE TODAY!' you know? 'fuck off!'

Js: I mean, corporations are kind of scary anyway in that sense – in the kind of 'no accountability' sense – but Blockbuster in particular really kind of freaks me out in the way that no one seemed happy. No one in that whole corporation seemed like they cared about what they were doing at all – from the bottom to the top. When I met the executives, they'd come and occasionally tour the branches, they weren't happy about being in the shops.

Cs: Go and have a look at the little guy over the bridge. We're taking two grand a week off him. He just sits there in the back, a little bit like betting shops, sits in the back, cos you never see the person when you walk in, you just see ends of rows, don't you? Bins full of discarded shit, you never see a person. Here – first thing you see? People!

Js: Absolutely!

Cs: I think it's… why is there Waitrose? Why is there John Lewis? Department stores close down left, right and centre every week. Why is there a John Lewis? Because people would rather buy their laptops there than at PC World! Even though it's exactly the same price. Exactly the same product. They just prefer it.

Js: Brand loyalty?

Cs: It's just nice! You know, it's just nicer! People like to go. If I'm stressed and I really can't face going to Asda, I just go to Waitrose. Don't even have to find a pound for the trolley, it's just nice. They trust you for that. We put all our chocolate on the counter, you take the actual product home, you can wander around here half-pissed at quarter to twelve at night, if you like. You know?

Js: I agree with that completely and that's what we are and that's what we try to be. I'm just worried that the product itself is being devalued to the point where people object to paying £3.50 for a film for a night.

Cs: Yeah.

Js: And that's what's been taken away from us! If me and you had our shops ten years ago, we would be kings, like we would be making a lot of money.

Cs: Just shows you how stupid I am, doesn't it? One of my mates said 'Why the fuck did you open a *video* shop?'

(Both laugh)

Js: I feel a measure of guilt as well, man. Because the time when we were speaking was right when I was opening Cowley Road and I was just in my most optimistic phase. I was like 'This is brilliant! I've proved it! We opened in Summertown! Everything's perfect! This is a winner!'

Cs: Yeah, but if Blockbuster go, I know there's the Warners thing too, but that could go either way. Things could easily be great for us for a couple of years.

Js: Nah. The one thing that we'll never get back that we had as an industry – which I don't think *you* even ever had – was the exclusivity, the six months between a film being released for rental and being released to buy and that's gone forever.

Cs: We still get first-day excitement about certain titles.

Js: Yeah, but it's not the same. The people have changed. The point is that at that point we had everyone, there was nowhere else they could see those films for that period. They certainly couldn't download or rip things to give to their friends. It wasn't in the cinema anymore, it wasn't available to buy and that was what the industry was built on. By closing that gap – and I can see why they closed that gap because you can almost look on it and say 'why was that gap even there for as long as it was there anyway?', the studios would have made a lot more money just by selling copies of this stuff. That's my biggest fear – is that we'll get done out of New Releases. Because it's already... Warner Bros, I hate. I phoned them, I've been screaming down the phone to them and I've given up – which is a terrible thing to admit. I've given up on it. The first point when they started sending us those thin cases, I was livid.

Cs: Yeah, I remember.

Js: Because they're saving fuck-all money on that and they're not even printing the titles on the spine. What are we supposed to do with that? It looks like shit and the fact that they're putting them in the big boxes for the retail market – with two discs – that's a fucking insult. That is actually an insult. They were the first ones to close that gap anyway – to do rental/retail on the same day and then it feels like a big fuck you – you know, rental you get a tiny little thin box and one disc, everyone else gets two discs, they get a nice big box and it's cheaper.

Cs: So you don't think there's any future in it at all?

Js: No. I think Warner Bros are market leaders and they dictate how it goes.

Cs: Well, we've had this discussion – there are online rental companies and they do have hard copies, so something has to be available for someone and I imagine the simplest thing for them to do is just so away with the distinction – it'd be cheaper manufacturing and we'd all have the same product – which'd make it half the price for us.

Js: I hope so. I really hope so.

Cs: Well, otherwise it's restricted practices, isn't it?

Js: No, because there's nothing that says they have to make things available for rental. There's nothing that says they have to do that.

Cs: It'd be a really interesting case – I'd certainly take it up.

Js: I think they see us as parasitical. I really do think that. I think that of Warners in particular.

Cs: But this is like the art world – you know, we had computers, we had projectors, in some cases it was cheaper to buy a projector, but we had projectors and we'd rent them – two rentals, we made our money back on the projector. Because people didn't want to buy them, they didn't want to deal with them, that sort of thing. I know it's slightly different but...

Js: Well, no, that's the same with anything – if you own something, you should be able to rent it out – because you own it. But film is different.

Cs: I'd certainly look into it from a legal point of view and I'd continue to trade. I certainly wouldn't lay down straight off just because they told us to. I would just buy their retail ones and put a sign up saying 'no rental copies were available, so if you get a warning at the beginning of the film, that's what it is – don't worry about it.' But there's only a few people who do that. 'If you've rented this, they've stolen it!'

Js: Well, Warners do it and they're the biggest. They still have the biggest films, it tends to be.

Cs: I'll just keep on renting until such time it's proved that I couldn't. I don't know if they've got the will to do that.

Js: I don't know what I'm going to do. I don't know how I'm going to wrap this all up. That's something I think about a lot.

Cs: I'm not ready to give up on it yet.

Js: I'm not ready to give up on it but I feel I'm being forced into a position.

Cs: It's two situations – with Warners in particular and with Blockbuster. If Blockbuster would show a little bit of clear blue sky, which I've been waiting for, we don't know which way it'll go.

Js: I hadn't thought about that until you mentioned it. The idea that Blockbuster closes down and then we have a perfect period where we're the only people renting stuff.

Cs: We could be the only people doing it. Imagine if we gave up and then Blockbuster went, however many months, a week later! I left my house, wanted to watch a film, where would I go? There'd be a lot of people wandering around doing that! I haven't got a 10mb thing and I don't want to watch some hooky copy I bought from Liverpool St station of whatever the next thing is.

Js: Absolutely. Although, my fear is that something as big as Blockbuster disappears, Tesco or Sainsburys are going to do it. They'll incorporate it.

Cs: I honestly don't think they would.

Js: Really? I still think that when a market leader disappears, someone's going to try something.

Cs: Well, the only thing I've noticed, reading through Cue and surfing around the net, is these automated ones. But I've seen them pop up and disappear in London.

Js: Yeah, me too. There was one on Marylebone which went very quickly and I looked into that as well. I was going to do that about six months after we opened Cowley Road, I was seriously looking into it cos I thought we could get one of those in Kidlington and some different areas – besides the fact that I really just wanted to call it 'Videosyncratic-o-matic'

(Everyone laughs)

Js: Which for me was reason enough to just do it. But they want a lot of money for those machines. If you buy them outright they're a fortune and if you rent them, you're giving them a huge percentage of your take. I just didn't think I should do it and the fact that the one in Marylebone disappeared so quickly really made me think they're not sustainable.

Cs: I don't want to change the subject but if you think of it in these terms; so, the big chain stores don't do vinyl anymore. They're all CD, cassettes have gone. Specialist record shops – in somewhere like Cambridge, always seems to sustain. They always seem to fuck up as well – certainly in London because the market is so fragmented into jazz and soul and that sort of thing, Rough Trade and all that –they're doing well, they're making money.

Js: Are they really making money?

Cs: Honest Johns, where I used to work in London, has just doubled its size. And they just sell old records and newly-issued stuff but very specialist types. So it doesn't really translate but it sort of does. That the specialist thing that we'd be having is that we'd have DVDS that you can rent and take home in our shop. Because no one else has. And there will be a market for that to sustain us for a couple of years if they go.

Js: I'm just worried about it all dwindling.

Cs: Well, it *is* dwindling, but you're getting a bigger share of a dwindling market! And you know, if Blockbuster go, we've got all of it! People are still going to go to Tesco and buy Casino Royale but a lot of people aren't.

Js: It could be an amazing glory period.

Cs: I've always thought – before I was doing this – I don't want a house full of DVDs. That's unusual! Most people want to watch a film once and that's it.

Js: OK, one last question, and Mark can be a part of this as well. With all the negative stuff that's there, all of the facts that we're not taking the money as an industry that we want to, that we're being ignored, that the things that we try so hard to do get ignored, what's the good thing about having an independent video shop?

Cs: Well, you get laid, don't you?

Mark: Yeah, you get laid. I have to roll myself in dog shit before I walk down the street sometimes. Just to thin it out some.

Js: Is that true?

Both: Yes!

Mark: Not the dog shit bit.

Js: It's been worth it.

Cs: Yeah, of course it's been worth it.

Mark: Yeah, it's been cool. Even the bad things about the shop are nothing, you know, like 'oh, it's so annoying when that happens' but nothing is ever like.... You don't ever go home and go 'for fuck's sake!'

Js: And you never go home resenting a day's work.

Cs: No, I mean, I come in here to relax sometimes. Everyone drops in, whether they're renting or not, just people you know – everyone knows where to find you. It's sort of like a bar, this place. I mean, you know, if there is a finite life to this business, and if we confront the problems that we've got, and if we are going to make it through to any clear blue skies that might or might not be, we may as well have fun doing it!

If you enjoyed this book, please tell people about it and give it a positive review.
Thanks!

This book is dedicated to a group of incredible individuals.

The roll call below represents the disparate group of miscreants and geniuses who worked the tills of Videosyncratic over the years.

Between them, they supported, maintained, furthered or attempted to destroy my vision of Video Shop Utopia.

TEAM VIDEOSYNCRATIC

HUMPHREY ASTLEY
JIM BARTLE
DAN BOND
SAM BRANTON
CHRIS BRUNNER
NICKY COPELIN
JOHN DAVIES
STEVE DUVAL
JAMES FLOWER
DAVE FRAMPTON
GEZ GERRARD
TIM HARDING
ELLIOT HOLMES
ROWENA HOWIE
LIAM INGS-REEVES
CODY JAMES
LAURA KENDALL
BEN LLOYD
MAYUR PANT
ZOE PARSONS
KLARA REPIKOVA
NICK ROBERTS
CHRIS STAMAS
JAMIE STUART
RICHARD WALTERS
HANNA WIGGINS-THIRKILL
MARTIN WILKINSON
SHELBY WILLIAMS

Honourable mentions go to our favourite customers
RICH MORLEY
and the sadly no-longer-with us
TONY EASTERBROOK and DAVID K. LORD

Ultimately, however, this book can only really be dedicated to the funny little man who, since 1976, has encouraged, indulged, supported or been dragged into my increasingly wild schemes with a detached air of mild confusion and amused frustration. My brilliant dad.
MICHAEL SPIRA

Huge thanks also go to:

Sam Jordison and Jacqui Barr for their editing prowess and telling me when I sounded like too much of a dick.

Susie Dent for the ace foreword, her years of patronage and being a deeply appreciated particitrousers in this project.

Chris Stacey – my video shop brother-in-arms

Jen Kirstein and Hank Starrs for unstinting support and encouragement

Ross Lawhead, Bernard Gowers, Matthew Engel, Simon Rosenberg, Stuart Barr, Dan Lentell and Miguel Rodriguez for kindnesses and enthusiasm

My Blockbuster crew – Gina Cotterill, Gez Gerrard, Nick Robinson & Becky Slorach for factual analysis and memory-jogging

and everyone who features in this book, in name or pseudonym.
Well, maybe not *everyone*.

The original Videosyncratic logo and associated branding was designed by Heather Weil for Videosyncratic Ltd.

The publishing of this book was funded entirely by people backing the Videosyncratic campaign on Kickstarter. I'm eternally grateful to all of my backers, especially the following beautiful people, who were particularly supportive and generous:

AARON CATTERMER / AARON WENDEL / ADAM PARKER-EDMONDSTON / ALAN THAGARD / ALEX KIDD / ANDREW GAMBIER / ANDREW ROPER / ANDREW SELZER / ANDREW STRINGER / ANDY MALT / ANGELA MARCHI / ANTHONY LAWRIE / ANTON BITEL / ARRON CAPONE-LAGAN / ASHLEY REBECCA COPELAND / BEN LAVINGTON MARTIN / BOAZ HALACHMI / BRYAN SCHUESSLER / CATHERYNE 'LITTLEJOHNS' HILL / CHASEN R. CHANDLER / CHRIS EAST / CHRIS GEORGE / CHRISTIAN MONGGAARD / CHRISTOPHER SERPICO / CHRISTOPHER STACEY / CLINT WILLIAMS / COLIN V. / CORMAC DONNELLY / DAN BOND / DANIEL C. HODGES DANIEL TREMBIRTH / DARREN NUTTALL / DARREN SAVAGE / DARREN WHITING / DAVID COLE / DAVID ELVIS LEEMING / DAVID STARNER / DAVID STEWART / DEADLY / DEREK J. BALLING / DEREK VICKERS / DERYN O'SULLIVAN / DOUGLAS GREENSHIELDS / ELLIOT SUTHERLAND / EON DAVIDSON / ERICA PRATT / FIONA MOREY / FRU JEUNE / GARRETT COAKLEY / GAVIN WILSON / GEOFF D. BLOGG / GEOFF DANNATT / GEOFF WAUDBY / GURDEEP SAMRA / HANK STARRS / HELEN BRENNAN / HORRIBLE IMAGININGS FILM FESTIVAL / IAIN POTTER / IAN GARRETT / J HARKER / JACOB W. FLEMING / JACQUI BARR / JAMES / JAMES GREENE / JANIS BEST / JASON AMISS / JEFF THOMAS / JOHN DAVIES / JOHN MAZZEO / JOHN ROOSTER FORD / JON CARTER / JONATHAN THETFORD / JULIAN STERN /

KEVIN C KUENKLER / KEVIN CHETTLE / KEVIN MAYLE / KRISTOPHER DAVIDSON / LAURA BURSON / LIAM DUNNE / MAGNUS SELLERGREEN / VIDEOGRAM / MALCOLM CLEUGH / MARK BROWN / MARK HATFIELD / MARK SHADDOCK / MARK TALBOT-BUTLER / MATT JONES / MATT RODABAUGH / MATTHEW SEARLE / MATTHEW STANOSZ / MICHAEL A JACOBS / MICHAEL J. ROBERTS / MICHAEL MASSEY / MICHAEL WOODRING / MIKE AND CAROLYN HAUSHALTER / MIKE KENT / MOVIELANDDOM / NEIL "BADGER" ROBERTS / NEIL KENNY / NICK DEAKIN / NICK HARTLEY-SMITH / NIGEL POWELL / NORMAN PRIMROSE / ONLINE STREAMING KILLED THE VIDEO STORE STAR / PANAYIOTA PANTELI / PAUL DRING / PAUL MOODY / PAUL SAX MAN SPENCE / PETER HEARN / PROF GN MARTIN / PHIL CLEMENTS / PHIL JACKSON / PHILL WARREN / REVEK / RICHARD BOWN / RICKY 'AFRAID' STEVENS / ROB IRWIN / ROBERT 'WEASELSPOON' WELLS / ROO RAYMOND / ROSS LAWHEAD / SACHA MOORE / SAM JORDISON / SARAH PALING / SCOTT BISHOP / SCOTT LYMAN / SCOTT SHAW / SETH MANHAMMER / SHAUN SULLEY / SIMON BLEASDALE / SIMON NIKLASSON / SIMON ROSENBERG / SIMON TRIGWELL / SIMON WHITE / SPINDLES / STEPHEN COX / STEVE HALL / STUART ARNOTT / STUART HEANEY / STUART NAISMITH / SUE LLOYD / T. SHEETZ / TALL MAN WITH GLASSES / TALLY & METZ / THOMAS LARKIN / TIM ELWELL / TIM SHIELDS / TODD BOWMAN / TOM LAVINGTON MARTIN / TYLER GOODISON / WARREN LAPWORTH / @P3RF3KT

Follow Jon Spira at www.kickstarter.com to find out first about future projects.

ABOUT THE AUTHOR

Jon Spira lives in North London with his partner, cat and several thousand DVDs. He is a documentary filmmaker with two feature films to his name; ANYONE CAN PLAY GUITAR and ELSTREE 1976. Between 2013 and 2016, Jon was the in-house documentary filmmaker for the British Film Institute. Over the years, Jon has been a film student, film tutor, film blogger, screenwriter and spent many years hanging out in, working, running or owning a wide variety of video shops. He has written for The Huffington Post, BFI, Daily Telegraph and many crappy websites and blogs. This is his first book.

You can follow Jon on Twitter @videojon

To receive occasional information about my future books and films, please sign up to my mailing list at:

http://eepurl.com/cD6-jX

You can check out my other work at:

www.jonspira.com